ORIGINAL SELFISHNESS

This book defends a startling idea: that the age-old theological and philosophical problems of original sin and evil, long thought intractable, have already been solved. The solution has come from the very scientific discovery that many consider the most mortal threat to traditional religion: evolution.

Daryl P. Domning explains in straightforward terms the workings of modern evolutionary theory, Darwinian natural selection, and how this has brought forth life and the human mind. He counters objections to Darwinism that are raised by some believers and emphasizes that the evolutionary process necessarily enforces selfish behavior on all living things. This account of both physical and moral evil is arguably more consistent with traditional Christian teachings than are the explanations given by most contemporary "evolutionary" theologians themselves.

The prominent theologian, Monika K. Hellwig, dialogues with Daryl Domning throughout the book to present a balanced reappraisal of the doctrine of original sin from both a scientist's and theologian's perspective.

D0209798

In memory of
PIERRE TEILHARD DE CHARDIN, S. J.
(1881–1955)
Paleontologist
Visionary
Pioneer of evolutionary theology

Original Selfishness

Original Sin and Evil in the Light of Evolution

DARYL P. DOMNING
Howard University, USA

with Foreword and Commentary by

MONIKA K. HELLWIG
Georgetown University, USA

ASHGATE

Published by
Ashgate Publishing Limited
Gower House
Croft Road
Aldershot
Hampshire GU11 3HR
England

Ashgate Publishing Company
Suite 420
101 Cherry Street
Burlington, VT 05401-4405
USA

Ashgate website: http://www.ashgate.com

British Library Cataloguing in Publication Data
Domning, Daryl P.
   Original selfishness : original sin and evil in the light of evolution.
   1. Sin, Original 2. Evolution (Biology) – Religious aspects – Christianity 3. Good and evil – Religious aspects – Christianity
   I. Title II. Hellwig, Monika
   233.1'4

Library of Congress Cataloging-in-Publication Data
Domning, Daryl P.
   Original selfishness : original sin and evil in the light of evolution / by Daryl P. Domning ; with foreword and commentary by Monika K. Hellwig.
      p. cm.
   Includes bibliographical references (p.   ) and index.
   ISBN 0-7546-5315-3 (hardcover : alk. paper)
1. Sin, Original. 2. Evolution—Religious aspects—Catholic Church. 3. Selfishness.
4. Theodicy. I. Hellwig, Monika. II. Title.

   BT720.D66 2005
   233'.14—dc22

2005012662

ISBN-10: 0 7546 5315 3

Typeset by Saxon Graphics Ltd, Derby
Printed and bound in Great Britain by TJ International Ltd, Padstow, Cornwall

Contents

List of figures   vii
Foreword
     Monika K. Hellwig   ix
Acknowledgments   xi

Introduction   1
     Daryl P. Domning

Part One   The historical and theological background of original sin
     Monika K. Hellwig
1   The classic teaching on original sin   11

**Part Two   Why the pre-critical understanding of creation and original
           sin is no longer tenable**
     Daryl P. Domning
2   The Genesis cosmogony disproven: the universe is ancient and large   19
3   Life has evolved: how Darwinian evolution works   23
4   Objections to the Darwinian view of nature   32
     4.1   Is evolution theory or fact?   32
     4.2   Is evolution a matter of chance?   33
     4.3   Is natural selection a tautology?   35
     4.4   Is natural selection creative?   36
     4.5   The rarity of favorable mutations   37
     4.6   Are there alternatives to natural selection?   37
     4.7   Micro- vs. macroevolution   40
     4.8   Has macroevolution ever been observed?   44
     4.9   Can we know what happened in the past?   47
     4.10   Competition and cooperation   48
     4.11   Is evolution wasteful and cruel?   51
     4.12   Evolutionary ethics vs. human values   54
     4.13   Descent from animals and human dignity   56
     4.14   Can evolved intelligence be trusted? Is freedom an illusion?   60
     4.15   Does evolution exclude God, meaning, and "purpose"?   63
5   No more Adam and Eve: science refutes monogenism   71
6   How suffering and death fit into evolution   75
7   Are we going anywhere? A static or cyclic universe versus an
     evolutionary universe   83
     7.1   The Bible as the mother of science – and of evolutionary thought   83
     7.2   Is there "progress" in evolution?   89

Response to Part Two
     Monika K. Hellwig   94

Part Three   Towards a new understanding of original sin
Daryl P. Domning
8   Evolution and human behavior   101
    8.1   The selfish behavior of primates and other animals   102
    8.2   Selfishness and its evolutionary consequences   104
    8.2.1 Parsimony, homology, and primate behavior   104
    8.2.2 The roots of sin   107
    8.2.3 Nature: the good, the bad, or the ugly?   108
    8.2.4 Does God need to "guide" evolution?   110
    8.2.5 Is the experiment of life repeatable?   112
    8.3   The challenge of reductionism: self, soma, and culture   113
9   Evolution and human ethics   117
    9.1   The moral divide   117
    9.2   The evolution of ethics   119
    9.2.1 Ethics among animals   119
    9.2.2 Human ethics before and after Jesus   121
    9.3   The theme of adoption in Scripture   128

Response to Part Three
Monika K. Hellwig   136

Part Four   Original selfishness: a contribution to evolutionary theology
Daryl P. Domning
10 Adam and Eve reinterpreted   139
    10.1   A new interpretation of original sin   139
    10.2   Advantages over the "cultural-transmission" and other
           interpretations of original sin   142
11 The meaning of salvation and the "Fall"   149
    11.1   Semantic difficulties   149
    11.2   The world as a work in progress   153
    11.3   A good or a "fallen" creation?   156
12 Reprise: What about suffering?   160
    12.1   Are there fates worse than death?   160
    12.2   Is there an alternative?   162
    12.3   A humble or a disciplinarian God?   166
13 Teilhard's synthesis and its fruits: a critique   172
    13.1   Teilhard and original sin   172
    13.2   Evolutionary theology today   174
14 Summary and conclusion   181

Response to Part Four
Monika K. Hellwig   188

Rejoinder
Daryl P. Domning   190

Bibliography   193
Index of scripture references   207
Index of subjects   211

List of Figures

Figure 10.1   The composite origin of "original sin"   141
Figure 10.2   Timelines of human ontogenetic development   144
Figure 12.1   The common origin of, and the causal relation between,
               physical and moral evil   163

Foreword

Monika K. Hellwig

This book has a history that will alert readers to what they may expect to find in it. About seven years ago my friend, Daryl Domning, a theologically knowledgeable Catholic paleontologist, explained very briefly in conversation the problems he had as a scientist with the Church's handling of the doctrine of original sin. He was then thinking of preparing an article presenting his own way of reconciling the doctrine with his scientific understanding of evolution. As we discussed it further, I suggested setting it out in more detail in book form, whereupon he invited me as a theologian to collaborate in such a book in a dialogue of alternating chapters. I had been extensively in conversation with the late Piet Schoonenberg, S.J., who had made a detailed study of the history of the doctrine. I was at that time the Landegger Professor of Theology at Georgetown University and had times in the academic year available for research and writing. It seemed a good project and I agreed to collaborate. Shortly thereafter, however, I moved into an administrative position that gave me little or no time for any continuous scholarly work.

While Domning continued to work on the project with passionate persistence for more than six years, Hellwig offered nothing but brief sketches for chapters, in spite of constant gentle reminders. Hence Domning not only refined and expanded the scientific components of his argument, spinning off some journal articles on the way, but read a great range of theological authors, past and present, on this topic. He came to formulate theological arguments and very definite conclusions of his own at some length (subsequently somewhat condensed and rewritten). This changed the type of dialogue possible to one in which the theologian contextualizes the discussion at the beginning, and responds with agreement or disagreement at several points in the text. Hence that is what is offered here.

Because Domning worked alone so long and so thoroughly, this book is entirely different from any of the many books that have come out in the last several years dealing with the doctrine of original sin in the context of Neo-Darwinian evolutionary theory. What the reader will find is a committed scientist setting out step by step the difficulties as they appear to him and the possibilities he sees of reconciling his scientific knowledge with his much-studied faith tradition.

He is very consistent in his pursuit. Therefore he is not able immediately to isolate the question of original sin, but finds he must first deal with the doctrine of creation in which there is tension between traditional Christian beliefs and contemporary evolutionary science.

In Part Two of this book, Domning defends the truth of the theory of evolution and its compatibility with Christian faith. In Part Three he deals with human instinctual behavior and the moral question in the evolutionary context. In Part

Four Domning deals with a number of theological issues as he understands them, and at the end there is a rejoinder to the theologian's comments.

The complexity of the discussion arises from the very different ways in which science and theology use language and conduct argument, and from the very different questions that are the subject matter of science and theology. Questions of compatibility of scientific and religious claims arise largely because for long centuries both scientists and theologians failed to recognize or acknowledge these differences in the subject matter and the rules of discussion.

Original sin, like most Christian doctrines, has a history reaching back several thousands of years. It is a tortuous and not always univocal history, which lends itself to variations of interpretation. As most people in the Christian tradition are less tolerant of ambiguity or subtlety in their faith than are, for instance, Jews or Hindus, churches have commonly taught simplified versions of a complex and subtle tradition. Hellwig's response to Chapter One tries to explain this history of the doctrine sufficiently to ground a sense of how the tension between faith and science arises.

This book will not be very helpful to those who have already made up their minds either that evolutionary theory threatens their faith and must be rejected or that Christian faith cannot be reconciled with what is obviously scientific truth so that faith must be rejected. This book will, however, be enormously helpful to those who are trying to reconcile the two, but struggle with a great number of specific issues that leave them puzzled. Domning has worked these out for himself with great patience and knowledge. Hellwig agrees with most of his work but has remaining reservations. Neither author claims to have a definitive or logically necessary answer. Readers are invited into the conversation to form their own conclusions.

Acknowledgments

I thank Robert Brungs, Steve Edwards, Dennis Hamm, John Haughey, John Haught, Donald Keefe, Thomas King, the late P. R. Masani, Joseph Murphy, Mike O'Mara, the late Karl Schmitz-Moormann, and Joseph Wimmer; the participants (including some of the above) in the annual Cosmos and Creation Conferences at Loyola College, Baltimore, and in the Washington Theological Consortium Religion-Science Discussion Group; and the participants in the RCIA program at St. Camillus Parish, Silver Spring, Maryland, for exchanges of ideas that helped greatly to clarify my thinking on various points. Donald Buggert, Steve Edwards, Thomas King, Robert Merikangas, Janet and Ronald Nimer, and Joseph Wimmer steered me to literature I would otherwise have missed. Peter Dodson gave the entire manuscript a critical reading and made further helpful suggestions.

Of greatest importance was the generous encouragement I uniformly received from John Haught, the faculty of the Washington Theological Union, and most of all Monika Hellwig. Without the open-minded and gracious acceptance that these eminent professional theologians extended to an unknown amateur and outsider, I would scarcely have ventured to persevere in publishing this work. Of course, these social influences in no way diminish my own culpability for its remaining imperfections!

For their moral and spiritual support, I owe much gratitude to my fellow members of Christian Life Community – and among these, most of all to Kathy my wife, for her patience and encouragement through year after year of days and evenings I spent on this project at our family's expense.

Short summaries of the main ideas presented here were previously published by me in the *ITEST Bulletin* (Institute for Theological Encounter with Science and Technology) 24(2), Spring 1993; in the *Call To Action: Baltimore* newsletter, Winter 1999 ("Why is there evil? And why didn't they tell us this sooner?", pp. 3–5); in *America* 185(15)(4547), Nov. 12, 2001 ("Evolution, evil and original sin: putting the puzzle together", pp. 14–21); in *Christian Life Communities Harvest* 35(1), Spring 2002 ("The Two Standards: a fork in the road of evolution"; pp. 6–8); and in an article posted on the website of *Science & Spirit* Magazine <www.science-spirit.org>, July 2001.

With great sadness I must record that Monika Hellwig passed away suddenly on 30 September 2005, while I was correcting the page proofs of this book. In her the Church and the world have lost a great treasure, and I have lost a great friend. *Requiescat in pace.*

DPD

Introduction

Daryl P. Domning

Does an evolutionary perspective bring any light to bear upon theological anthropology, the meaning of the human person as the imago Dei, *the problem of Christology – and even upon the development of doctrine itself?*

Pope John Paul II[1]

This book is addressed to those who ask whether Christian belief and acceptance of evolution are compatible. (They are.) More particularly, it seeks to show how the Christian doctrine of original sin can be understood in an evolutionary world-view, and why this view actually does away with the otherwise insoluble theological and philosophical problems of evil and suffering. Written from a standpoint and presupposition of religious faith (specifically, that of Roman Catholicism and of non-fundamentalist Christianity in general), this book does not seek to win over the skeptic to a belief in God or in other Christian doctrines. It follows instead in the theological tradition of "faith seeking understanding," to show what Christian faith can look like when it takes fully into account the present state of knowledge about human origins. Intellectual honesty requires no less of any believer; and I submit that this particular understanding requires no compromise in the essentials of that faith. I argue, in short, that there is no more reason now than in centuries past to think that the Book of Nature contradicts the Book of Revelation.

The acceptance of an evolutionary worldview nonetheless poses acute problems for many Christians. For example, after the 1996 statement by Pope John Paul II which acknowledged that evolution is now "more than a hypothesis," a man wrote the following in a letter to *The New York Times*:[2]

> Pope John Paul II's acceptance of evolution touches the doubt in my heart. The problem of pain and suffering in a world created by a God who is all love and light is hard enough to bear, even if one is a creationist. But at least a creationist can say that the original creation, coming from the hand of God, was good, harmonious, innocent and gentle. What can one say about evolution, even a spiritual theory of evolution? Pain and suffering, mindless cruelty and terror are its means of creation. Evolution's engine is the grinding of predatory teeth upon the screaming, living flesh and bones of prey. ... If evolution be true, my faith has rougher seas to sail.

Nor does this existential dilemma cause merely interior struggles in the hearts of believers: it is the main driving force behind a public policy debate that has dragged on for generations, with profound implications for education, especially in the United States, but increasingly in other countries as well. In the creation-evolution controversy,

... we are faced with a deeply-held conviction that evolution inevitably includes the rejection of God and morality, and further greases the slippery slope leading to the ultimate destruction of civilization. If we were able to defuse this line of reasoning without compromising or soft-pedaling evolution, imagine how much would the quality of science education improve when we could devote our efforts to the task at hand?[3]

One of my hopes for this book is that it may contribute to achieving this goal, by showing Christians that evolution is not a threat to their most deeply held values, but rather a vantage point, firmly founded on the best available science, from which Christianity is actually seen to be more rationally coherent and compelling than it ever appeared before.

A century and a half of history, however, stands in the way of such a reconciliation between Christianity and evolutionary science. The revolution in worldview set in motion by Charles Darwin's *Origin of Species* in 1859 had quite divergent effects on the scientific and the theological communities. By the end of the nineteenth century, the scientists had regrouped around the new evolutionary paradigm, embraced it more or less enthusiastically, and begun to build on it with new discoveries and insights that have continued to the present day. The Christian churches, on the other hand, emerged from the nineteenth-century ferment over evolution in comparative disarray. Not only had science and religion in the West lost their previous unanimity on the subject of origins; these winds of intellectual change exacerbated the theological divisions among Christian denominations, and left them scattered from horizon to horizon like a fleet of ships after a storm at sea. At one extreme, some clung to biblical literalism, while others accepted the new scientific findings to varying degrees and found ways to reconcile them with their theologies. Many individuals, meanwhile, concluded that the Bible was hopelessly falsified by science and abandoned Christianity altogether.

The Roman Catholic Church started out near one end of the spectrum but moved gradually toward the other.[4] Its first statement on evolution (in 1860) rejected as "completely contrary to scripture and the faith" the idea that the human body is derived from lower forms; and the First Vatican Council (1869–70), had it not been interrupted, would very likely have defined as a dogma of the faith the descent of all humans from a single couple. This negative attitude toward evolution was understandable, given that the evolutionary thought of the time was preeminently "the instrument of atheistic and materialistic propaganda; hence, to accept evolution in the form of that time really constituted a danger to the faith."[5] However, a more open spirit cautiously made itself felt over the ensuing decades of scientific progress; and by 1950, the year of Pope Pius XII's encyclical *Humani Generis*, the magisterium (the teaching authority of the Church) had officially accepted in principle (albeit within certain limits and with various strictures) the possibility of organic evolution of the human body.

Nonetheless, pockets of hostility to evolutionary thought have persisted among some Catholic clergy and laity, doubtless due in part to the fact that that papal approval was hedged with significant qualifications. These were three in number: insistence on the immediate divine creation of each human soul; denial that the fact of human evolution had yet (by 1950) been demonstrated; and insistence on the descent of all humans from a literal Adam and Eve (monogenism) and our inheritance from them of the effects of original sin.

These reservations, which were repeated as recently as 1966 by Pope Paul VI,[6] have been a source of concern to those Catholic thinkers who have sought to incorporate the evolutionary worldview into Christian theology as thoroughly as scientists have absorbed it into their science. The works of the Jesuit paleontologist, theologian, and mystic Pierre Teilhard de Chardin, for example, were suppressed because he was suspected (rightly or wrongly) of undermining the Church's strictures on evolutionary speculations, in particular concerning the origin of the soul. Indeed, *Humani Generis* was issued largely to counter the spread of Teilhard's ideas.

It was not until the 1980s that the official Church, through its Pontifical Academy of Sciences[7] and statements of Pope John Paul II,[8] declared its acceptance of the fact of human evolution. With John Paul's further acknowledgment in 1996 that evolution is now "more than a hypothesis," Pius XII's second stricture has explicitly been laid aside.

Pius's first concern, the origin of the soul, is also being addressed through contemporary reinterpretations.[9] Even some highly orthodox Catholic theologians, such as Karl Rahner,[10] have seen no need to insist on the special creation of the human soul by a direct divine intervention in history. A widely favored approach today is that of process theology, wherein the human mind is seen as an emergent product of evolution, rather than a distinct substance as implied by the dualistic term "soul."[11] It is worth noting that the idea of the soul in the Christian tradition actually comes from pagan (Neoplatonic) philosophy; the word "soul" does not even appear in the traditional Creeds, which instead profess faith in the "resurrection of the body." For example, Fr. W. J. Ong, S. J., points out that:

> ... insistence upon the survival of the soul after death is not a distinguishing feature of divine revelation. Most of the Old Testament is silent about such survival, and in the New Testament, while this survival is supposed, it is enveloped in the strategically more important Christian doctrine of the resurrection of the body. Fascination with the survival of the soul is a mark of certain pagan philosophies. The resurrection of the body – born of this universe – is an article of faith distinctively Christian. ... The pagan may look forward to getting rid of his body and hence of this universe. The Christian does not look forward to this at all.
>
> The world view which is opening out before us in our post-Darwinian world is thus one eminently congenial to a follower of Christ.[12]

It seems to me that what the Christian faith really affirms is the immortality of the individual human *personality*, embodied in some sense, and not necessarily well described by the ontological categories of ancient or medieval philosophy. But this is a subject outside the realm of science, and will not be pursued further here.

Original sin, however, and the doctrine of monogenism which it has seemed to demand, do touch on certain fields of science, and have remained sensitive issues for those who would bring the religious and scientific strains of Western thought back into harmony. Can science, particularly evolutionary biology, say anything new on these subjects? At least one informed observer (biologist David Sloan

Wilson) thinks so, basing his judgment on current ways of thinking in the social sciences in general:

> ... I will venture the following prediction: Take *any* subject that is relevant to human behavior, and study it in the way that a behavioral ecologist or an evolutionary game theorist would study the subject in nonhuman species, and that approach will be largely new from the standpoint of the human social sciences.[13]

G. K. Chesterton remarked nearly a century ago that original sin is "the only part of Christian theology which can really be proved."[14] Given the great advances since then in anthropology, evolutionary biology, psychology, and related sciences, one might have expected more efforts to determine how much truth Chesterton's quip actually contains. However, the subject has been neglected by scientists, despite its obvious importance as an intersection between science and theology. Late-twentieth-century theologians, for their part, have shown continuing interest in original sin.[15] Yet, despite their voluminous studies, even the new *Catechism of the Catholic Church* (1994) admits that the doctrine remains problematical:

> How did the sin of Adam become the sin of all his descendants? The whole human race is in Adam "as one body of one man" [St. Thomas Aquinas, *De Malo* 4, 1]. By this "unity of the human race" all men are implicated in Adam's sin, as all are implicated in Christ's justice. Still, the transmission of original sin is a mystery that we cannot fully understand...[16]

An earlier statement by Joseph Cardinal Ratzinger, then Prefect of the Vatican's Congregation for the Doctrine of the Faith (and now Pope Benedict XVI), put the matter even more starkly:

> The inability to understand "original sin" and to make it understandable is really one of the most difficult problems of present-day theology and pastoral ministry.[17]

This echoed the still earlier words (dating from 1947) of Pierre Teilhard de Chardin:

> It is no exaggeration to say that, in the form in which it is still commonly presented today, original sin is at the moment one of the chief obstacles that stand in the way of the intensive and extensive progress of Christian thought.[18]

Granted, the new *Catechism* does not do justice to the insights that Scripture scholars and theologians have gained in this area since the Second Vatican Council (1962–65).[19] (For instance, the *Catechism*[20] seems to adhere to belief in a literal Adam, Eve, and Garden of Eden.) Biblical exegetes have come to see the creation narratives of Genesis 1–3 not as attempts at history in our modern sense but as allegories or parables of the moral struggle inherent in all human existence, and specifically in the life of the community that produced these scriptures. The Garden of Eden is best understood not as the original state of humanity but as a vision of what

God desires for us in the end: as Carmelite scholar Carlos Mesters summed it up, the Eden narrative is "a prophecy of the future, projected into the past."[21] This vision, moreover, has a practical rather than a theoretical purpose: to help us attain this paradise by indicating to us where lies the root of the evil we must first overcome. "If the Bible points out the origin of the evil or the *original sin*, it does so not to show how the evil began, but to show how the evil may be ended."[22]

As for new theological insights, perhaps the most widely accepted is the view (for example, of Jesuit theologian Piet Schoonenberg) that original sin is transmitted culturally, as a necessary result of each individual's birth and acculturation into a sinful human society. Of course, such transmission undoubtedly takes place: as sung in the Rodgers and Hammerstein musical *South Pacific*,

> ... to hate all the people your relatives hate,
> You've got to be carefully taught!

But this view is hard to reconcile with the scriptural and patristic tradition which insists that original sin is transmitted (again quoting the 1994 *Catechism*, no. 419) "by propagation, not by imitation"; that is, that its transmission is in some mysterious sense biological or genetic and not merely cultural or learned.

Among the many harmful notions of sin that have come down to us from various religious and secular sources is a naive belief that sin is a weed with shallow roots, hence easily eradicated: if sin is simply a matter of wrong choices made through individual free will, then proper upbringing or social engineering should suffice for individuals to freely choose good over evil.[23] The classic doctrine of original sin, stating that evil is bigger and older than all of us, served as a corrective to this false idea. The recent reinterpretations of the doctrine by Schoonenberg and others have repeated this caution while casting it in social terms, with our social milieux seen as the medium through which sinfulness is universally transmitted. In this book, however, it is argued that sin is rooted much deeper even than that, not just in human history, sociology, and psychology, but in the farthest depths of evolutionary time and in the mechanics of the evolutionary process itself. Far from undermining the concept of original sin, therefore, the evolutionary perspective underlines both its truth value and its practical relevance as never before.

A clear case of this practical usefulness is in studies of aggression and its counterpart, reconciliation, as illuminated by primatologist Frans de Waal in his book *Peacemaking Among Primates* (1989). He deplores the lack of study of interpersonal reconciliation behavior in humans, blaming it on social scientists' optimistic belief that aggression can be eliminated from human life altogether, and therefore need not and should not be integrated into our lives under the control of checks and balances:

> I recently asked a world-renowned American psychologist, who specializes in human aggression, what he knew about reconciliation. Not only did he have no information on the subject, but he looked at me as if the word were new to him. ... He reflected on my remarks, yet the concept had evidently never taken center stage in his thinking. His interest turned to irritation when I suggested that conflicts are inevitable among people and that aggression has such a long evolutionary history that it is logical to expect powerful coping mechanisms. He

did not see what evolution had to do with it and argued that the most important goal is to understand and remove the causes of aggressive behavior.[24]

This book does not try to "prove" theism or Christianity from scientific evidence, nor to "prove" evolution based on the testimony of religion. Rather, I take science and theology as independent sources of insight standing on their own feet, and point out ways in which their independent conclusions are convergent and compatible. In particular, from my vantage point as a professional biologist and theological layman, it appears to me that the older Catholic tradition – regarding original sin as something literally transmitted by biological propagation – expresses elements of truth that the "cultural-transmission" understanding of original sin, despite its undeniably valid insights, has been too hastily discarded. Moreover, the elusive biological mechanism of "transmission" seems to me transparently simple, obvious, and straightforward (though apparently unfamiliar to theologians, who in most cases seem little acquainted, and often uncomfortable, with contemporary evolutionary biology). I argue below that this interpretation renders moot the entire issue of monogenism, and lays to rest the theological need (still strongly felt by many Christians) to postulate a literal Adam and Eve. This interpretation also suggests a way to resolve some other differences of theological opinion, such as the present tension between "creation spirituality" (not to be confused with special creationism!) and the traditional Christian theology of salvation.

By thus shedding some light on the nature and origin of original sin, I hope to help move the discussion of this topic out of the unhealthy rut in which it has long languished – that is, focused on the past (indeed, a mythical past) rather than the needs of the present. The original aim of theologians, after all, was to account for the evil we see in the world, "and justify the ways of God to men".[25] The myth of Eden was long ago put to use for this purpose; but ironically, this ad hoc "solution" of the problem, now reified to the point that many consider it as firm a fact as evil itself, has become equally an intellectual problem with the problem of evil it was supposed to solve, absorbing just as much explanatory energy.

More recently, the "cultural-transmission" school has gone to the opposite extreme, abandoning the search for the true historic origins of evil, and attending only to how it inflicts itself on each person newly born into the world. I also wish to avoid this error of too *little* attention to (pre)history, and steer a course between these extremes – back to a point from which the existential problem of evil can once again be addressed, without the burden of either a false history or a lack of any history. As Mesters emphasizes,

> ... in our past thinking on original sin, we lost our sensitivity for its real, personal aspect. We posed the problem almost exclusively in terms of time and history, limiting ourselves to asking, "How did this vice enter the human race? What has come down to us as a result and consequence of the sin of our first parents?"[26]

To the extent that these questions can actually be answered, perhaps some of our natural curiosity about our past can be laid aside so that we can (as Mesters wants) deal more forthrightly and realistically with the personal sin we commit today.

A comprehensive revision or even review of this area of doctrinal theology and its voluminous literature is beyond my abilities and the scope of this book.[27] I wish, rather – in addition to the more urgent goals set forth above – to sketch what I see as some of the boundary conditions that modern biology sets to future theological discussion of this issue: to show how, in other words, certain scientific data might constrain, inform, or possibly even inspire theological reflection on the subject of human origins and the human condition. This book, therefore, stands solidly in the spirit of engagement between evolutionary science and evolutionary theology as envisioned by Catholic theologian John Haught.[28]

A few years ago, Michelangelo's great frescoes in the Sistine Chapel, including the famous scene of God's creation of Adam, were given a thorough cleaning and restoration. Suddenly, centuries of soot and varnish were removed from pictures that generations of viewers had been accustomed to see in dull, muted hues. The world was astonished (and some art experts were even scandalized) to learn what vivid colors Michelangelo had actually used, and how bright and cheerful his compositions truly were.

In the same way, the traditional notions about original sin that have come down to us remain murky at best and, to many people of good will, dispiriting to the point of being repulsive. I feel, however, that the story of the creation of our world and our species is really much brighter, more hopeful, and more coherent than much of our tradition has painted it. It is time that Adam's portrait had a good cleaning.

Notes

1. John Paul II 1988.
2. *New York Times*, Nov. 3, 1996, quoted by S. J. Gould in *Natural History* 106(2): 62, March 1997.
3. Hunter 1998.
4. Alszeghy 1967; see also Haught 1998b.
5. Alszeghy 1967, 31.
6. Neuner and Dupuis 1975, 133.
7. See Lowenstein 1982.
8. For example, John Paul II 1985.
9. Cf. Edwards 1999, 74–77; Wiseman 2002, Chap. 4.
10. Rahner 1958.
11. Korsmeyer 1998, Chap. 5, concisely summarizes this line of thought. Johnson 1996 and Clifford 1998 also take this position. See also Murphy 1998 on the history of "nonreductive physicalism."
12. Ong 1960, 146.
13. Wilson 1998, 267.
14. Chesterton 1924, 24.
15. Cf. reviews by Connor 1968, McDermott 1977, Duffy 1988, and Wiedenhofer 1991.
16. *Catechism of the Catholic Church*, 1994, no. 404.
17. Ratzinger 1985, 79.
18. Teilhard 1971, 188.
19. Cf. Acker 2000.
20. *Catechism of the Catholic Church*, 1994, nos. 374–379, 390, 396–412. Compare the comment on the "Dutch" Catechism (Dhanis and Visser 1969, 537; quoted here in Chap. 13, note 32), which frankly admits that this seeming literalism persists in official teaching simply for lack of any better idea.

21. Mesters 1974, 77.
22. Mesters 1974, 41.
23. For a sharply contrary view, see Niebuhr 1960.
24. De Waal 1989, 233–234.
25. J. Milton, *Paradise Lost*, book 1, line 26.
26. Mesters 1974, 111.
27. A useful and very readable short introduction to the subject, as well as an understanding of original sin broadly in agreement with my own, is provided by Korsmeyer 1998, which appeared after this work was already near completion.
28. For example, Haught 2000, Chap. 3.

Part One
The historical and theological background of original sin

Monika K. Hellwig

CHAPTER ONE

The classic teaching on original sin

The Christian doctrine of original sin is a troubling one to contemporary believers or would-be believers who are educated and thoughtful. In order to approach the apparent conflict, however, it is necessary first to disentangle the doctrine from misrepresentations of it. The Protestant, Orthodox and Catholic strands of Christianity are not entirely agreed on the interpretation of the doctrine and have developed their theology of it in somewhat different ways. Hence in setting out the meaning for purposes of this book we want to make it clear that we are situating ourselves in the Catholic strand of Christian tradition.

The doctrine of original sin is rooted, as are all Christian doctrines, in biblical narrative, basically in the third chapter of the book of Genesis. As with all ancient texts, the meaning must be discovered by looking at the story in its own historical, cultural, and linguistic setting. As with all historical texts, this is a task for well-trained experts. Just as the classification, identification, and assembly of scattered remains of ancient bones is not something anyone can do casually by common sense, so ancient texts cannot be classified, identified, and assembled casually by anyone who is devout. In the first place, even the reconstruction of manuscript evidence passed on over the centuries has been challenging. Words in the ancient Hebrew may have become obscure, and manuscripts from which the transmission was made may have been damaged. Hence, often text has been reconstructed from circumstantial evidence, such as comparison with parallel or related texts, other literary remains of the time, knowledge of the history, culture, economy, and so on, of the time, and the place and function of the text in the subsequent living tradition. In the case of a narrative it is important to know the literary genre, whether for instance it is intended as a literal account of something that happened, or an embellished, interpretive account of something that actually happened, or as a moral tale whose worth is not dependent on its having happened, or something in the nature of myth. Myth, not in the popular but the basic meaning of the word, is a narrative which interprets the human situation in general by presenting a particular and very concrete event, image, or story. People who shape myths are not naive, they are using analogical reasoning, and often they use it in very subtle ways. One thing they do not do is ask the question, "Is it literally true? Could a camcorder have made a record of it? Is it in principle empirically verifiable?" Oddly, to our contemporary Western, post-Enlightenment way of thinking, they do not ask those questions because such questions seem to them both irrelevant and uninteresting. In practice they deal appropriately with questions that require empirical verification, though myth-making peoples seldom have familiarity with such vocabulary. It seems quite obvious in practice to more traditional peoples which kinds of statements and stories do not require such empirical verification because they serve a different purpose.

In the light of the foregoing, the Genesis 3 story about the couple in the garden and their encounter with temptation might be retold in non-mythic language (thereby losing something) somewhat as follows. The human person (Adam) finds him or herself in an ambivalent situation. Created by God for fellowship, relationship, community with others, this person nevertheless finds that others also bring temptation and distortion. This is the source of the figure of Eve in the story: her name is interpreted as "mother of all the living," and she represents society as it relates to the individual. The creation narrative had made it clear that the human being is essentially relational and cannot become fully human except in relationship with others. Yet what we all experience is that our parents, our community, our tradition offer us both good and bad influence, guidance, and empowerment. This is clearly a fact of life. The very tradition that teaches us loyalty to family, ethnic or other group, or country carries with it the tendency to exclude or despise others as outsiders, less worthy of respect, care, and attention. Our mentors teach us a certain amount of mistrust, inherited hostility, cupidity and competition for wealth and privilege, sometimes hatred and revenge, acceptable patterns of bullying others, and much more. The question that arises is this: if we need relationships with others to become fully human, yet we cannot totally trust those others and their values and perceptions, are we not betrayed by the very God who created us?

The thrust of the Genesis 3 story is a reassurance that we are not in an ultimately absurd dilemma to which there is no solution. Evil (the serpent of the story) comes from within God's creation, but is not as such a creature of God. The serpent of the story is really a question mark. We cannot pinpoint the origin of evil. Yet the story also alludes to extra-biblical legend which tells of an earlier creation of pure spirits, in other words, beings of pure freedom, of unfettered power of self-determination. Freedom cannot exist as predetermined, and therefore it cannot be guaranteed a happy outcome. Freedom is risk. The story about a prior creation is really a reflection about the nature of freedom. The serpent comes into the garden as the possibility of misusing freedom, that is of using it destructively, in independence of the creator and therefore of the order of creation. The temptation inherent in human, situated, freedom is to seize it as though it had no limits, as though one person or group is free to ignore the claims of others for sustenance, space on earth, human dignity, and full participation in human society. That is why the story has the tree at the center of the garden which is absolutely and without exception the prerogative of God. But human freedom is in fact not pure freedom in dependence on God the creator. Human freedom emerges slowly from the developing infrastructure of the biological organism, and tests and tutors itself in interaction with others, first parents and authority figures, later peer groups and chosen reference figures, gradually the culture and its traditions and norms. If in fact these are distorted by prejudice, fear, promptings of hatred and revenge, lasciviousness, cupidity, and so forth, the emerging human freedom of the human being is crippled from the outset, though not killed or defeated. It can still develop to great purity and intensity but only by dedication to discernment and asceticism.

What has been set out here so far is an interpretation of ancient text with the help of modern scholarship, that is, careful detailed work on the available manuscript evidence, contextual historical studies, comparative mythology, and so on. The situation for Christian believers is, however, more complicated than that. Most Christians, including many of the clergy and the guardians of orthodoxy, have not been introduced to this type of scholarly search for meaning. Their understanding of the doctrine of original sin is the outcome of an historical development that begins with Paul in the New Testament. Paul wrote "As in Adam all men die, so in Christ all will be brought to life; but each in his proper place: Christ the first fruits, and afterwards, at his coming, those who belong to Christ." (1 Corinthians 15:22–23) To understand this text properly, it is important to know that the title "Christ" is used by Paul both to indicate the individual Jesus and to refer to the corporate personality of the Risen One, which includes the community of his followers. With this understanding it is clear that Paul is speaking of a common involvement in sin to be redeemed by a common involvement in grace, and he is expressing this by the juxtaposition of two heads of corporate identity.

In subsequent Christian centuries the subtle ambiguity of the figure of Adam was lost, and Adam seems to have become simply an individual at the beginning of the human race, chosen as champion by whose decision the fate of the human race would be decided, while the figure of Eve became utterly problematic as an individual woman who sinned first but was not significant for the fate of the race, being female. This latter point did not trouble Christians for a long time, because the status assigned the female figure in the story reflected the status of women in society generally, especially after the Constantinian establishment of the fourth century in which the structures of the pagan empire were largely reproduced in the structures of the churches. The role of Adam did, however, trouble Christians, as exemplified in the Pelagian movement which maintained that the sin of one man could not implicate others unless they followed his bad example.

As is well known, the opponent of this Pelagian position was Augustine of Hippo, whose sense of the absolute power and freedom of God was such that he accepted, apparently without a qualm, the notion that the great mass of humankind was, through no fault of their own, a doomed multitude. Augustine saw the heritage of Adam's sin as transmitted by the physical act of procreation, and therefore inescapable for all human beings.

While eastern (Greek, Coptic, and Syriac) Christianity never settled for quite so simplistic an explanation, the Latin West continued Augustine's explanation with a slight nuance. The transmittal of sin was not to be seen as indicating that sexual intercourse was in itself evil, or even that the transmission of sin was due to a lack of total purity of intention in the procreating couple. In fact, the emphasis seems to have been far more on the notion of an initial decree against Adam that universally embraced his offspring for all generations, than on individual transmission.

A voice far ahead of its time was raised against this in the twelfth century by Peter Abelard. Deeply committed to moral rather than ontological or judicial explanations, Abelard pointed to the ways people are observably drawn into either destructive or redemptive behavior by complex moral causality of which example is one, but other lines of influence also come into play. This was bitterly contested in his time as giving too little credit to God's absolute power and freedom in judgment or to God's grace in redemption. Even in the midst of this struggle and for many centuries after, the whole matter was always discussed in terms of the individual and in what ways individuals were morally disadvantaged by the sin of Adam.

The way this disadvantage was and continues to be discussed (at least in the Catholic context) is interesting and insightful. The question is put: what is it that is lost by the sin of Adam? The answer is that there are so to speak two levels of loss: the first level has to do with the relationship to God as source, meaning, and destiny of human life; the second level has to do with the integrity that rightly belongs to human existence. The language used is technical. At the first level it is sanctifying or habitual grace that is lost, and it has been maintained that this is recovered by faith and baptism into the community of the risen Christ. At the second level it is described as a fourfold loss or diminishment: a loss of the clarity with which the truth of situations, relationships, and options in human life are seen; a loss of the appropriate operative hierarchy of values by which choices and commitments are properly directed to their ends; a loss of freedom from unnecessary and unprofitable kinds of suffering; and finally, a loss of that quality of life which is not threatened or defeated by death.

There is an assumption underlying this inventory (which we inherit from medieval times), which bears reflection. It is assumed that for a human life to be ultimately coherent it has to be focused to a transcendent goal, God. Furthermore, it has to be lived unflinchingly in the light of truth; its choices and decisions have to be in a hierarchy of values fully consistent in themselves and fully expressing what it is to be human; it should be a life that does not create unproductive suffering for itself or others; and it must be lived free of the constant shadow of fear – fear of one's own mortality and vulnerability. This is, of course, a modern and rather abstract way of presenting what has been known traditionally as the loss of preternatural gifts, but it may help to clarify what it was that preoccupied medieval and subsequent theologians.

In the traditional presentation, the story line of Genesis was preserved. Hence this theology proposed that at a more basic level people are created with finite ends, the risk factor of human free will, and the prospect of muddling along, by no means guaranteed freedom from ignorance, prejudice, and self-deception, or freedom from confused motives and inappropriate hierarchy of values and choices, or from causing themselves and one another a lot of unnecessary suffering, or finally from living lives distorted by the fear of death and all sorts of injury. The theology then supposes that a general human discontent with this situation is due to the fact that at the beginning (perhaps simultaneously with creation) there was an enhancement of human nature, which the theologians called the supernatural state, and which consisted of such intimate relationship with the source of all being that it drew human lives into a higher and privileged integration. This line of thinking was used to interpret the story of the garden: in the narrative God walked and talked with the people in the cool of the evening, a privilege that was more than natural, and God had provided a garden, a place of harmony, that preceded any effort on their part to organize their lives or make sense of their world.

Basic to the interpretation supplied by traditional theology is the understanding that this heightened (supernatural) mode of existence did not and could not remove freedom. Such a removal of freedom would not lead to a supernatural but rather to an infranatural existence. But because freedom remained, risk remained, for the two are inseparable. Therefore the theology continues to follow the Genesis 3 story: the risk of freedom has in fact been realized in destructive ways, and this does not remain an individual matter but is communicated across the generations because we realize our freedom relationally. We all become the heirs of what theology came to call original sin – the sin or state of sin in which each human being originates, not because of the immediate parents but because of the whole deeply entrenched flawed use of human freedom from the beginning.

Again, this is a contemporary and abstract way of explaining what the medieval theologians and their successors were expressing in their more technical language and with a kind of realism which our contemporary sense of reality does not allow us to adopt. One aspect of this realism is that they seem to have assumed without critical question that what they were describing was really a historical, or rather pre-historical, unfolding of events in the past. Contemporary analysis of biblical narrative and imagery has pointed out that there is a kind of symmetry in the way that the beginning and the end are described. A golden era is projected into the remote past to justify and explain what it is that is hoped for the ultimate future. As will be evident from the way the theology has been set out here, we can readily see a reflection on what is actual human experience in history as compared with the conditions that would need to be met if the promise inherent in human nature were to be realized.

Theological attention in the twentieth century has largely focused on another aspect of the question. The discussion throughout the centuries had been concerned with the condition of each individual, and had assumed an actual historical event at the root of the problem in which each individual is placed with respect to the challenge to live a fully and responsibly human life. A preliminary clarification allowed attention to be drawn rather to the social situation and acculturation of human beings and to the problem of structures that express distortion of values and goals. This preliminary clarification concerned the literary genre of the stories on which the doctrine of original sin had been based. Through much of Christian history the story of Genesis 3 had been understood quite literally, at least in the West, that is to say in those churches that derived from the Latin-speaking culture of the ancient Mediterranean. With the advance of scripture scholarship in modern times it became possible for theologians to raise the question of the historicity of Genesis 3, given that the original authors do not seem to have intended the narrative in a literal sense.

Once the historicity of the foundation story was undermined, it was possible to search the tradition of the earlier Christian centuries for the meaning of the doctrine of original sin. The position was suggested and in the course of time almost universally accepted among theologians and theologically knowledgeable people that what is meant by original sin is grounded in the common observation that each of us is greatly diminished by what has happened prior to our own decisions and actions.

We are not concerned, therefore, with one event that took place somewhere near the beginning of human history which somehow queered the pitch for all that followed in human history. Rather we are concerned with the cumulative effect of choices and actions which were less than worthy of human freedom and community. Each action has consequences that tend in greater or lesser degree to make it more difficult for others afterwards to act justly, truthfully, compassionately, constructively. Cumulatively many such actions build values, expectations, and whole cultures and societies in which it is very difficult to see the reality of relationships and behavior because there is an elaborate and subtle network of complicity in place. Thus the individual, who is born a bundle of potentialities realized and shaped through relationships with others, is at the mercy of the heritage of confusion of values. It must, of course, be said that each individual is also immeasurably indebted to those who preceded for the good values that have been established, the constructive actions that have shaped society, the progress in culture and civilization that has been made.

Strange though it may now seem to thinking people, there was at first considerable resistance to the notion that the "sin of Adam" or original sin did not refer to one specific action at the beginning but rather to cumulative distortion. There was opposition, as might be expected, from those who for denominational and other reasons were committed to a fundamentalist interpretation of scripture. But there was opposition also from those who thought that this suggestion somehow undermined the universality of the need for redemption, and therefore undermined the whole Christian understanding of the human situation. The response to this has been that the need for redemption is even more clearly universal if we are dealing not with some sort of heavenly book-keeping but with the observable facts of life, namely that those growing up within a prejudiced environment of any sort will have great difficulty extricating themselves from the culturally accepted prejudices, that those born and bred among hostile and suspicious people, or among habitually violent people, will with great difficulty establish for themselves a set of attitudes different from their environment and a style of life and behavior that is not like those of the social context.

With this in place, the attention of theologians in the recent past has been drawn to the question of the social expression and cultural embodiment of the distortions due to destructive and evil deeds in human society. The focus has been on the notions of "social sin" and "sinful structures" as the real issue of the traditional doctrine of original sin. What is meant here is that the behavior of individuals in society may be far more destructive than is coextensive with their personal culpability. The complex structures of our societies set limits to what we can see, understand, and choose to do. We are caught in the web of relationships, expectations, economies, cultural activities, acculturation to particular contexts, political and administrative arrangements which seem to take on a life of their own, larger, more enduring, and more resistant than the efforts of any individual or group of individuals to change or act in opposition to such forces. Here, then, is the concrete presence of original sin or the sin of Adam, the force for evil that precedes the choices of those who appear to be choosing, preempts the actions of those who appear to be acting, and tends to crush out of existence any who persist in acting in critical opposition.

In this contemporary interpretation the doctrine of original sin appears to be not only defensible but even self-evident.

Part Two
Why the pre-critical understanding of creation and original sin is no longer tenable

Daryl P. Domning

The Genesis cosmogony disproven: the universe is ancient and large

The contemporary interpretation of original sin outlined in the previous chapter is indeed defensible; far more so, indeed, than the pre-critical, traditional, or "classic doctrine of original sin,"[1] based on some degree of biblical literalism, which one still encounters in some Catholic and much Protestant catechesis. If this contemporary understanding were as widely known and accepted in Christian circles as it should be, the doctrine would not be the stumbling block that it still is for so many. Nevertheless, I wish to argue that this contemporary understanding can still be improved on. Although it does not conflict with modern ideas on evolution, neither does it make any explicit or constructive use of them; whereas such use, I suggest, is not only possible and necessary but highly fruitful. Indeed, the Darwinian account of our origins is nothing less than "a great gift to theology."[2] Still more can the older, literalist interpretation be improved on; and this latter task, as well as the more modest former one, are the aims of this book.

For the reader with detailed concerns about whether Scripture conflicts with science's present view of the cosmos, I enthusiastically recommend a recent book by two authors raised as evangelical Protestants: a paleontologist and his brother-in-law, a Baptist minister (Godfrey and Smith 2005). They jointly and movingly recount their separate faith journeys from young-earth creationism to an understanding of Christianity much like that offered here. Indeed, Godfrey and Smith end just about where the present book begins, and theirs can be read as a very effective prologue to this one.

I realize that these and other books will not convince every believer for whom a literal interpretation of the Bible in general, and Genesis 1–3 in particular, is an essential (even the most essential) article of faith. Such believers I can only invite to meditate on the First Commandment. Scripture, after all, even Scripture understood to be the Word of God – let alone any mere human understanding of that Scripture – is still distinct from, and subordinate to, God's own Self. When we here at the base of the mountain put Scripture, Tradition, or any other *thing* on a pedestal and worship it as *the* essential ingredient of our faith, we risk forgetting the *Person* who speaks to us from the mountain top. In every age let us above all else seek God, disdaining no person, place, form, or idea in which God's Spirit may reach out to us.

The twentieth-century theological developments just summarized by Monika Hellwig have come about as a result of both insights within theology itself and discoveries in the natural sciences. These latter, especially discoveries in geology, physics, cosmology, biology, and paleontology, have swept away the ancient conceptions of a youthful, static universe which colored the biblical accounts of creation, and replaced those conceptions with radically different ones of an ancient, dynamic, and evolutionary sort.

Given the technical complexity of the science involved, and the unfortunate bouts of hostility between some scientists and some religionists that continue to erupt even today, it is natural that theologians, most of whom are not trained in the relevant scientific disciplines, have proceeded slowly and cautiously in exploring the terrain of this new evolutionary paradigm and in working out its theological implications. Scientists, for their part, tend to be even less sophisticated (typically less by far) in their grasp of theology than theologians are in science. Hence the present transitional period of tension between scientists who have become accustomed to think in terms of an evolving universe, but have scant knowledge of or sympathy for theology, and theologians who accept intellectually the fact of evolution, but do not yet feel at home in this new landscape and remain understandably uneasy about what dangers may lurk in its often-impenetrable thickets.

But we have been through all this before; and just as Christian theology, through the work of St. Thomas Aquinas, was able to profit from the intellectual advances of the thirteenth century, it is safe to say that theology will continue to profit from the scientific achievements of the present age and beyond. The message of this book is that the present understanding of evolution in particular is not merely capable of being reconciled with Christian theology, but is a positive, valuable, and indeed indispensable resource for doctrinal development.

Before developing this constructive line of thought, however, it is first necessary to sketch the ways in which evolution has come to be (mis)perceived as destructive to the Christian worldview. I take the position that science is revealing to us the physical reality of the universe and how it works, and that the truths of science cannot ultimately contradict the truths revealed in the spiritual order. In both realms, however, truth is less than fully comprehended in the formulations and dogmas of any one moment, and formulations too long left unexamined are apt to become outdated as progress is made in other areas. This, I believe, has happened to our understanding of original sin.

As was made clear in the previous chapter, biblical literalism is not the present viewpoint of orthodox Catholic or many other Christian theologians, and exegetes.[3] Nevertheless, it is a persistent concern of many sincere Christians and even entire denominations, especially in the United States. Moreover, even some Catholic writers[4] compartmentalize their thinking to the extent of accepting geological time, evolution, and even human evolution, while simultaneously retaining belief in a literal Adam, Eve, and Garden of Eden. But such a hybrid view (reflecting the persistent influence of *Humani Generis* but also older than that) depends on an untenably superficial understanding of evolution and its pervasive theological implications. Therefore it will be useful to a wider audience, of Catholics and non-Catholics alike, if I start at the beginning and outline at some length the scientific insights that have taken us beyond biblical literalism to an entirely new way of looking at the created world.

Many people today have the impression that, in the Judeo-Christian tradition at least, belief in a literal six-day creation was universal down to the time of Darwin. The truth, however, is much more complicated. Many of the Greek and Latin Fathers of the Church, for example (including St. Augustine), understood the biblical "six-day" creation story metaphorically. A unique moment in history when all living things were directly and specially created, in the modern anti-evolutionist sense, was far from being insisted on. Indeed,

> ... for many centuries prior to the birth of modern science religious thinkers had no difficulty believing in the spontaneous creativity of physical reality. Today we may smile at the medieval belief that piles of dung could generate maggots and flies, or that heaps of grain could give birth to rodents, but there was at least an acknowledgement that creation can be spontaneously creative. Ironically, it was especially after the birth of modern science in the seventeenth century that the realm of "matter" came to be thought of as so passive – and so alien to life – that the need for "special creation" of life by God became more intellectually appealing. Today's creationists, who claim to be defending ancient teachings, are often implicitly upholding a very modern set of beliefs about the inert character of matter. Fortunately science itself is now returning – in a new way of course – to an awareness of nature's spontaneity that got lost in the modern period.[5]

Thus, as the natural sciences developed in the West in the post-medieval period, the account of the origins of the universe and of humanity given in the first three chapters of Genesis became (for lack of any obvious evidence to the contrary) accepted in more or less literal form both by natural scientists and by many theologians. The events of the Reformation and Counter-Reformation, including the Council of Trent in the sixteenth century and the condemnation of Galileo in the seventeenth, did nothing to encourage departures from this growing literalism, which remained the norm down to the nineteenth century.[6]

At that time, the discoveries in geology and biology associated with the names of Hutton, Smith, Lyell, Wallace, and Darwin brought about a major upheaval in our views of human nature and prehistory. The idea of a six-day creation mere millennia in the past was shattered once and for all, giving way to a timescale for creation measured in millions or billions of years. Later, discoveries in nuclear physics made possible the development of radiometric dating and the actual measurement of when, among all those billions of years, specific natural events had occurred. Included among those events were the most radical rearrangements of the Earth's surface, with seas, mountains, climatic zones, and even entire continents shifting about as easily as stage scenery in an ever grander and lengthier play.

As the details of this history became clear, the sequence of events recounted in Genesis 1–2 fared no better than their overall time frame, despite earnest attempts to harmonize the "days" of creation with sequential periods of geological time. The appearance of land plants (Third Day in Genesis 1) before creation of the sun (Fourth Day) or of aquatic animals (Fifth Day); the appearance of birds (Fifth Day) before "creeping things of the earth" (presumably including insects, amphibians, and reptiles; Sixth Day); and, contradicting the account in Genesis 1, the creation of man prior to the existence of land plants, animals, or even rain (Genesis 2:5–7, 19) – all these are irreconcilable with the actual history of the Earth as we know it from the geological and paleontological record.[7]

Meanwhile, astronomy and astrophysics vastly expanded the spatial as well as the temporal dimensions of the known universe, and came to acknowledge a gradual physical evolution of the whole cosmos, stemming apparently from an initial Big

Bang over thirteen billion years in the past. We and our home planet shrank to very small specks in a very big universe, whose beginnings were very far removed in every way from our present state of affairs. The notion of the Earth and humanity being in any sense the center of this geometrically centerless universe came to look less and less tenable.

With such ever-expanding gulfs of time and space inserted between the world's origin and ourselves, believers in a Creator began to think in terms of a creative *process*, in which natural laws rather than direct divine fiat had to play the role of proximate cause. The successful explication of these laws by Newton, Einstein, and the physical sciences in general drew around all of nature a firm line, within which God's direct tinkering was no longer required. If the Creator, in this view, had not necessarily lost interest in the material world, He or She had at least put its day-to-day operation on automatic pilot.

Notes

1. Schoonenberg 1965, 177.
2. Haught 1998a, 574; 2000.
3. See Brown 1985 for a centrist Catholic view of modern scriptural interpretation and its theological implications. See Matsumura 1995 for a compilation of position statements from various Christian denominations that accept evolution. See Williams 2001 for a detailed exposition of the untenability of a literal interpretation of Genesis in regard to original sin.
4. For example, Zimmerman 1998.
5. Haught 2001, 54. Another factor in this theological devaluation of matter, with ancient but persistent roots, was the influence of Neoplatonic and Gnostic ideas; see section 4.13 below.
6. Williams 2001, Chap. 4, compares Protestant and Catholic as well as Eastern Orthodox views of Genesis 2–3.
7. The "six days" of Genesis 1 actually form a logical schematization of the events of creation, divided into two phases: three "days" of progressive differentiation of the primeval chaos, followed by three "days" of population of the resulting parts of the cosmos, respectively; see Boadt 1984, 114.

CHAPTER THREE

Life has evolved: how Darwinian evolution works

Most unsettling of all, biologists and paleontologists discovered that, when viewed on a timescale of millions of years, the kinds of living things we see all around us are no more stable than the eroding rocks and moving continents beneath our feet. Far from having been specially created in anything like their present forms, all living things had evidently descended from one or a few common ancestors that likely resembled bacteria more than anything else we know; and from these unpromising beginnings, they had been slowly modified along constantly-splitting lines of descent to yield the exuberant diversity of life that exists today. Along the way, moreover, countless forms were ruthlessly eliminated: perhaps 99.9 per cent of all species that have ever lived are now extinct.[1] Even diverse groups of creatures that dominated the Earth successfully for scores of millions of years, such as the dinosaurs, ended up on the same fossil heap with the shortest-lived evolutionary failures.

Furthermore, although life has not yet actually been produced from nonliving matter in the laboratory, many scientists today are confident that this will eventually be achieved,[2] along with explanations of how life could have arisen naturally on the primordial Earth – and probably on countless other planets as well.[3] As the present situation was recently described:

> For those who are studying the origin of life, the question is no longer whether life could have originated by chemical processes involving nonbiological components. The question instead has become which of many pathways might have been followed to produce the first cells.[4]

In order to make clear just what evolutionists are and are not saying that is relevant to theology, a rather lengthy exposition of evolutionary theory is necessary.[5] In this exposition I will adhere to the twentieth- (and twenty-first-) century understanding of Darwinism embodied in the so-called "Neo-Darwinian Synthesis" or "synthetic theory of evolution," both for substantive reasons (because it is extremely well supported by scientific evidence) and for rhetorical reasons (because it is considered by many to be maximally threatening to the Christian worldview). (The terms "Neo-Darwinism" and "synthetic theory of evolution" refer to the synthesis, achieved in the early twentieth century, between Darwin's concept of evolution by natural selection and the understanding of genetics gained by Gregor Mendel and others.) I wish to show on the contrary that even this most uncompromising, hard-core version of evolution, allegedly the believer's worst nightmare, is entirely compatible with Christian faith. And although it turns out that neither the pattern nor the process of the unfolding evolutionary panorama seems to hold out much comfort to the traditional, anthropocentric view of divine providence, nonetheless the core mechanism of the evolutionary process has profound and fruitful implications for theology, especially the theology of original sin.

23

Given the overall factuality of evolution, we naturally seek meaningful patterns among the lesser facts of life's history that the theory, or "metafact," of evolution organizes and explains. But despite many earlier attempts to describe evolutionary patterns as showing orthogenetic (straight-line) trends which might suggest an underlying plan or purpose, by the mid-twentieth century it was hard for most biologists to see in the family "tree" of life anything but a bush that branched and spread more or less equally in many directions. Our large brains and self-conscious intelligence, however important in our own eyes, are now viewed by many as just the peculiar specializations of one evolving lineage among countless others, and no more nor less a cause for wonder than the longevity of the giant sequoia or the whale's mastery of the deep. Like water seeping into every pore of a sponge, life has evolved its way into every niche that offered the chance of survival. As a result, the dominant impression one gets from inspecting the organic world is that, in its production of such myriads of insect and other species, *diversity* seems to have been an end in itself. When asked by a bishop what he could infer from his study of nature about the attributes of the Creator, the great geneticist J. B. S. Haldane is said to have replied, "an inordinate fondness for beetles."

To those seeking purpose in nature, the *process* of evolution, as understood by Darwin and his modern disciples, has proven even more distasteful than its pattern. Given the fact of organic evolution (now long since well established by paleontology and other disciplines), a central problem of biology was to explain the *adaptations* of living things to their environments – why, in other words, the products of evolution are so well suited to their surroundings that they appear to have been specifically tailored to those surroundings by an intelligent Designer. Virtually all biologists now agree with Darwin that adaptations arise ultimately out of two basic processes, today called mutation and natural selection. (It was, in fact, the idea of natural selection that was Charles Darwin's greatest intellectual contribution, and not the idea of evolution itself, which was already widely discussed even before Darwin's time. However, the idea of evolution only became scientifically respectable when a plausible mechanism – natural selection – was proposed to explain how it might operate.)

"*Mutation*" denotes a variety of kinds of changes in the genetic material of living things: chromosomes and other gene-bearing structures within each living cell, and the self-replicating molecules, DNA and RNA, together with other "epigenetic" elements that make up the genes and store and decode the instructions for the assembly and functioning of the complete organism. Mutations are changes in the *genotype* (the genetic code of an individual) that result from accidental damage (caused by exposure to radiation, chemicals, or other agents) or from mistakes made in copying the code during the reproduction of the cells. They can be likened to typographical errors, or to the sorts of damage that can degrade the information stored on magnetic tapes or computer disks.

Mutations in themselves are considered to occur by "chance." This does not mean they do not have causes (some possible causes were named just above), but rather that their causes have nothing to do with the "needs" of the organism for adaptation to its environment at that moment: the changes are *random with respect to adaptation*. A mutation that would benefit a population of organisms is not more likely to occur simply because it would be useful. The vast majority of mutations are in fact harmful or neutral, as would be expected of changes made at random to any finely tuned mechanism (if you switched two electrical connections chosen at random in a computer, or two bits of code in its program, the change would be unlikely to make the machine run better!). Only rarely will such random changes result in a useful innovation. However, given that the dice are being thrown constantly, among hordes of members of each species in each generation, and continuously over millions of years, winning combinations are bound to occur with some frequency.[6]

Furthermore, in sexually-reproducing species, even many combinations that are not immediate winners can be kept on hand for possible future utility as part of the large hidden store of genetic variation that is held in every naturally-occurring population but not expressed "phenotypically," that is, in the outwardly-visible forms or functions (*phenotypes*) of the organisms. This stored variation, originally produced by mutation, is constantly (and randomly) being unmasked by the process known as *recombination*, and manifested outwardly in members of the new generation, potentially influencing how they live and how well they survive and reproduce. (Recombination is the exchange of genetic material between chromosomes – a sort of reshuffling of the cards in the genetic deck as part of the process of sexual reproduction.)

Mutation and recombination together create the aggregate of genotypic and phenotypic variations that characterize every natural population. The term "variation," however, may tend to perpetuate the misconception that these are mere departures from some ideal norm which constitutes the "essence" of a species. As discussed further in section 4.13 and Chapter Seven below, one of the key insights of Darwinism is that there are no such "essences": real species and populations are *nothing but* collections of variations, embodied in groups of actually or potentially interbreeding individuals, within which the "norm" is merely the statistical average of the individuals who are members of the group at a given moment. Precisely because it has no unchangeable metaphysical "essence," but only a shifting membership of varying individuals, the species' statistical "norm" is able to shift indefinitely, and the species is able to evolve. This Darwinian "population thinking" (which is really statistical thinking) was a revolutionary break with earlier concepts of the species, and is central to understanding how adaptive evolution occurs. (A species can't evolve just any way at all, however. Given the opportunities and limitations of how genes are translated into individual development, some changes are inherently much more likely, while others are simply impossible; so in this sense evolution is constrained – unable to go in certain directions.)

In Darwinian theory, adaptation (useful change to genetic information) results from interplay of the chance factors of mutation and recombination with an *anti-chance* factor: *natural selection*. This process is analogous to the artificial selection exercised by animal and plant breeders, who select organisms with desirable traits (desirable, in this case, to humans) and allow those, and only those, to serve as parents to the next generation. The genetic information responsible for the desirable traits is thereby perpetuated at the expense of genetic information that codes for less desirable traits.

In the case of natural selection, the role of the breeder is played by the environment itself – both the physical conditions to which an organism is subjected, and the other living things around it, including members of its own species. As Darwin himself outlined the process, every species can potentially produce far more offspring than can possibly survive on a finite planet, and therefore these offspring must compete (with each other and with other species) for limited resources. Since they virtually always vary among themselves genetically in ways that are relevant to success in this competition, it is inevitable (in an actuarial sense) that those which chance to be better endowed will tend to leave more offspring in the following generation. As a result, any heritable physical, behavioral, or other characteristic that enhances their number and survival will automatically tend to be preserved and to spread in the population with each successive generation. "Natural selection is simply a statistical bias in the relative rate of reproduction of alternative genetic units."[7]

Like artificial selection, natural selection can thus be described as the nonrandom reproduction of random variants: only the "fittest" survive and reproduce, with "fitness" or competitive ability defined pragmatically in terms of effectiveness of engineering and efficiency of function. (What Darwin called sexual selection – selection for traits whose function is to attract a mate – is a special case of natural selection in the broadest sense.)

This competition, however, is sometimes misunderstood in too narrow a sense. We naturally tend to visualize the Darwinian "struggle for survival" as an actual head-to-head conflict, or at least a match race: two bull moose with antlers locked in combat; the sickly zebra falling prey to the lion while the healthy members of the herd escape; the peahen choosing the showiest peacock for her mate over less colorful suitors; the faster-growing tree hogging the sunlight and leaving its slower-growing neighbors in the shade. But competition also takes more subtle forms, in which the competitors need never come within miles of each other, and the success of one need not always be gained through direct conflict with others. A well-camouflaged mouse in one valley will go unnoticed by the hawk who spots a more visible one in the next valley. The hawk with better eyesight, or more efficient aerodynamics, will bring more food per day to its hungry nestlings. Organisms are pitted not just against their conspecific rivals, competing species, predators, and parasites, but ultimately against everything in their environment that challenges their ability to survive and reproduce. As zoologist Michael Ghiselin put it in making some of the points above: "Struggle is not the basic element in natural selection, but only a description of the conditions under which natural selection does in fact occur. 'Natural selection' designates not the struggle, but the preservation of favored races accompanying that struggle. ... Natural selection is differential reproduction with its causes, nothing more."[8]

It is also important to keep in mind that classic Darwinian evolution involves processes operating simultaneously (in the simplest case) on at least three levels: those of the genetic material within an organism, the individual organism itself, and the population. The genes mutate; the individuals are selected; and as a result, the population evolves. An individual develops from conception to death, but it does not evolve; its genetic makeup is essentially fixed throughout its lifetime. Only through turnover of individuals in the population, and the birth or immigration of new individuals with new gene combinations, does the gene pool of the population change – until, with the passage of much time, the population's new range of variation may have little overlap with its old range, or none at all. A new adaptation starts with a single mutation in one individual, becomes more frequent as that individual leaves more descendants than its competitors, may be improved by additional mutations along the way, and eventually comes to characterize most or all of the members of a descendant population. This change of gene frequencies within a population, and this alone, is evolution.

The genetic code is constantly being revised, not by an intelligent designer but by that very set of environmental demands to which the organism must immediately adapt. The environment itself sees to it that only the adequately-adapted live and reproduce; therefore the survivors' level of adaptation to that environment necessarily remains adequate or even improves with time. It never, however, becomes "perfect"; natural selection can be expected to produce only adequate adaptations that are equal to or better than those of an organism's actual competitors. (In fact, less-than-ideal though still-sufficient adaptations, and examples of jury-rigged engineering compromises in living things, furnish some of the best proofs of evolution, contrasting with the ideal perfection that a divine designer should be able to create from scratch. This is the theme of Stephen Jay Gould's well-known essay, reprinted in the book of the same name, entitled *The Panda's Thumb*.)

Importantly, adaptation is only to present conditions, never to those of the near or remote future, which natural selection cannot foresee: it is narrowly focused on short-term advantage. Although the misleading word "preadaptation" has often been used by biologists for an adaptation that turns out in the long run to be useful in some way quite different from its original function, this comes about by pure luck, and the term "preadaptation" carries no implication that evolution was in any way "planning ahead."

This constant interplay between genetic code and environment can become quite complex, especially in species (like ours) that significantly modify their own physical and/or social surroundings: genetic tendencies can influence our behavior and thus the environments our behavior creates, whereupon these new or changed environments can then generate different selective pressures to which our genes must adapt. This process can create feedback loops of unpredictable sorts. (It also makes possible, in theory, the conscious control of our own future evolution.) Furthermore, the phenotypic development of the individual is highly plastic in many species, and is largely controlled by the immediate environment, which determines which of an array of genetic possibilities is actually realized. Among certain fishes, for example, if the resident male in a group leaves or dies, the dominant female can turn into a male – and then revert to a female if a larger male shows up. "In a sense, our genes are the means by which the environment regulates our development."[9] In such cases, natural selection has programmed the genes with alternatives that can be switched on or off to suit the conditions under which the individual develops.

The beautifully simple mechanism of natural selection is, in the Darwinian view, all that is required to produce, from the raw material of chance genetic variation, all the adaptations of all the living things we observe. Indeed, it functions automatically in every system that involves imperfect copying of information and exposure of the results to competition for survival and reproduction. Not confined to living systems, natural selection has been modeled successfully in computer simulations,[10] and is even being put to use directly in the design of industrial products and computer software. For example, genetic algorithms (automated design processes based on natural selection) have already generated computer programs that can maneuver a spacecraft or control a prosthetic hand better than any software yet devised by human programmers; they have designed engine turbines for the Boeing 777 airliner, created simple robots, streamlined the scheduling of industrial production, and are finding many other engineering applications.[11] They can even invent totally novel, outside-the-box solutions that their programmers never anticipated – like the genetic algorithm that was intended to produce an oscillator from simple electronic components, but which unexpectedly achieved the same goal by evolving a radio receiver instead![12]

There is no doubt that natural selection works, and no way to stop it from working in natural populations – as shown by the rapid evolution of resistance to antibiotics on the part of disease-causing microbes, and of pesticide resistance on the part of insect pests. Natural selection is a force of awesome power in nature, and consequently a principle of unexcelled explanatory power in science.

According to Darwinian theory, therefore, individuals do whatever they can to ensure their own survival in the broadest sense: not only (and not necessarily) by maximizing their own lifespans, but by maximizing the numbers of copies of themselves in the next generation. (The technical expression for this is maximizing one's "Darwinian fitness.") In most cases this is best done by producing more offspring (each of which typically embodies half or more of a parent's genetic information). However, even a very incomplete copy of one's own genetic code confers more immortality than no copy at all; hence, outwardly altruistic behavior that benefits an individual's siblings, their offspring, or even more distant relatives can also help to perpetuate that individual's own genes, in proportion to the degree of genetic relationship (that is, similarity). In other words, by promoting the survival and reproduction of close kin, an individual perpetuates copies of some of its own genes as well, and maximizes what biologists call its "inclusive fitness" – a more subtle and "farsighted" manifestation of "Darwinian fitness." This refinement of natural selection is known as *kin selection*.[13]

In some species having genetic systems different from ours, such as bees and ants, it turns out that a female actually shares more genes in common with her sisters than with her own offspring; and in such a case kin-selection theory dictates that she should forego reproduction entirely and put all her energy into raising her nieces and nephews. This is precisely what happens in a beehive or ant colony: only one female (the smallest number possible) reproduces, and all the others devote themselves to raising this "queen's" progeny, thereby maximizing the replication of their own genes.[14]

Not even genetic relatedness, however, really sets aside the calculus of self-interest. Siblings compete, notoriously, despite their close kinship. A mother of any species readily sacrifices her life for a single offspring when it is the only one she has any hope of leaving; but in other circumstances, the interests of mother and young can be opposed, and the same Darwinian logic can dictate a different strategy. In time of famine, for example, a young female may not only suppress ovulation but may spontaneously abort or abandon (or even eat) an offspring whose nutritional demands jeopardize her own survival, if she can thereby gain the chance to live and breed again another day.

The reproductive strategies of parents can likewise conflict. For example, the father's genetic interests may be best served by large, robust young; but the mother who has to bear and nourish said young may incur less risk to her health and her own genetic investment if the young are smaller. Both sexes choose mates with an eye to their own reproductive advantage; but even where females have limited control over their choice of mates and are coerced into copulating, they may still have numerous ways to control which sperm of which males fertilize their eggs, or which eggs or offspring develop to maturity.[15] The result: a dynamic state of competition, compromise, and coevolution of reproductive attributes by each sex in response to adaptations in the other. "Recent research has provided dramatic demonstrations that reproduction occurs neither for the good of the species nor as a mutually beneficial interaction between males and females," writes biologist Tim Birkhead. "Sexual reproduction is anything but cooperative."[16] Competition, in short, is pervasive; an individual cooperates with another only when (and only to the extent that) this promotes its own interests better than any other option.

Cooperation, in consequence, is also pervasive in nature, because it is very often an advantageous competitive strategy for all concerned. Many cases of cooperation, especially in "higher" animals, can be explained by *reciprocal altruism*: I'll scratch your back because you scratched mine yesterday and may do so again tomorrow, even if we are unrelated. This kind of "doing unto others" is quite in accord with selection theory, since it is obviously motivated by self-interest; but in contrast to kin selection, it involves an essentially economic rather than genetic exchange, and is therefore less direct and more vulnerable to abuse by individuals who accept benefits but don't reciprocate.

This insistence on the role of *individual* advantage is perhaps the most distinctive characteristic of the neo-Darwinian explanation of evolution. Scientists continue to argue about whether, or to what extent, selection can ever favor the interests of groups at the expense of the individuals in those groups. Classical neo-Darwinism, however, is extremely skeptical of this possibility, to say the least. To the neo-Darwinian, the individual organism is the most important, if not the only, unit on which selection acts; and individual self-interest accordingly dominates the evolutionary process.

Putting it in the most general terms possible, *each living organism, even the simplest, consciously or unconsciously seeks (in competition with others) to maximize its own share and control of the available energy and resources, and to apply these to its own survival, growth, and reproduction*. It has been programmed to do this by that influence of its environment called natural selection, which (as explained above) is the "designer" or "programmer" that has gradually "written" the genetic code of its population and continues to maintain and upgrade it as environmental conditions change. If an individual's genetic program is such that it causes the individual to function in ways less successful in reproducing itself than are its competitors, then, in the course of generations, copies of that suboptimal program (and the individuals bearing them) will tend to decline in frequency and perhaps disappear from the population altogether.

   Thus, this powerful force of natural selection has, from the very dawn of life, worked constantly and automatically to create, and then to enforce, biological functions and behaviors that are directed toward *self-perpetuation*, in the broadest sense, on the part of all things living. (Indeed, a "living" thing is often defined as one having the capacity for self-replication.) The innate, genetically-programmed drive to perpetuate oneself and one's posterity, and to sustain this effort by arrogating to oneself as much energy and resources as possible, is the most basic and necessary of all instincts. Because this drive is patently self-centered and ultimately (in a world of finite resources) succeeds only at the expense of others, there is no violence to language in calling it, in the simplest, most objective, non-psychological and non-pejorative sense, *selfish*.[17]

Notes

1. Raup 1991.
2. Indeed, it was reported in July 2002 that a virus (which most scientists do not consider to be "alive") has already been made from scratch in a laboratory.
3. For recent discussions of this subject, in particular the inevitability of the chemical evolution of life, see de Duve 1995 and Bruteau 1997, Chap. 6.
4. National Academy of Sciences 1999, 6.
5. For up-to-date presentations of the whole breadth and depth of the evidence for evolution and its mechanisms, see current college textbooks such as Price 1996 or Futuyma 1998. The eminent evolutionary biologist Ernst Mayr (2001) sets forth the Darwinian understanding of evolution in what he calls "an elementary volume that stresses principles and does not get lost in detail." For concise popular summaries of this subject, especially useful to secondary-school teachers, see National Academy of Sciences 1999 (available online at <www.nap.edu>) and Pojeta and Springer 2001; Zimmer 2001b provides a longer treatment. Scotchmoor and McKinney 1996 and Scotchmoor and Springer 1999 are resource books for K-12 and K-16 teachers, respectively. "Teaching Evolution: An Online Course for Teachers" at <www.pbs.org/wgbh/evolution/educators/course/index.html> is designed for in-service and pre-service high school biology teachers, or anyone else interested in learning more about evolution and how to teach it. Some other useful websites devoted to evolutionary biology, supported by the National Science Foundation and endorsed by professional scientific societies, are <www.evolutionandsociety.org> and <http://evolution.berkeley.edu>. For a detailed study of the genesis, philosophy, and logic of Darwin's theory, see Ghiselin 1984. Bruteau 1997 goes into much more detail than the present volume concerning the physics, chemistry, and biology of cosmic as well as organic evolution, and compellingly portrays all of cosmogenesis as the incarnation of God. Miller 2001 gives a useful anthology of writings on the science as well as the theological implications of evolution, while Catholic theologian John Haught (2001) lucidly addresses "101 questions on God and evolution."
6. Raup (1991, 51) usefully defines "random" events in natural systems as "events that are unpredictable except in terms of probability."
7. Ayala 2001, 235. This is a broad use of the term natural selection, which more strictly is the *process* (the interaction between organisms and environment) that *results in* the observed bias.
8. Ghiselin 1984, 74. Cf. Chapter Two, note 5 above.
9. Dusheck 2002, 53.
10. For example, Zimmer 2001a.
11. Gibbs 1996, Petit 1998, Taubes 1998, Lipson and Pollack 2000, Wakefield 2001, Koza et al. 2003.
12. Graham-Rowe 2003.
13. Dawkins (1989) gives a lucid explanation of kin selection.

14. See, for example, Hölldobler and Wilson 1994, 96–101. A similar sort of social system ("eusociality") can result simply from a high degree of inbreeding, as in the case of the naked mole rat.
15. Birkhead (2000) describes these often amazing strategies in detail.
16. Birkhead 2000, x.
17. Of course it is equally defensible to make verbal distinctions here and to restrict the term "selfish" to moralizing contexts – an option for which Rolston (1999), for example, strenuously argues. But such distinctions, conventional as they are, would shed no new light; whereas my aim is to draw attention to the real but generally overlooked homology and *historical continuity* between the amoral self-centered behavior of non-human life and our own morally "selfish" acts. This justifies my consistent use of "selfish," understood in a non-moral and non-anthropomorphic sense, for this entire spectrum of phenomena. Cf. the parallels and connections between the self-centeredness of the physically starving and that of the love-starved, and the need of both for rescue or salvation, as sketched by Hellwig 1992, Chap. 1.

CHAPTER FOUR

Objections to the Darwinian view of nature

To many people, however, this beautifully simple mechanism of Darwinian natural selection seems too simple, and anything but beautiful. A long list of objections to this account of how evolution works is regularly raised by those who find the idea profoundly disturbing. Among these objections are the following.[1]

4.1 Isn't Evolution Just a Theory, Not a Proven Fact?

In common parlance, a "theory" is often no better than a guess, and hence the weakest of assertions – what a scientist would call a mere "hypothesis." But there is a broad spectrum of senses in which the word "theory" is used; and at the other, most "scientific" extreme, a theory is just the opposite: one of the *strongest* of assertions, so well tested and supported by so many facts that it is actually more worthy of belief (and harder to refute) than any single "fact," that is, any single observation (which is more likely to be mistaken than the entire mass of other observations that support the theory). A theory in this sense could even be called a "metafact," a fact about facts: it is not only factual in itself (true beyond reasonable doubt), it explains and gives meaning to a multitude of relatively trivial, seemingly unrelated facts (individual observations or data points).

Thus, the atomic theory, the theory of gravitation, the theory of relativity, quantum theory, the heliocentric theory, the cell theory, and the germ theory of disease are correctly spoken of as theories, and at the same time are among the biggest, best-supported facts we know. They are true only within limits (relativity and quantum mechanics will someday be subsumed under a more general theory; the sun is only the center of our solar system, not of the whole universe; some but not all diseases are caused by germs), but within those limits they are incontrovertibly true.

Likewise the theory of evolution (Darwin's "descent with modification"): it is both a theory in the strictest sense, and a rock-solid fact, that all organisms living today have evolved from past ones that were very different. Darwin's theory of natural selection (his explanation of *how* evolution occurs) is also a well-tested theory, as well as a fact as far as it goes (natural selection does occur and does result in adaptation and evolution); the only thing biologists still argue about is whether it explains *all* adaptive evolution. Observations, facts, hypotheses, and theories in science always remain, in principle, subject to rechecking, retesting, and fine-tuning; but once theories have passed as many tests as Darwin's, they are fully entitled to be ranked among the best-established *facts* we have.

4.2 Chance Alone Could Not Possibly Account for the Complexity of Life

Correct: it doesn't. As explained above, chance is only one component of the process. The dominant component, and the one that does generate adaptive complexity, is natural selection, which, though it is unconscious and impersonal, is the very opposite of random. It is therefore completely mistaken to characterize Darwinian evolution as essentially random, or to describe its products as simply the results of chance.

A currently popular version of this objection is couched in terms of information theory: where could the (genetic) information embodied in living things have come from, if not from an intelligent designer? The question, however, answers itself if only we pause to specify what this information is *about*. The information any organism needs for its survival (including the genetic information that generates the organism itself) is, at bottom, information about what works in its own immediate environment, the one in which it has to survive; and the most authoritative source of information on this subject is obviously the environment itself. The environment thus acts as a template against which natural selection "presses" the genetic makeup of the populations of organisms that inhabit it. Their gene pools thereby have automatically "impressed" on them the very information most relevant to their continued survival – not by accident, nor chance, nor micromanagement by an "intelligent designer," but simply because in the natural order of things this could not be avoided. Together with the occasional improvements introduced by favorable mutations (which, although individually random, are statistically certain to occur over the long haul), this simple, direct, reliable, nonrandom process of natural selection, continued over countless generations, has gradually raised the complexity of living things to the levels we now observe.

These considerations allow us to see why critiques of Darwinism such as the following are misdirected: "Though it is clear that mutations occurred, creating new information that was selected on, and though we understand fairly well the process of selection, we still have no explanation for the appearance of selectable information."[2] The trouble with this statement is that random mutations by themselves do not "create information," any more than a monkey with a typewriter creates a Shakespearean sonnet. Information cannot usefully be said to exist in the genetic code until after selection has acted. The occasional favorable mutation which ultimately enhances the information in an already-existing gene sequence is, at its origin and to the best of our knowledge, always random with respect to adaptation (that is, it is an accident), which means its occurrence does not need to be explained in terms of adaptation. Moreover, it cannot even be recognized as favorable until it has proven itself in the crucible of selection. It is only the exposure of mutational "raw material" to the test of survival in the environment that carves this random input into new "information" (which, remember, is *about* nothing other than survival in that very environment, and is thus a "report" from the field to future generations about what actually worked).

In short, the necessary and sufficient "explanation for the appearance of selectable information" is simply that the information was created (in the form of order in the population's gene pool) by the previous action of selection, which imposed an environmental "reality check" on initially random mutations in individuals.

Once created, that information continues to be selected (for or against) in each new generation, as long as that piece of genetic code survives in any living thing. Because selection has been acting since the origin of the first simple, self-replicating molecules (probably simpler by far than DNA or RNA), which presumably originated by chance combinations of chemicals, this explanation does not involve an infinite regress of causality.

Here's another way to look at this bugaboo of chance in evolution. Suppose you are writing a computer program to perform some complex mathematical calculation. At some point in the computation a random number is needed, so you incorporate a set of instructions called a random-number generator into the program and go on writing the rest of it. Do you now, upon reflection, suddenly start to look askance at or distrust your handiwork because it contains an element of randomness and unpredictability? Do you worry that this randomness will, in some mysterious way, start to seep from one line of computer code into another, and eventually propagate, virus-like, to turn all your data into gibberish and shut down your whole system? Or do you fret that the answer obtained at the end of the computation will be seen as merely the result of blind chance and not as your own intellectual achievement?

Of course not. The bits of code that generate the random numbers have been given a precise and clearly circumscribed role to play in an overall process that itself is highly ordered and anything but random – a process in which the random numbers are mere raw material. In this case, the order is consciously supplied by you, the programmer. In evolution, it is supplied by the impersonal, unconscious action of the environment via natural selection. Or, if you demand a conscious First Cause for this order, you can identify this with a God who creates the unconscious natural laws and proximate causes involved in the evolutionary process (including the opportunity for chance mutation), and then works through them.

The point is that random *factors* in the evolutionary or creative process do not render the *whole process* random in a destructive sense. The outcome may, within certain limits, be unpredictable, at least from our limited perspective; but if in our own lives we tolerate and even prize a measure of indeterminacy (in the form of free will), we can hardly complain if the history of life as a whole is not rigidly predetermined. For example, I would judge that, given enough time, the evolution of the universe was bound to produce intelligent life in some form, but that many details of the anatomy of those intelligent creatures – such as their exact number of teeth, toes, or chromosomes – were matters of historical accident and of no consequence to their Creator (see also section 8.2.5 below). Chance has a role to play in life and its evolution, but it is not the dominant role.

More generally, randomness in nature is in no sense incompatible with laws of nature; on the contrary, it is an important (and maybe even the only) source of variety and novelty (see also section 11.2 below). As Catholic theologian Elizabeth Johnson says, "chance is not an alternative to law, but the very means whereby law is creative."[3] John Haught argues that, in fact, a materialistic version of evolution (such as Daniel Dennett's) actually betrays the idea of evolution, because it reduces evolution to the fatalistic, deterministic working out of physical laws and thereby rules out the emergence of genuine novelty.[4] So, while "chance alone" does not account for the complexity of life, from this point of view we can appreciate, without apology, the value of chance as the ultimate source of the novelties which selection eventually molds into new adaptations. Even entropy – the universal tendency to disorder that manifests itself in genetic mutations – can thus be harnessed by selection to create opportunities for new and greater forms of order.[5]

I suspect, however, that when many people object to the supposed role of "chance" in evolution, they are really expressing discomfort with a different attribute of nature: what philosophers and theologians often discuss under the term *autonomy*, the world's apparent ability to operate and evolve on "automatic pilot," governed only by its own natural laws. Thus, many people have extreme difficulty accepting what physicist Brian Swimme described as follows: "Thirteen billion years ago, the universe began as hydrogen. Left entirely to itself the hydrogen became rosebushes, giraffes and humans."[6] Even if this process is acknowledged not to be purely the result of chance (that is, it involved natural selection as well), it is still hard for many to believe that "mere" inanimate matter and impersonal natural forces, without supernatural intervention, could accomplish such a thing. (The pagan, rather than biblical or Christian, roots of this skepticism will be discussed in section 4.13 below.) So perhaps it will help, here as in other sections below, if I offer a Scripture-based argument in support of the naturalistic evolutionary view.

> "Which is less trouble to say, 'Your sins are forgiven' or 'Stand up and walk'? To help you realize that the Son of Man has authority on earth to forgive sins" – he then said to the paralyzed man – "Stand up! Roll up your mat, and go home." (Matthew 9:5–6)

In like fashion: Which is easier, for God to become a human being, or for hydrogen to become a human being? To help us realize that the Son of God can also be a son of man, God has laid before us the physical evidence that, impossible though it may seem, the sons and daughters of men have arisen, by natural means, from matter that seemed as inert and powerless as a paralytic. In literal fact, *while respecting nature's autonomy and acting through natural laws,* God *has* raised up children to Abraham from the very stones (Matthew 3:9).

4.3 Natural Selection is Tautological: Those Who Survive are Said To Be "The Fit," but "The Fit" are Defined as Precisely Those Who Survive!

This misconception arose from the methodology of experimental geneticists early in the twentieth century, who were not seeking to test the logical basis of Darwinism but, assuming the reality of natural selection, merely seeking to measure its power in the laboratory. They therefore took it as a working assumption that survival reflected fitness, and used observed survival as an empirical measure of or proxy for fitness, introducing terms like "Darwinian fitness," as defined above (= representation of one's genes in the next generation). In reality, as already explained, true fitness (competitive ability) is the result of "good engineering" of the organism (however difficult this may be to measure in practice).

Those who survive are the competitively able, and the competitively able are the well-engineered: there is no logical circularity.

4.4   Natural Selection is Purely a Negative Force: It Only Removes Less-fit Individuals and Gene Combinations from the Population, so it Cannot Create Anything Genuinely New

But even a negative process can still be creative: Michelangelo carved his "Pietà" by merely removing pieces from a block of marble, yet his creativity is not questioned. It is precisely because evolution is change in a population (an interbreeding group), rather than change in an individual, that it can result in novelties: populations with different genetic character. What changes under the influence of selection is the overall genetic makeup of the population – the relative frequencies of different gene combinations in the population.

In particular, natural selection generates novelty by increasing, in stepwise, ratchet-like fashion, the probability of combinations of genes that by themselves are extremely improbable. Geneticist Francisco Ayala describes a simple experiment with the bacterium *Escherichia coli* that illustrates this. A strain of *E. coli* that cannot reproduce without the amino acid histidine is grown for a few hours on a culture medium that contains this substance, until several billion bacteria have been produced. Among these, about one in 100 million will have spontaneous mutations for resistance to streptomycin. Adding this antibiotic to the culture will kill all but the few dozen resistant cells. A few hours later, their several billion descendants are all resistant to streptomycin. Of these, about four in 100 million will carry spontaneous mutations enabling them to reproduce in the absence of histidine. These will now be able to grow in a culture with streptomycin but with no histidine – the opposite of the starting conditions. Note that the experimenter manipulates only the environments in which the bacteria breed, rather than selecting the individual bacteria that breed best in each environment, as is the case in animal and plant breeding. Thus it is truly natural selection that has, in two steps, brought into existence a population with two traits absent from the original bacterial strain. "The probability of the two mutational events happening in the same bacterium is of about four in ten million billion ($1 \times 10^{-8} \times 4 \times 10^{-8} = 4 \times 10^{-16}$) cells. An event of such low probability is unlikely to occur even in a large laboratory culture of bacterial cells. With natural selection cells having both properties are the common result."[7]

Together with this kind of constant input of wholly new variations from mutation, the selective removal of variations from the gene pool over long periods of time can bring about almost unlimited change. The Darwinian process is therefore less like marble sculpture than like clay sculpture: that which is being "carved" or shaped (the gene pool) is not static or fixed in stone, but endlessly changeable, malleable, and constantly being added to as well as subtracted from. The recurrent biblical image of the Creator as a potter or worker in clay (for example, Genesis 2:7, Isaiah 64:7, Jeremiah 18:2–6, Romans 9:21) is thus an extremely apt image of the evolutionary creative process through which we can envision the Creator working.

4.5 Favorable Mutations are Too Rare to Provide Sufficient Raw Material for the Evolution We Observe

Although mutations are the ultimate source of the variation on which selection acts, the immediate source is usually recombination, which can at any moment newly (and repeatedly) expose to selection a mutation that actually occurred many generations before. Indeed, it should normally be the case that a favorable mutation becomes available not just in the nick of time, when an organism's need for it is acute, but during a period when the organism is quite adequately adapted to its surroundings and the novelty merely improves its functioning in some way, over and above the minimal demands of survival. Moreover, when a mutation is first exposed to selection, it may be selectively neutral (hence not eliminated), and only become favorable when circumstances change – due to environmental change, or to the mutation's being placed by recombination in a different genetic context. Therefore the "window" of time within which an ultimately favorable mutation has to occur before it is needed may actually be quite generous. As microbiologist Christian de Duve expressed it:

> Chance does not exclude inevitability. Of critical importance are the constraints within which chance operates. One is the number of options. There are only two possibilities when a coin is flipped, six when a die is cast, 36 when a roulette wheel is spun and 5×10^{28} when a hand of bridge is dealt. The number may be large, but it is always finite. So it is with possible mutations. Their number is not only limited, it is not even extremely large, relatively speaking. This point is readily corroborated by experience.
>
> Antibiotic-resistant bacteria, chloroquine-resistant malarial parasites, DDT-resistant mosquitoes and herbicide-resistant weeds all have appeared in the course of a few decades – not thanks to fluke mutations but because the spread of the drugs has suddenly given banal mutations an opportunity to prove beneficial and be selected. If wide-ranging changes of this kind can take place in such a short span, evolutionary times of millions of years are likely to allow for almost every useful eventuality. Contrary to a widespread notion, evolution does not so much follow the vagaries of chance mutations – although this may occasionally happen – as do mutations wait, so to speak, for an opportunity to affect the course of evolution.[8]

4.6 Aren't There Other Mechanisms of Adaptive Evolution Besides Natural Selection, as well as Adaptations that Natural Selection Can't Account For?

Biologists continue to debate whether ordinary natural selection among individuals within populations suffices to explain all of evolution, or whether any special mechanisms, such as selection choosing among different species, are involved in evolution above the species level ("macroevolution"). Indeed, most so-called critiques of Darwinism are not arguments against evolution itself, but rather for one or another such supplemental mechanism. However, these supplemental mechanisms continue to bear the burden of proof; and given the evidence that ordinary selection can produce genetic change far faster than what would be needed to explain macroevolution, additional mechanisms seem superfluous.

A conservative view of the issue would be that, just as inches add up to miles, so-called micro- and macroevolution (see section 4.7 below) form a continuum, and it is artificial and misleading to draw a sharp distinction between them.

Sometimes particular differences between taxonomic groups have seemed to require qualitative "leaps" in genetic organization beyond the scope of ordinary mutations (and therefore beyond the scope of selection acting on such mutations). However, it is by no means proven that such "leaps" are ever really necessary, and the examples that have been proposed (such as the evolution of the eye) have typically been shown to be explainable by small intermediate steps well within the power of mutation and selection.

In many cases, the crucial steps are not "forward" but "sideways," when something adapted to one function takes on an additional, quite different role (and then perhaps loses the original function) – as when reptilian jaw bones became additionally involved in sound transmission and then turned into mammalian ear bones.[9] There are probably few if any truly complex adaptations in which this basic pattern of innovation via change of function has not played a part. Failure to take this possibility into account is a central, and fatal, flaw in the reasoning of "intelligent design" theorists such as Michael Behe (see below).

On the nuts-and-bolts level, mechanisms are known that can greatly expedite such innovation. For example:

> While biochemical complexity has many sources, one of the key concepts underlying our current understanding of biochemical evolution is that of *gene duplication*, a process whereby a gene is doubled in a genotype. As a result of this process, one gene can continue the old function, while the duplicate is freed up to be co-opted to serve novel functional ends – the duplicate gene acquires mutations that change its activity. These mutations may be preserved or eliminated through the operation of natural selection. If preserved, these mutations can lead to new functions. More importantly for our purposes, gene duplication is also a central evolutionary source of some of the *redundant complexity* we actually observe in biochemical systems...
>
> It is a hallmark of many evolved biochemical systems that there are typically multiple causal routes to a given functional end, and where one route fails, another can take over.[10]

Since our understanding of the genetic code is still in its infancy, it may turn out that there are more efficient though still purely natural ways of bringing about complex adaptations in addition to classical Darwinian selection. Here again, though, those arguing for unknown evolutionary mechanisms in addition to selection are themselves in the position of making conjectures, and do not have parsimony on their side. This includes, as well, all those who would postulate intangible vitalistic or finalistic forces in evolution, or (as in the case of biochemist Michael Behe) some direct divine intervention or "intelligent design" which guides organic evolution on certain desired paths or creates adaptations of allegedly "irreducible complexity."[11] In fact, natural explanations for such complexity are available:

> Natural evolutionary processes give rise to the redundant complexity we observe in biochemical systems. But these redundancies may also provide, in

concert with extant functional systems and structures, the *biochemical scaffolding* to support the gradual evolution of systems that can ultimately manifest irreducible complexity when the scaffolding is reduced or removed. By the operations of natural selection, some of these *biochemical arches* [by analogy with stone arches built with scaffolding] will be retained for further evolutionary elaboration, while others will be eliminated. In effect, *irreducible complexity* results from the evolutionary reduction of redundancy in *redundantly complex* systems – systems that are themselves the fruits of evolutionary processes.[12]

In short, adaptations thought to be irreducibly complex may have evolved by *simplification* from conditions that were actually *more*, not less, complex – a possibility overlooked by proponents of intelligent design.

An example of how complex adaptations to novel environmental circumstances can quickly be assembled from pre-existing parts is provided by certain bacteria that have evolved a metabolic pathway to degrade a man-made pesticide, pentachlorophenol (PCP), which did not exist in nature before 1936. This pathway was patched together using parts of other pathways that originally had different physiological functions. As one might expect for an adaptation that is less than a century old, this one is still rather inefficient and is presumably still an evolutionary work in progress![13]

A much older and far more consequential example of "molecular tinkering" is the assembly of the Krebs cycle, the most important biochemical pathway of metabolism, from "'pieces' of chemical steps previously functioning for amino acid biosynthesis." In this case, what evolved was not merely a workable system but the best possible chemical solution to the problem. Moreover, this "achievement of the fundamental steps of the Krebs cycle was not difficult at all. Almost all of its structure previously existed *for very different purposes* (anabolic), and cells had to add *just one enzyme* … to convert a collection of different pathways into the central cyclic pathway of the metabolism. This is one of the most clear cases of opportunism we can find in evolution."[14]

In somewhat the same position as "intelligent design" theorists are so-called neo-Lamarckians, who postulate natural mechanisms that would permit the inheritance of adaptive characteristics acquired by an organism during its lifetime.[15] New mechanisms of heredity and gene function continue to be discovered, and some of these do involve ways for the genetic code to be heritably modified apart from mutations of the classical sort. One example is "horizontal transfer" of genes from one species to another, such as from a bacterium to a plant or animal (multicellular organisms, however, do not seem able to use this trick among themselves). But none of these mechanisms has so far been demonstrated to reliably and consistently produce *adaptive* changes to the code, and that has always been the critical point. At this writing, and despite periodic claims to the contrary (for example, reports of such highly controversial phenomena as "directed mutations"), natural selection still remains the only proven sculptor of organic adaptation. All other known mechanisms of genetic change appear to be at least partly random with respect to the organism's needs, and therefore function as "mutations" in the broadest sense. (Historical aside: It was Darwin's own ignorance of the mechanisms of heredity that forced him to treat the subject largely as a "black box," leaving the details unspecified, and fortuitously gave his theory much of its great robustness in the face of later discoveries of the genetic details.[16])

A mechanism of inheritance, in other words, is not the only thing needed. To appreciate what else any would-be substitute for selection would have to provide, suppose that the bigger muscles developed by a blacksmith could be inherited by his sons:

> The inheritance of acquired characteristics [would] thus appear to explain adaptation. But when it is examined more closely, the appearance turns out to be deceptive. In truth, the theory takes the whole problem of adaptation for granted. That the blacksmith should make an adaptive response, growing larger muscles when larger muscles are needed, has been assumed; it has not been proved. But it needs proof. Why should a blacksmith's muscles grow larger when exercised? They might just as well grow smaller, because they are being used up. *In fact* they grow larger, but the fact itself is what needs to be explained. The extra growth is an adaptation, which the theory must explain, not take for granted.
>
> To explain the adaptive response of the blacksmith's arm the theory of the inheritance of acquired characters would have to fall back on some other theory that actually did explain adaptation. Natural selection is the only known theory that does. To grow bigger muscles when they are needed is an adaptive response. If that trait enabled the blacksmith's ancestors to reproduce more than competitors who lacked it, then it would have been favoured by natural selection. Even if acquired characters were inherited, therefore (which they are not), the true explanation of adaptation would have to come from the theory of natural selection. ...
>
> All theories of 'directed' variation must suffer from the same defect. They all lack an explanation of how the directed variations manage to be adapted to the environment in which they must live. They must either fall back on natural selection to explain adaptation, or fail to explain it.[17]

4.7   Mere Change of Gene Frequencies Within Species, or "Microevolution," is Not Sufficient to Account for Evolution of New Species or Higher Categories ("Macroevolution")

Darwin himself based his explanation of macroevolution on a simple and admittedly conjectural extrapolation from microevolution. However, no evidence discovered since gives serious reason to doubt the validity of this extrapolation.

That's the short answer; but before giving a longer answer to this objection, we must take a critical look at the terms of the objection itself. It is worth remembering that the distinction between micro- and macroevolution has actually been observed only in the writings of evolutionists and their critics, and never "out there" in nature. It is just as much an interpretation of the actual data as was Darwin's own extrapolation from micro- to macroevolution (though he did not use these terms). It is, in other words, a distinction *hypothesized* by people with an axe to grind, either theoreticians debating about evolutionary mechanisms (and postulating qualitatively different mechanisms for these two supposed modes of evolution) or creationists denying the existence of macroevolution altogether. Not all evolutionists agree, moreover, that the distinction is valid or worthwhile.

Revealingly, the distinction is often made according to a sliding taxonomic scale – particularly by creationists, when they speak of the supposed "created kinds" within (but not between) which they are willing to concede some amount of (micro)evolution. When they are talking about humans and what evolutionists view as our closest relatives, the "created kind" is always a species or (at most) a genus; but on branches of life's family tree more distant from us, the "created kind" is typically a group that taxonomists rank as a family, order, class, phylum, or even kingdom. This semantic dodge (which exploits the average layman's fuzzy notions of biological classification) conveniently allows the creationist to claim, when confronted by evidence of macroevolution within such a major group (that is, between slightly less major subgroups), that "the bacterium is still a bacterium," "the worm is still a worm," "the fish is still a fish," "the horse is still a horse," and so on – glossing over the tremendous differences among different kinds of bacteria, worms, fish, or horses. But heaven forbid the conclusion (which the same reasoning and criteria of comparison would require) that we are still apes!

Even more revealing is the creationists' simultaneous insistence that no species has ever been observed to give rise to another species (but see section 4.8 below). By this they imply that no species *could* evolve into another; but then, *every* living species would have to represent a separately created "kind." Even creationists, however, don't really go this far any more, at least in their more sober moments. In practice, nowadays they are willing to admit evolutionary diversification at low taxonomic levels and at a safe distance from our own ancestry, as noted above. For example, they allow that within the "dog kind" (roughly the taxonomic family Canidae, to an evolutionist), animals conventionally classified in different genera, such as dogs and foxes, have evolved from a common ancestor. (A recent creationist publication, while narrowly defining "dog" as the single species *Canis familiaris*, even goes so far as to include *hyenas* in the list of so-called "dog varieties." This is a howler of an admission, implying that most or all of the entire Order Carnivora – which also includes cats, bears, weasels, seals, and so on – must have evolved from a single ancestor, since no competent zoologist would classify hyenas anywhere near the dog family, let alone in the dog species![18]) Another creationist writes:

> By "evolution" I mean "macro-evolution", or *big changes* such as the transformation of a fish into an amphibian or a dinosaur into a bird or an ape into a man. ... Evolution means that dogs evolved from a non-dog ancestor. Today we observe dogs with many adaptations, even having *speciated* into domestic dogs, wolves, coyotes, etc. ...[19]

Here, "macroevolution" *doesn't* mean just change from one species to another, but something much greater; whereas one species (the created ancestor of modern dogs, foxes, and so on) has admittedly given rise to ("*speciated* into") all the other, living species of the Canidae. So, as the creationists' rhetorical need dictates, macroevolution can mean the origin of merely a new species, or a new class (such as fish to amphibian), or anything in between. This constant shifting of the ground of their argument, however, cannot be reconciled with trying to hold the line at the species boundary in other contexts – such as human evolution, or their claim that evolution beyond a species boundary has never been observed. Observed or not, creationists themselves are conceding that new species *have* originated and something more than microevolution *has* occurred, simply by admitting that those dogs, wolves, and foxes all had a common ancestor. But they are betting that their audiences won't notice that small inconsistency!

Catholic critics of Darwinism typically use the micro- versus macroevolution dichotomy in a similar but more philosophically sophisticated way. This is based on the metaphysics of Aristotle and the Scholastics, which has been considered normative to varying degrees in the Catholic Church since the fourteenth century, but especially since the nineteenth-century neo-Thomist revival. As discussed further in Chapter Seven, this philosophy holds that different "kinds" of creatures have different, unchanging "essences." Hence, evolutionary transitions between these "kinds," if they occur at all, are *by definition* beyond the power of merely natural forces like selection, and require a boost, in the form of divine intervention, in order to cross the otherwise-insuperable thresholds separating the "kinds." This system of thought logically leads to a type of theistic evolutionism in which God is periodically obliged to act in nature (as a "secondary cause," not just as a "prime mover" or immanent ground of being) to keep evolution moving and on the desired course – above all in two cases: the origin of life, and human emergence from nonhuman ancestors. Theistic evolutionists of this ilk often advocate, as explanations of apparent "gaps" between "kinds," a process of evolution by "saltation": sudden "leaps" to new levels of complexity, brought about by means that remain mysterious (and are, by implication, supernatural).

The trouble with all this is that the revolution in thought sparked by Darwin has done away with unchanging biological "essences," and instead sees the species as a segment of a continuum. It is a population of potentially-interbreeding individuals, varying among themselves in a wide range of traits, and grading backwards and forwards in time into more or less different ancestral and descendant populations, while remaining more or less sharply delimited from contemporary species. Species related as ancestor and descendant are thus to be visualized, not as discrete beads on a string, but as successive sections of a twig on a branching bush: the "boundary" between one section of a twig and the next section of the same twig is basically arbitrary, and if drawn at all it is only drawn by humans according to human-chosen conventions and for human convenience. The twig is real, but the boundary line drawn on it is artificial, like political boundaries on the Earth.

To use a different metaphor, a species is part of a genetic river flowing through time, with well-defined banks on either side, but no sharp boundaries upstream or downstream. Any observation of a species at a given moment is like a snapshot of a section of a river: a turbulent mass of moving water molecules (= a population of interbreeding individuals) in continuity with the water upstream and downstream (= ancestral and descendant species), though separate from other rivers (= unrelated species lineages). The river meanders across the landscape, passing through some towns rather than others, somewhat as a species evolves in the course of time along a narrow path through the universe of different possible forms, taking on some characteristics and not others.[20] The river (= species lineage) is real, but boundaries between species and their immediate descendants (recognized by humans long after the fact) have no more reality to the evolving organisms themselves than a state or county line drawn on a map matters to the water molecules in the river that crosses it.

Some biologists prefer to draw species boundaries at points where a single lineage branches into two, as a river branches into distributary channels to form its delta.[21] This criterion, based on a geometric metaphor, gives greater objectivity to species definitions, but it does not make the boundaries any more real to the organisms themselves, or necessarily effect any immediate change in them that would be apparent to an observer – just as we, drifting downstream on a foggy night aboard Huck Finn's raft, would remain unaware that we had been carried into one channel rather than another.

With this background, we can tackle the more substantive issues raised by the (obviously loaded) question of micro- versus macroevolution. First, can "microevolutionary" processes (mutation and selection) by themselves really produce major change?

New research on embryological development proves that simple mutations in regulatory genes (genes that control the action of many other genes) can in fact bring about radically new body plans of animals. For example, a single dominant mutation suppresses the development of some of the many legs found in crustaceans to yield the three pairs of legs seen in insects.[22] This is a clear case of how a simple micromutation in a gene that controls major aspects of development can produce a "macroevolutionary" phenotypic change (provided, of course, that it passes muster with natural selection).

Most differences between species, however, are much less dramatic. They can generally be described as quantitative differences (differences of degree); and the rates of selection-driven quantitative evolution produced in the laboratory, or observed in nature today, are far more than sufficient (by up to seven orders of magnitude![23]) to account for the slow "macroevolutionary" changes we observe in the fossil record. In fact, microevolutionary change in natural populations is so rapid (sometimes being measurable from decade to decade and even from year to year[24]) that it has even been (misleadingly) called "irrelevant" to the patterns of life's history shown by fossils.[25] It is "irrelevant" only in the sense that the profits or losses on any one day in a large business have little effect on, and are therefore largely irrelevant to, the company's year-end balance. Microevolution (driven by selection, which can only reflect immediate adaptive needs) tracks short-term ecological changes, which are often reversed within a few years, decades, or centuries (as in the familiar textbook case of industrial melanism among peppered moths in Great Britain[26]). In contrast, the fossil record, coarse in resolution as it typically is, usually filters out such rapid zigzags and only displays patterns of net change that have been averaged over much longer periods (tens of thousands to millions of years), as in the equally familiar example of body size increase in some (not all) lineages of fossil horses. In sum, the rate of macroevolution reflects the (generally slow) rate of long-term net change in the environment, not some inherent limit to the power of natural selection itself (which can produce much faster change).[27]

The supposed micro- versus macroevolution dichotomy is sometimes expressed by anti-evolutionists as a contrast between "adaptation" and "real evolution (across species boundaries)." Although these expressions misrepresent the reality of evolution, they actually make resolution of the difficulty even easier, by underlining the fact that natural selection only aims at, and can only produce, short-term adaptation to immediate needs. If those needs never changed, selection would quickly achieve the best adaptations readily attainable, and evolution would largely cease. (This is the case with so-called "living fossils": organisms lucky enough to have found ecological niches that have remained relatively stable for many millions of years.) But the target is often a moving one: many environments change over the long haul. As a result, there is no end to the task of adapting, and no limit (at the imaginary "species boundary" or any other boundary) to the amount of change that natural selection can eventually bring about.[28]

4.8 Has Macroevolution Ever Actually Been Observed, in the Fossil Record or Elsewhere?

Here again it is important to notice the biases built into the question. The premise imputed to evolutionists is that if (a) a species living at time 1 is ancestral to one living at time 2, and if (b) we were to watch carefully during the entire period from time 1 to time 2, then at some point we would see something dramatic happen: macroevolution!

But failure to see something dramatic ("to see a new species evolve today") is in fact not a valid test of the Darwinian paradigm, which has quite different, non-essentialist premises. As explained above, we no more expect necessarily to see something happen when one species "turns into" another than we expect to find a waterfall at every point where a river crosses a state line. We humans draw these artificial lines separating ancestral and descendant species, and we do it only in hindsight, after we notice that enough change has accumulated to warrant recognition of a new species. Different paleontologists will certainly disagree over when and how these arbitrary decisions are to be made. (In practice, we usually take advantage of temporal gaps in the fossil record as convenient places to draw the lines – because in parts of the record where there are no gaps, we most often find either no change or continuous change, and choosing where to draw a line becomes much harder!)

As pointed out by paleontologists who favor the "punctuated equilibrium" hypothesis, rates of evolution indeed vary widely: long periods during which little or no net change in a species occurs (presumably because there is little or no net environmental change to disturb its adaptive "equilibrium") may be "punctuated" by much shorter periods of relatively "rapid" change. But this change is "rapid" only to a paleontologist – that is, it is too quick to be observed in the fossil record, coarse-grained as the latter is. If viewed on an ecological time scale (such as the scale of a human lifetime) rather than a geological time scale, the rate of change during one of these "punctuations" would still seem very slow indeed (and probably well within the capability of natural selection), with no dramatic, "macroevolutionary" breaks that would catch our attention. (For this reason, the idea of "punctuated equilibrium" is in no way inconsistent with neo-Darwinism.)

Some theorists argue *a priori* that most evolutionary change should occur at the origin of new species, due to sudden reorganization of the gene pool. This doubtless occurs in some cases, at least when observed on ecological time scales. But when applied to the fossil record, this reasoning is liable to be circular. When marked change does coincide with species boundaries, in practice it's likely to be the other way around: only where change is observed has someone been able to demarcate a new species!

Does all this mean we can never catch macroevolution in the act? No. In special circumstances, new species have been seen to appear, as in the case of plants in which new species can arise in a single generation by means of polyploidy (multiplication of sets of chromosomes). But even leaving aside that genetic trick, which is not involved in the origins of most species, we can certainly identify cases where large numbers of new species have evolved in the (relatively) recent past, and most likely are still evolving today (though without any dramatic discontinuities being visible to us). These cases of "species swarms" include hundreds of species of cichlid fishes in East African lakes, and of fruit flies (*Drosophila* spp.) in the Hawaiian Islands – species found nowhere else on Earth.[29] These "species swarms" have demonstrably evolved within the last few thousand or last few million years, because the lakes and islands in question did not exist earlier. For example, all of the 300–500 species of cichlids in Lake Victoria have originated since about 12,400 years ago, because the lake was nearly dry before that time.[30] It has also recently been shown, in both fish and fruit flies, that the kind of reproductive isolation that separates species in the wild can be directly produced by natural selection, and within as little as a dozen or so generations.[31]

Similarly, a new species of tree sloth is known to have evolved in Panama since 8900 years ago, because the island on which it lives only became separated from the mainland at that time.[32] Mosquitoes living in the subway tunnels of the London Underground, most of which were built less than 100 years ago, have already evolved so many differences from the surface-living mosquito population that gave rise to them that some (though not all) biologists would consider them to already represent a different species.[33] Indeed, such disagreements among biologists are to be expected, because we find in nature today every gradation of species separation – from freely interbreeding local populations of a single species, to subspecies or "semi-species" that have only a limited ability to hybridize, to completely distinct species that cannot interbreed at all – just as the Darwinian view of gradual species differentiation predicts we should find.

Macroevolution has also left its footprints in the bodies of now-living creatures, in the form of vestigial organs that obviously were once functional but are no longer. These include the greatly reduced wings of flightless birds like the kiwi, the tiny hind-leg bones occasionally found attached to the pelvis in whales and manatees, and the human coccyx or tail bone. Tiny skin muscles, which erect individual hairs to increase the insulating ability of the fur or to create a visual display in other mammals, do nothing for us nearly-"naked apes" but give us "goose bumps."

Finally and most conclusively, countless instances of macroevolution are clearly documented in the fossil record, despite the creationists' impassioned denials. Although the fossil record was just beginning to be explored in Darwin's day and gave him little direct support when his ideas of evolution were first proposed, fossil documentation of macroevolution is now so routinely reported in the scientific literature (and so little remarked upon even there) that it seldom attracts any attention from the popular press. The remaining "gaps" between genera, families, orders, classes, and other major categories of living things are steadily being filled in by fossil finds every day. This is true throughout the realm of paleontology, but some of the most dramatic cases (and those best known to me) involve discoveries of fossil marine mammals in which my closest colleagues and I have been privileged to play a part.[34]

For example, a 15-million-year-long sequence of fossils from the margins of the North Pacific Ocean now documents all the significant stages by which ancient tropical sirenians or sea cows resembling the living dugongs and manatees gradually evolved into the Steller's sea cow: a strikingly different animal, several times larger, cold-adapted, and so bizarre that even a creationist could scarcely classify it in the same "created kind" with a modern dugong or manatee. This course of evolution involved the origin, not just of new species and genera, but of a new subfamily.[35]

Other intermediate fossils are now known that largely bridge the gaps which formerly separated various fully land-dwelling mammals from sea cows,[36] from whales,[37] from sea lions,[38] and from seals[39] – transitions which respectively resulted in the origins of two new orders and two new families of mammals. These four independent returns to the sea by different groups of land animals are striking instances of macroevolution by any standard. Within each of these and other major groups of marine mammals, fossils also now demonstrate many of the detailed pathways of macroevolutionary descent leading to particular genera and species of sea cows, whales, dolphins, sea lions, walruses, seals, and so on.[40]

Former gaps between entire vertebrate classes, such as between bony fish and amphibians,[41] reptiles and birds,[42] and (especially) reptiles and mammals,[43] have become so crowded with diverse intermediate fossils that the difficulty now often lies in picking out the true ancestors of the descendant groups among all the collateral fossil lineages that are candidates for the honor.[44] Any paleontologist can cite similar examples from his or her own field of specialization – not least among them the increasingly well-documented evolution of humans.[45]

Many of the highest-level connections (such as among the phyla of invertebrates, and among the kingdoms of other living things) may very well never be demonstrable by fossils, because the connecting "links" were soft-bodied, often microscopic creatures that were seldom if ever fossilized. (These connections, however, can be traced to a large extent by analysis of these groups' DNA.) Other, lesser gaps in the evolutionary record, even that of fossilizable organisms, may never be filled in, because not every species has necessarily left fossils to record its passage, and not all fossils that exist get discovered. This obvious limitation of the fossil record, however, should give creationists no comfort: more than enough fossil examples of macroevolution have already been found to forever dispose of the canard that evolution beyond the supposed "boundaries of the species" never occurs. (After all, it takes only one example to disprove "never"!) Of course, creationists refuse to concede this fact so fatal to their position. But their refusal to acknowledge the obvious continuity between species has no more sense to it than arguing that the footprints forming a single trail through the snow were each made by a different creature, because there are gaps between the footprints!

This is the testimony of the fossils. As to my own testimony: I accept (macro)evolution as a fact, not just because I was taught it, not just because it makes sense to me, but because I myself have dug evidence of it out of the earth with my own hands, time and again, in many parts of the world. I wish everyone could have, in person, this awe-inspiring and humbling experience. But even those who cannot dig up the fossils themselves can still find out, in books and museums, what we scientists have discovered – if they choose to do so. Those who have eyes to see, let them see.

4.9 Regardless of What Sorts of Evolution We May Observe Happening Today, We are Still Not Entitled to State as Fact What Happened in the Distant Past, When No One (or No One but God) Was Around to Witness It

If this argument were logically valid, we would have to make some pretty radical changes in our legal system, which routinely (even increasingly) sends convicts to prison, or even death, in the absence of eyewitness evidence. Physical evidence, in the form of fingerprints, DNA, autopsies, ballistics, and many other kinds of scientific data, is rightly considered sufficient in principle to meet the legal standard of proof "beyond a reasonable doubt" even regarding events for which no human witnesses are available. Similarly, skilled hunters, like Indian scouts in the old West, can often tell from animal tracks and other signs what sort of creature passed a spot and how long ago – and then prove it by tracking down the creature itself. And any of us can walk into our own homes and in a single glance, with all the certainty we need, tell something from the changes since our last visit about what our family members or pets have been doing there. It doesn't take a Sherlock Holmes, let alone divine revelation, to see into the past; merely an understanding of the ordinary processes and behavior of nature and society.

Natural science is no different. Although the "historical" sciences like geology and paleontology rely much less on human manipulations of nature (hence much less on eyewitnessing of events) than the so-called "experimental" sciences like physics, chemistry, and much of biology, their conclusions are no less certain. The reason is that there *was* in fact a witness to the distant past, as far back as the Big Bang itself, other than God; and unlike God, that witness can be hauled into court to testify. That witness is the physical universe itself, which has from the first moments of its existence been recording its own history in its own ever-changing form and substance. Countless "experiments" have already been done, by nature itself, and cosmologists, geologists, and paleontologists have only to observe the results. The record is not complete, of course; but it is more than complete enough for us to figure out the essentials, including not only the fact of evolution in general but many of its details as well, and to establish them as proven beyond reasonable doubt.

Related to this objection about our knowledge of the past is a more sweeping objection of fundamentalists about our knowledge in general: as a result of Adam's Fall, human intellects have allegedly become so "darkened" that we can't trust them to figure out much of anything, and hence we have to rely on divine revelation even about natural things (certainly including the possibility of evolution).

The odd thing about this objection is that it is never raised in regard to areas of human activity other than the study of our origins. How odd that geologists seek oil and gas miles underground, and reliably find enough of it to keep their companies in business – but they can't be trusted to calculate the age of the Earth and not be off by a factor of a million. How odd that biologists profitably breed plants and animals and even create a whole industry of genetic engineering – yet when it comes to how evolution might work, they don't know what they are talking about. How odd that every day, humans manage all sorts of complex tasks like repairing cars, programming computers, launching moon rockets, doing brain surgery, winning lawsuits, and even preparing their own income tax returns – and somehow the "darkening" of their intellects precludes none of this. Only when we turn to the study of evolution, it seems, do the shades come down on our brainpower.

The limitations that evolution might or might not have imposed on our brains themselves are discussed further in section 4.14 below. The sciences that reveal our evolutionary origins, however, are no more mysterious, no more beyond the average person's understanding than any of these other achievements. They all require study and effort to master, and every student has days when the intellect seems darker than others; but the methods are open to public inspection, and the methods work.

4.10   Stressing the "Selfish" Qualities of Living Things Ignores the Abundant Evidence of Cooperative, Even Altruistic Behavior in Nature

This is a crucial point, as understood clearly by Darwin himself, who stated in *The Origin of Species* (1859): "If it could be proved that any part of the structure [or, by implication, the behavior] of any one species had been formed for the exclusive good of another species, it would annihilate my theory, for such could not have been produced through natural selection."[46] So far, no such case has been found. Destructive exploitation of one species by another, via predation or parasitism, is ubiquitous, and almost equally so are cases where the interaction benefits one species while leaving the other unaffected (commensalism) and cases where both species benefit (symbiosis or mutualism). But wherever a trait of an organism benefits another species, it is found also to be somehow of use to its possessor.

Instances of cooperation among members of the same species are also common, and long posed a puzzle to evolutionary biologists until they worked out the genetic and mathematical principles of kin selection. Most cases of cooperation prove on examination to involve close relatives; and, as noted above, one's close relatives carry many genes identical to one's own.

Lions, for example, are famous for their cooperation in hunting and in rearing their young. But on closer study, the lions in a cooperative group are nearly always closely related, and even then the extent to which they actually cooperate turns out to be strictly determined by degrees of genetic relationship within the group and, ultimately, by the genetic self-interest of individuals. Wildlife biologists Craig Packer and Anne Pusey report that "[m]ale lions form lifelong alliances with anywhere from one to eight others – not out of any fraternal goodwill but rather to maximize their own chances for reproducing. Most companions are brothers and cousins that have been reared in the same nursery group, or crèche... . Once matured, these coalitions take charge of female lion groups, called prides, and father all offspring born in the pride during the next two to three years. After that, a rival coalition typically moves in and evicts them... Male lions display their greatest capacity for teamwork while ousting invaders – the situation that presents the greatest threat to their common [reproductive] self-interest." As for the maternal sex, "[a]lthough female lions do nurse the offspring of other females, they try to give milk primarily to their own cubs and reject the advances of other hungry cubs." The latter succeed most often when the female is asleep after an exhausting hunt. When females do allow nursing by cubs not their own, they are "most generous when their crèchemates are their closest relatives."[47]

As previously noted, many other cases of cooperation can be explained by reciprocal altruism; and all seem to be grounded ultimately in self-interest. The issue of how rarefied this self-interest can become and still account for (seemingly) altruistic behavior through natural selection is now a lively topic of research; but so far, no well-studied case seems to violate Darwinian principles. On the contrary, computer simulations and experiments in game theory show that cooperation can be a highly adaptive strategy even in a strictly Darwinian environment, and may even have played a role in prebiotic molecular evolution.[48] In other words, natural selection can promote cooperativeness as well as competitiveness, and the latter can even take the form of the former.

Although "cooperation" and "altruism" are sometimes used as nearly interchangeable terms, these observations indicate that more precision is needed. Probably no one set of rigorous definitions would win universal assent; but the following clarifications might serve for the present purpose. "Cooperation," to me, implies that all the cooperating parties benefit, at least potentially; none is expected to behave self-sacrificially. This would embrace both kin selection and reciprocal "altruism." True altruism, in contrast, requires that a benefit be rendered to another at some net cost to the agent's inclusive fitness. But controversy rages over whether such altruism really occurs in either humans or other organisms, or is merely an illusion that consciously or self-deceptively conceals self-interest underlying all behavior. Pope[49] provides a recent review of this topic, and dissects the complex levels of behavior involved, at least in the case of human nature (for example, stated reasons for actions, conscious and unconscious motives, and biologically-based drives). To avoid an overlong discussion of this subject here, perhaps the best strategy is to stipulate for the moment that all behavior should be presumed to be selfishly motivated until selfish motives are ruled out. This point will emerge as important later on (in section 8.2.1 and Chapter Nine).

As evolution has advanced, cooperation has in some cases increased in importance relative to the cruder forms of competition. A special and highly refined form of cooperation that occurs in the higher primates (monkeys, apes, and humans) is reconciliation behavior: limiting the escalation of arguments, and making up afterward. Frans de Waal, who has pioneered the study of peacemaking in our primate relatives, emphasizes the individual self-interest that, in fact, ultimately motivates it: "The goal of conflict settlement is not peace per se; it is the maintenance of relationships of proven value."[50]

Although de Waal properly cautions against assuming that selfish genes (he prefers to speak of "self-promoting" genes) necessarily promote selfish behavior,[51] the fact remains that self-interest and self-seeking are central to the evolutionary process – even when behavior is not *overtly* "selfish" and motives are not *consciously* "selfish." If I persist in broadly applying the term "selfish" even to these latter cases where finer distinctions of terminology could potentially be made, it is to keep the focus of this discussion clearly on the nature of the evolutionary process as a whole and its theological implications.

In short, the origins of cooperation and apparent altruism seem explainable in terms of selfishness, and selfishness may have been accompanied (and facilitated) by cooperation right from the beginning; but no one has managed (or, so far as I know, even tried) to explain the origins of selfishness itself in terms of altruism, or shown how cooperative units could persist in the absence of self-preserving behavior. Evolution is most plausibly viewed as following the same course as our individual development: we each started out in life totally self-centered, and only later learned to work and play well with others. Selfishness would thus appear to be the more primitive and fundamental condition, with altruism (if it arises at all) as its later-appearing derivative.

Nonetheless, it has been argued (for example, by mathematician and cybernetics theorist P. R. Masani) that the lives of animals are somehow morally superior to our own, as though they preserved vestiges of an Eden of cooperation in silent reproach to our fallenness. Masani regards us humans as having undergone at the time of our evolutionary emergence a "behavioral degradation (conceitedness, deceitfulness, murderousness, hypocrisy) – in moral terms a fall." He bases this opinion on the novel argument that behaviors such as intraspecific killing, infanticide, and cannibalism in nonhuman species are not only rare and abnormal, but are actually artifacts of "human intervention in the animal domain... In short, animal wickedness is man-made."[52] However, modern field studies, such as those cited above and in section 8.1 below, have not tended to support these assertions; and we will find no more eloquent rebuttal to such a view than these words of Craig Packer, long a student of African lions, baboons, and chimpanzees, as he muses here on Joseph Conrad's novel *Heart of Darkness*:

> We set such high standards for each other that we find ourselves constantly disappointed, and we become increasingly cynical as we grow older. But to claim that humankind is uniquely vile belies a tremendous naïveté about animals that is as misplaced as the most bizarre form of religion. Animals focus narrowly on short-term selfish gains, on instant gratification, on exploitation and fierce competition.
>
> By studying cooperation in other species, I have watched animals at their kindest. But what have I seen? A handful of helpers exploited by their elders, a few individuals cooperating to make war. The darkness is the behavior of animals. This is what Conrad feared. He placed it in the Congo, but the darkness lies coiled in all our hearts.[53]

4.11 No Process as Wasteful as Darwinian Evolution Could Be Part of a "Good" Plan of Creation

Many have pointed to the inconceivable numbers of organisms that have had to live and die throughout the ages in order for the present living world to evolve. How can a process so prodigal of life be seen as efficient, let alone morally tolerable?

I think the answer hinges on what we mean by "wasteful." Central to our ordinary idea of waste is the notion of *purpose*: something is wasted only when it fails to fulfill its potential or its reason for being. Spilled milk is regretted because it was supposed to have been drunk. But central in turn to this notion of purpose is our own egocentricity: we humans see the spilled milk as wasted, but the cat that laps it up sees it differently. Purpose and its accomplishment are very much in the eye of the beholder.

We can distinguish between purpose as the intended goal of an agent, and purpose as the intended function of a useful tool or resource. Some things have goals, some have functions, and some have both. In either case, "intention" in some sense is involved, implying some agent or "designer" (maybe just natural selection) to do the "intending." An agent may start out with its own goal; but then it may also become the tool or resource of another agent, and may end by having its original goal thwarted, so that it is no longer anything but that tool or resource. Yet (and this is the relevant point) it is never without its *uses*, even if we may not wish to apply the term "purpose."

We say, for example, that a life is wasted if it fails to fulfill its potential: a person may feel that her life is wasted if the purposes that she has envisioned for her life are not attained. But what are the "true" purposes – or uses – of a life? Suppose we could ask this question of another kind of creature – say, a mouse. A serious-minded mouse, acquainted with Darwinian theory, might reply that its purposes in life are to live long and leave behind as many offspring as possible. Therefore its life would be wasted if it were sterile, or to the extent that it was cut short before the end of a mouse's normal reproductive lifespan.

But now our informant's fellow mice offer an opinion. Don't take so narrow a view, they say. Even a mouse without any offspring of its own could still make itself useful *to us* by helping us rear our own litters. Or it might save one of our lives, however unwittingly, by attracting away the attention of a predator. Even a mouse who dies very young may not die for nothing. If its death is a "selective death" – that is, the result in some way of natural selection acting to remove less-fit individuals from the population – then future generations of mice will benefit from the removal of its inferior genes from the gene pool.

A cat, overhearing this interview, interjects that the question really has a much simpler answer than that. The "purpose" of a mouse, obviously, is to feed a cat; the only wasted mouse is the one that lives, dies, and decays without being eaten or engendering more mice.

But still other voices now interrupt from the soil below. We will have the last word, say the worms, bacteria, and fungi: it is *our* purpose in life to ensure that even that which decays is not wasted. Even teeth, bones, and shells that we cannot eat go to make up the fabric of the Earth and enter into its chemical and geological cycles, which help to sustain all that lives. We bear witness that nothing that lives is ever wasted!

So it seems, from this quick opinion survey, that if we take the largest view – the view of the planet's biosphere as a whole, the entire ecosystem of evolving life – there is no such thing as waste. Everything is somehow recycled, as thoroughly as the laws of thermodynamics permit. If a biological process has a "waste" product, some organism is likely to evolve the ability to use that product as a resource. Dung beetles use the manure of mammals to nourish their larvae, and the oxygen we breathe is a waste product of plant photosynthesis. Even residues that go unused by life return to the supporting Earth itself, as fossils (some even destined to be fossil fuels!).

Ultimately, even the supposedly inescapable Second Law of Thermodynamics gives back something to the cycle of life – and something indispensable. The universal energetic inefficiency that we call entropy, which constantly tends to drag ordered systems toward disorder, shows up on the microscopic scale as well, in the inevitable errors that occur in the copying of DNA. And without these mutations to serve as grist for natural selection, life could not evolve. The circle is complete: the law responsible for the ultimate "wasting" of the universe, the entropic loss of heat that on the grandest scale destines the physical cosmos to a cold, dark future, at the same time stokes the fires of life with ever-new variety and promise.

Each individual and species on our planet, then, may have its own "purposes" and potentials, but failure for one is success for another. Each, no matter how it participates in the cycles of life, helps to keep those very cycles, and hence the creative process of evolution, going. A vivid example is offered by bison on the Montana plains, where droughts strike every five to ten years:

> It seems hard. For each buffalo the shift in weather meant hunger, less chance of reproducing, more chance of dying. For the bison as a species, it meant a shrinking population. But the dry years were what kept the prairie a grassland. If every year were wet, trees would grow, the grass would go, and the bison would follow. That's not to say that those who suffered in the droughts did so for the greater good of bisonhood; they were just unlucky. But their bad luck was an inescapable part of the boom-and-bust cycle of all temperate grasslands. And it's the bust part of that cycle that ensured that the minerals from their bones nourished a grassland covered with living bison and not a woodland haunted by their ghosts.[54]

All things, then, have their uses, and living things have their individually-intended goals as well; but as theists, we can say further that all things (together with their own individual goals, if any) find their ultimate function – their highest purpose – in the intent of their Creator. If we believe in a unitary act of creation, or even in a single Creator, then the purpose that really counts, in the eyes of the Creator, is the overall purpose of the biosphere as a dynamic whole and of its ongoing cycles – whatever that purpose may be. What we see as "waste" – because it does not seem to advance our own narrow purposes – the Creator may even regard as exuberance and fecundity, and as a worthy end in itself.

In this light it is hard to see how Darwinian evolution, as an inevitable result of those natural cycles, can properly be called "wasteful," if nothing in fact is being wasted; and equally hard to see what alternative could possibly be more efficient. A similar response can be given to the charge that evolution is "cruel." If this means merely that it involves suffering, this is certainly true; but (as I will argue in Chapter Six below) it seems impossible to imagine life governed by known physical laws yet without suffering and death. "Cruelty," however, connotes the infliction of suffering unnecessarily, gratuitously, for no good reason. The relevant question then becomes: Are the results of evolution worth the suffering it necessarily entails? To which I reply: Does a mother consider her child to be worth what she suffers to bring it into the world?

Even if evolution's achievements are deemed to justify its costs, however, still another aspect of evolution that scandalizes some believers is the sheer amount of time involved: would an efficient Creator need *billions* of years of such suffering and death to accomplish his or her purpose?

Our impulse is to answer "No"; but, if we are honest, do we (any more than Job) really know enough about the business of creating worlds to make such a judgment? (Cf. section 12.3 below.) Suppose that I, in my ignorance of cookery, am scandalized to learn that roasting my Thanksgiving turkey will take four and a half hours. I decide, based on nothing in particular besides my impatience, that half an hour should suffice for the job, and order the cook to turn up the heat. Needless to say, I will be driven from the kitchen with the derision I deserve. Recipes simply cannot be hurried in that fashion. By the same token: starting with only some simple molecules, and the surface of an initially hot planet for a skillet, who are we to say that four and a half billion years are too long to cook up a human being?

And consider further: the Gospel traditions record at least 42 generations between Abraham and Jesus; since the resurrection of Christ, nearly 2,000 additional years have passed; and yet the Reign of God is still not perfected. Clearly we are dealing with a God who is in no hurry, who is willing to let things take their course according to the natural pace of this world. Perhaps a few billion years of preparation were not out of proportion to two Christian millennia that have seen so little progress on the part of us Christians. Perhaps, even, we live now in the Seventh Day of Creation, and it is impertinent of us to disturb the Creator's day off with our impatient complaints about the state of the world, when our own assigned tasks remain so far from completion!

A still more basic reason, however, has been suggested for why creation is taking so long:

> For theologian Karl Rahner the fundamental theme in Christian faith is that the infinite mystery of God pours itself out unreservedly into the creation. But since the Infinite cannot be received by a finite creation in any single instant, the world must undergo an ongoing self-transcendence, an expansion and intensification of its own being simply in order to receive this infinite gift. In its depth, therefore, evolution is *really* the world's adapting to the mystery of endless Love.[55]

When someone objects that Darwinian evolution is cruel and wasteful, therefore, we must ask: Compared to what? To my knowledge, no one has ever suggested another practical way of making a functioning, coherent material universe. Even if God used the short cut of special creation, thereby avoiding billions of years of evolution, the result would be only a patchwork of genealogically unrelated pieces that were fundamentally alien to each other, and not a unified, coherent whole, let alone a community – indeed, a family – that we should prize and protect (see also section 11.2 below).[56] And if God's intention was to have that universe bear fruit in a magnificent diversity of interrelated forms of life, including intelligent beings capable of love and able to enjoy into eternity a personal relationship with their Creator, then it is surely possible to argue that the result is worth the cost, and the wait.

4.12   The Darwinian Idea of "Survival of the Fittest" Provides Too Ready a Justification for the Elimination of Human Individuals or Groups who are Deemed Inferior, Due to Physical or Mental Handicaps, Ethnic Prejudice, or Other Reasons, and is Incompatible with Christians' Belief in the Dignity and Unconditional Worth of Each Person

It is true that Darwinism has been used in this way, for example by the Nazis, to excuse some of the worst atrocities in history. More generally, creationists blame evolutionists for having fostered racism and most other social ills (even though racism in the US today is more typically associated with creationism and opposed by evolutionists).[57]

But is it proper to lay the blame for such things at Darwin's door, or have the authors of these atrocities misapplied his ideas? Darwin sought merely to explain how evolution has managed to bring living things to their present state (and he explained this quite successfully); he did not try to impose some draconian ideology on society. There remains a great logical chasm between the descriptive statement that life up to now has evolved through natural selection, and the prescriptive or normative statement that human beings should consciously attempt from now on to control their own evolution according to the same principles, through artificial selection (or, at the very least, that they should shed no tears if poor or marginalized people somehow fall by the evolutionary wayside).

Unfortunately, some biologists, philosophers, and others (such as "Social Darwinists"), in their zeal to harvest fruits from evolutionary science for the supposed benefit of humanity, have been all too eager to make precisely this illogical leap, and to derive their morals from biology itself. Although some (such as T. H. Huxley[58]) have seen evolution as flatly opposed to morality – or (with G. E. Moore) have found in evolution no relevance to morality at all – many others, like Herbert Spencer, Petr Kropotkin, Julian Huxley, and E. O. Wilson, in their very diverse ways, have considered our morality to be itself a product of evolution, even a sign of evolutionary progress. Although the resulting attempts to construct systems of "evolutionary ethics" have generally been unsatisfactory, the subject still occasions lively debate.[59] Such attempts most often suffer from the "naturalistic fallacy": the logically problematic notion that "is" implies "ought to be." If "the survival of the fittest" has governed all past and present evolution, then by this reasoning it is the only proper principle by which to steer our own future course.

This error is easy to understand: if no other data than those of evolutionary biology are deemed relevant to the development of an ethical system, it is hard to agree on an alternative to simply extrapolating from the role selection has played in our past to the role it should play in our future. Even given the empirical fact that ongoing human evolution today operates by different rules than in the past (specifically, our evolution is now mainly cultural rather than genetic), and given that the laws of ordinary natural selection are therefore no longer applicable to our situation (let alone normative), it is not clear from science alone what other laws we should regard as normative. Some versions of evolutionary ethics, it is true, have been made to yield humane dicta that are at least consistent with those of traditional religions;[60] but other systems, like that of the Nazis, endorse ruthless elimination of the "unfit" as an ideal for human society. Which ethical inferences from evolutionary biology are correct?

Of course, other data, other "givens" besides those of biology, are arguably relevant. As discussed below in section 9.2, human and even nonhuman societies evolved ethics long ago, without any conscious knowledge of evolution; and among the many "givens" that eventually went into forming human ethics were those of revealed religion. For example, in the Judeo-Christian tradition, the dignity and worth of the individual are rooted in the revelation of the sovereign authority of the Creator and of that Creator's personal concern for the individual human creature, who has in some sense been made in God's own "image" and "likeness" (Genesis 1:26). This concern was early made manifest in God's Covenant with Israel. Christianity later expressed this in the doctrine that each individual human has a soul directly created by God. Some contemporary neuroscientists, such as Malcolm Jeeves,[61] prefer to say (in line with the non-dualistic, Hebrew and early Christian view) that each human being *is* a soul. But however this belief may be stated, its implication is that human persons have a value that individuals of other species do not.[62]

An interesting philosophical question is whether this conclusion can be justified without recourse to revealed religion. Darwinian population thinking, with its anti-essentialistic stress on the uniqueness of the individual in any species, certainly provides a good start in this direction (see also section 4.13 below). Beyond this, self-conscious intelligence itself may confer a greater dignity on the members of species that have evolved it than is possessed by those that have not. Is this a merely arbitrary assertion, or does it follow in some way (given the unquestionable survival value of greater intelligence, other traits being equal) from our strictly biological understanding of evolution? Many biologists would probably reply that questions of the intrinsic "dignity" or "value" of organisms lie outside science altogether. Others might say that if any product of evolution deserves to be called "good" in some objective sense, it is intelligence. If one draws this conclusion, a theological consequence might be that God values humans because we have intrinsic worth, and not vice versa. But I will leave this for others to debate.

In any case, it is empirically clear that the laws of Darwinian evolution are superseded in the case of humans, who now adapt to their environments mainly through cultural mechanisms. This, I think, relieves biology of the sole responsibility of providing us with our ethics, and shifts most of that responsibility onto these cultural mechanisms, which include systems of belief such as Christianity. As biologist F. J. Ayala summed it up succinctly, "the capacity for ethics is a necessary attribute of human nature and thus a product of biological evolution; but ... moral norms are products of cultural evolution, not of biological evolution."[63]

Although John Dewey[64] thought that Darwinism shifted this burden of establishing moral norms in what might be thought of as the opposite direction (from the supernatural to us), our subsequent experience has made it ever more clear that Darwinism itself is not likely to shoulder much of the load, however helpful the advice it offers. Attempts to derive satisfactory ethical systems from evolutionary principles alone are unlikely to succeed,[65] and I think the effort in any case is basically misguided. Darwinian theory is best viewed as morally neutral – though it can shed valuable light on human behavior and provide a useful background to discussions of morality.[66] In particular, by exposing the role of selfishness in our evolution, it provides a powerful antidote to that very selfishness:

> The new [Darwinian] paradigm strips self-absorption of its noble raiment. Selfishness, remember, seldom presents itself to us in naked form. Belonging as we do to a species (*the* species) whose members justify their actions morally, we are designed to think of ourselves as good and our behavior as defensible, even when these propositions are objectively dubious. The new paradigm, by exposing the biological machinery behind this illusion, makes the illusion harder to buy.[67]
>
> … Martin Luther … said a saint is someone who understands that everything he does is egotistical…. [I]t is certainly true that Darwinism, by this measure, can help make a person saintly. No doctrine heightens one's consciousness of hidden selfishness more than the new Darwinian paradigm. If you understand the doctrine, buy the doctrine, and apply the doctrine, you will spend your life in deep suspicion of your motives.[68]

In the end, there is more to human existence than human biology, and therefore no reason to rely on biology alone to supply our ethical needs. Our complex social and conceptual worlds are not reducible to purely biological causes, and in seeking ethics to govern these worlds, we should not look for them where they are not to be found. Likewise, there is more to morality than just the altruism which has preoccupied evolutionary biologists, as philosopher Elliott Sober[69] points out: sometimes morality calls for altruism and sometimes it doesn't. As enlightened evolutionists, therefore, we should seek our ethics elsewhere than in Darwinian selection. In particular, those of us who are also Christians are to follow the very different road revealed to us through the incarnation of Christ; and along this road it is never permissible to leave our unwanted by the wayside as "evolutionary waste."

4.13 The Claim that Humans are Descended from Mere Animals is an Affront to Human Dignity

I wonder why people who raise this objection never seem to look at it the other way: if the animals gave rise to us, doesn't that enhance their dignity? This reply may seem flippant, but it has serious implications, especially for Christians.

Call to mind two Scripture passages that I think are relevant. The first is the parable of the unforgiving servant (Matthew 18:23–35). A servant who was forgiven a great debt by his master turned around and refused to be similarly generous to a fellow servant who owed him a paltry sum, and he was punished for his hard-heartedness. With this story Jesus was making a point about forgiveness, but also enunciating the more general principle that we who have received generosity from God should imitate God's generosity in our turn.

Now juxtapose this with Paul's famous panegyric to Christ in Philippians 2:6–7: "Though he was in the form of God, he did not deem equality with God something to be grasped at. Rather, he emptied himself and took the form of a slave, being born in the likeness of men."

Christians view God's nature as infinitely exalted above our own or that of any other creature; whereas the difference between humans and other animals, however great, is still finite. If God thought enough of us to step across an infinite chasm and take on our human nature, while we despise our inferior fellow creatures even to the point of denying any kinship with them, are we truly imitating Christ? If our God is a humble God, are we not deluded if we pride ourselves on bearing that God's "image and likeness"?

A related theological argument is made by John Haught:

> It is especially in its capacity for intense interrelationship that the organic world as a whole bears the imprint of its Creator. God, after all, is distinct from the world not by being unrelated to the world, but by being the most intimately related Being of all (as implied in the Christian doctrine of the Trinity). Our own bearing of the image and likeness of God, therefore, also means our having the capacity for intense relationship. We show forth God's image and likeness not by separating ourselves from the wider circle of life on earth, but by intensifying our relationship to it. Evolution helps us to understand and appreciate this communion. If anything, it supports rather than undermines the biblical sense of our being created in God's image and likeness.[70]

In a similar vein, Benedictine theologian James Wiseman argues that the idea of other creatures being also in some way "images of God"

> … need not derogate from the special place that the Judeo-Christian scriptures allocate to human beings but would simply recognize that there is a whole spectrum of ways or degrees in which creatures might image forth their Creator. Accepting the existence of such a spectrum (a term which itself implies a continuum) could allow one to affirm a genuinely soul-like aspect to creatures other than humans and so avoid the need to posit the kind of "ontological leap" that Pope John Paul II referred to when noting the pronounced physical continuity that natural science affirms between human beings and other organisms.[71]

These theological considerations, however, leave unanswered a philosophical question: if human dignity depends on the uniqueness of our rationality (or the uniqueness of our creation in God's image), and if Darwinism demonstrates a continuity between humans and other animals, then doesn't Darwinism undermine the idea of our uniqueness and distinctness, and therefore undermine our dignity? Can our dignity, in other words, be shared with other species without fatally diminishing it?

For a start, we would do well to acknowledge that the similarities between other species and our own – for example, the similarities in behavior and psychology between us and the great apes – are no mere figments of Darwinian imagination. Like it or not, these resemblances are demonstrable, incontrovertible facts. Indeed, no scientific discoveries of the last half-century have shed more light on human nature and its origins than these.[72] Great apes of all species (orangutans, gorillas, bonobos, and chimpanzees) have highly individual personalities, rich emotional lives, and complex social relationships; at least some can learn systems of symbolic communication (such as American Sign Language), teach it to others, and even use it to talk to themselves; they display empathy, conciliation, and love as well as surprisingly sophisticated political intrigue, deceit, and aggression. At least some ape species even possess distinct behavioral and material cultures in different geographic regions.[73] Clearly, we have grossly underestimated them in the past; and while their intellects and cultures are certainly inferior to our own, we must admit that we have yet to plumb accurately the depths of their inner lives, or to determine the true limits of their abilities. In all honesty, we do not yet know precisely how different, or alike, they and we really are.

As for Darwinian theory, it is indeed opposed to the "essentialist" view, harking back to Plato and reflected in modern creationism, that different species have fundamentally different, eternally separate and unvarying "essences." Living species instead consist of populations of unique individuals that vary in countless ways, and this very variability is the raw material of evolution. In this sense, as Bradie says in discussing James Rachels's ethics of "moral individualism," Darwinism "promotes the importance of individual differences" in contrast to species differences, and challenges the idea that humans are in a special moral category.[74] (At the same time, of course, this stress on individual uniqueness potentially enhances the dignity of individual humans, as distinct from humanity as a whole.)

Moreover, a property such as "rationality" (or "intelligence") is made up of many distinct traits and abilities, all of which vary among human individuals and are shared to various degrees with non-human animals. Even if we seize on a single one of these traits (such as self-consciousness, or an ability to reflect on moral choices) to define what is "uniquely human," it is difficult to imagine that that trait came to characterize the human population by other than a gradual process, making the "animal–human" boundary irreducibly fuzzy.

But a boundary need not always be absolutely sharp in order to be real. A difference in degree can also be, or become, a difference in kind. After all, "because there are sometimes fuzzy lines between species and varieties (subspecies) does not mean that the concept of a species should be abandoned; there are no sharp boundaries between the colors in a rainbow, but color is nevertheless an important tool when negotiating traffic signals!"[75] We recognize so-called "emergent" properties in all sorts of developmental processes and hierarchical systems, both living and non-living. Continuity across boundaries, and threshold effects at those boundaries, are complementary, not contradictory, aspects of evolution. A simple rise in temperature changes ice to water to steam, with profound consequences for physical properties. A tadpole transforms itself imperceptibly into a frog; a caterpillar becomes a butterfly. The invention of computers has shown that the attainment of a certain kind and level of "mere" physical complexity can yield "intellectual" abilities (such as solving math problems or playing chess) equaling or far exceeding those of humans. If improvement in some or all of the abilities making up "intelligence" might even cross the threshold to self-conscious moral reflection, then why might evolution not give rise to moral agents? Even if it did, a distinction between morally reflective and morally non-reflective beings would still be defensible for us today – or at least no more problematic than the task of distinguishing degrees of moral responsibility among defendants in our courts of law, when questions of immaturity, insanity, or mental impairment are raised. As for our extinct, "subhuman" ancestors at the evolutionary boundary between non-human and human, as a practical matter we are not called upon to judge their actions.

The extinction of these intermediate forms that once connected our species to others has left a significant gap in the continuum of traits that once existed. This gap is convenient for the practical purposes of our classifying and moral philosophizing today, notwithstanding its having come about by historical accident (or even if, as many suspect, our early ancestors widened the gap by giving our closest primate relatives a premature push off the family tree, as we may soon do to today's apes). In any case there is today a clear boundary between human and non-human abilities, making us unique among *extant* species on this planet. If human dignity requires uniqueness, there it is. If one allows that our dignity as a species can be a matter of degree as well as kind, then we can still retain our moral stature and responsibilities while acknowledging the dignity of our fellow creatures and our commonality of descent with them. As two students of chimpanzee culture put it:

> ... we found some people quite disturbed to realize that the characteristic that had appeared to separate us so starkly from the animal world – our capacity for cultural development – is not such an absolute difference after all.
>
> But this seems a rather misdirected response. The differences between human customs and traditions, enriched and mediated by language as they are, are vast in contrast with what we see in the chimpanzee. The story of chimpanzee cultures sharpens our understanding of our uniqueness, rather than threatening it in any way that need worry us.[76]

Although Darwinism in one sense regards humans as a species like any other, it also emphasizes the differences among species that arise out of the variations among individuals. The differences, especially in our case, are as obvious and important as the similarities, and Darwinism helps explain how those differences came about. If Darwinism does not assert for our species a special dignity, it is because "dignity" itself is not part of the vocabulary of science; but we need not look to science alone to provide our sense of dignity, any more than our sense of ethics.

A final point about our common descent from "mere animals" is made by Lutheran pastor and theologian Steven C. Kuhl, who traces hostility to this idea back to the heresy of Gnosticism:

> Gnosticism is a pseudo-Pauline version of the Christian faith that first emerged as Christianity encountered Greek thought and Hellenistic culture. Gnosticism [posits] an absolute dualism in the nature of things: two Gods (one wrathful and evil; one merciful and good) and two corresponding worlds (one

material and evil; one spiritual and good) with humanity being essentially spiritual but caught in the material. Although Gnosticism was roundly rejected in the second and third centuries by what became known as orthodox and catholic Christianity, nevertheless, it keeps emerging perennially, in many and various forms, among Christian as well as other religious movements, not the least of which is the "New Age Movement." Gnosticism is a creation-denying spirituality in that it identifies essential humanity, not with the created world, but with the divine itself. In my judgment, the fact that many "Christians" today find the idea of "common descent" objectionable is due not to a genuine biblical, catholic and orthodox understanding of Christianity, but to the fact that "Christian Gnosticism" has once again reemerged in the hearts and minds of many people.[77]

When we disavow any genealogical relationship to "mere animals," in other words, we are implicitly denying that we (we spiritual beings!) are really part of God's material creation. Actually, this idea of the Gnostics (that the human body is alien to the human personality or soul) can be traced still further back, indeed to Plato and the Neoplatonics, who had great influence on early Christian thought, especially that of the Greek Fathers.[78] Like that other Platonic notion, essentialism, this one too is opposed to Darwinism – and to the orthodox, incarnational Christian faith. It is supremely ironic that such a dualistic, unbiblical stance should be taken by biblical literalists who insist on the importance to Christianity of the Genesis creation account – which unequivocally affirms that we were formed "out of the clay of the ground." (Genesis 2:7)

Ultimately, of course, whenever we allow ourselves concern over affronts to our dignity (whether as individuals or as a species), we are flirting with the sin of pride, rather than practicing the Christian virtue of humility (let alone imaging a humble God). But this is a moral issue on which evolution (contrary to fundamentalist opinion) is neutral. Biblical literalists feel that descent from "mere animals" diminishes our dignity; but the implications of evolution really cut both ways. For which is more flattering to my ego: to think that in making my species, the Creator spent only an instant (or six days at best); or to think that God was willing to devote *over thirteen billion years* to the task of bringing *me* into existence?

The Hasidic teacher Rabbi Simcha Bunam of Peshischa said, "A spiritual seeker should carry two stones in a pocket. On one should be inscribed, 'I am but dust and ashes.' On the other, 'For my sake was the world created.' And the seeker should use each stone as needed."

4.14   If Our Brains are Merely the Evolutionary Products of Blind Natural Processes, How Can we Trust our Own Thinking, in Science, Morality, or Anything Else? In Particular, What if our Religions Themselves are No More Than Useful Adaptations to our Environments, and Have No Objective Truth Value?

Some evolutionists (for example, the philosopher Michael Ruse) have indeed taken the position that selective advantage rather than metaphysical objectivity determines our patterns of thought. However, even Ruse concludes that "in real life this does not matter, for we have the world of common-sense reality... [T]he Darwinian epistemologist need not really fear even the deepest barbs of scepticism. Total deception of the kind that the metaphysical sceptic threatens is a far-from-plausible notion."[79]

The reason why the evolutionary origin of our brains does not vitiate our ability to apprehend truth, even theological truth, is simple: truth, in the sense of ambient reality, constitutes the ultimate criterion of evolutionary advantage, and not vice versa. It is illogical to think that just because some perception has survival value and has therefore evolved, it is for that very reason delusory. Just because we have evolved to perceive light does not mean that light itself is a delusion; on the contrary.[80] In natural selection, the condition of the organism is constantly referred back to and tested by the demands of the environment. The organism (via the mutation or genetic variant) proposes, the environment (via natural selection) disposes. In the long run, therefore, selective advantage lies in conforming oneself to the demands of objective reality, not in illusory systems having a merely subjective basis.

Suppose I see two hungry wolves approaching from my left and two more from my right. According to my personal conviction (or simple inability to add), 2 + 2 = 3. Confident that I am more than a match for any three wolves, I elect to stand and fight, though I would flee from four. My idiosyncratic mathematics costs me my life. In the long-term evolutionary struggle for survival, mental illusions cannot be useful.

An actual experiment shows that this argument does not apply to humans alone. In her studies of wild African lions, biologist Karen McComb played tape recordings of strange lions to groups of female lions defending their territories. She found that "females would attempt to repel groups of tape-recorded females only when the real group outnumbered the taped invaders by at least two. Females can count, and they prefer a margin of safety. Numbers are a matter of life and death..."[81]

From simple arithmetic to religion may seem like a large leap, but the same human brains perform both functions. Of course, any given system of belief may be erroneous, because the individuals who constructed it were fallible. Our nervous systems and sense organs can and do generate systematic errors, such as optical illusions. But the fact that our individual or collective powers of reason are themselves able to recognize and correct such errors shows that our basic cerebral equipment, used with due care, can be trusted. The truth value of our more complex belief systems is difficult to determine for reasons intrinsic to the belief systems themselves, not because evolution has wired the circuits of our brains to give deceptive results.

Ironically, it is the anti-evolutionists who are more vulnerable to doubts about whether we can trust our own intelligences. Fundamentalist Protestants (and maybe even some Catholics) continue to hold the doctrine (noted in section 4.9 above) that our minds are so clouded by the effects of Adam's sin that human reason (for example, in the form of evolutionary science) cannot be trusted and we must seek aid in a literal reading of the Bible to gain correct knowledge of worldly reality.[82] But this doctrine itself, of course, is an example of human reasoning (it is contradicted by Matthew 16:2–3 and Luke 12:54–56: "If you know how to interpret the look of the sky ..."), and consequently it undermines its own credibility, leading to a logical dead end. Evolutionists, in contrast, have a firm basis for trust-ing their own thought processes and (if they are so inclined) for appreciating them as part of the Creator's handiwork, and they need not fear this kind of logical paralysis.

Wait a minute, says the materialist skeptic. This is an intolerably naive view of how our brains work! Strong arguments, and even experimental evidence, can be presented to show that natural selection has molded us to behave in certain ways – altruistically, for instance – while remaining unconscious that our "true" motives are evolutionarily-selfish ones. In fact, sometimes it may even be positively advan-tageous for us to think our motives are exactly the opposite of the selective forces that really drive us.[83] Our mental processes may well include all sorts of mecha-nisms for self-deception aimed at getting us to behave in adaptive ways; after all, with natural selection it's our behavior that counts, not whether we understand it. Therefore, the objectivity of our thoughts is highly suspect at best, above all in matters of religious belief, which can often be shown to serve the selfish interests of individuals or social elites. And if our conscious minds are so thoroughly in the dark about how our subconscious is responding to Darwinian demands, then least of all can we believe any longer in so-called "free will," or the moral responsibility it implies!

The skeptic has a point. It is common knowledge that we often deceive ourselves, especially in imagining ourselves to be more benevolent, just, and saintly than we really are. This tendency is so deeply ingrained that it is doubtless a product of our evolution, and very likely it has some selective value. But beyond this point the skeptic's argument also undermines itself; and it is precisely the issue of free will that brings this fact into sharpest focus.

Everyone agrees that we *seem* to have free will: right now I can choose to move my hand right or left, up or down; I can entertain one thought in place of a differ-ent one; and no amount of introspection reveals any internal or external compul-sion to do either thing rather than the other. Still, for all I know this freedom could be an illusion, just as the skeptic says. But if it is, then my innermost mental processes are untrustworthy: even when I examine my own thoughts, divorced from any sense impressions from the outside, I cannot rely on my perceptions. Even less, then, can I rely on my thought processes when they operate on sensory data (which may themselves be subject to optical or other illusions) or when they are influenced by my social surroundings or political ideologies. Therefore I cannot hope to know what is really going on outside my head, any more than inside it; so truly objective empirical science is impossible. Science, like religion, is at best an illusion perpetrated by natural selection. But it was empirical science that discovered Darwinian evolution and generated the evidence for selection-molded self-deception! Thus has the skeptic's torpedo circled back to sink its launcher – just as did the fundamentalist's distrust of the "sin-darkened" human intellect.

My conclusion? As far as freedom is concerned, the philosopher may perhaps be permitted radical doubts about free will; but as a practicing scientist I have no such liberty. If I doubt so immediate a perception as my own free will, still less can I believe anything I think I see in nature, and therefore I cannot do science. Likewise for doubts about the capacity of human logic and intellect. Whatever deceptions about myself evolution may have programmed into my brain (and I am willing to grant they could be many and varied), science cannot, without destroying itself, go so far as to impugn mental functions on which our knowledge of the world depends.

Putting it another way, self-deception (like free will) belongs to the category of "higher" mental functions which are only manifested by the more intelligent and socially sophisticated creatures. Phylogenetically speaking, these "higher" functions are relatively recent add-ons to the much older, simpler, and presumably non-self-deceptive mental equipment with which less sophisticated creatures view the world. Self-deception in particular appears to be adaptive not in general but only in the narrow social context of attempts to deceive others: as Bradie phrases it, "[w]e are, in effect, self-deceptive about our practices of deceit."[84] Meanwhile, our old reliable perceptive equipment is still there in us, is used by us in most situations, and is accessible to us whenever we wish to take a truly hard, critical look at our own behavior.[85]

It has also been noted that "our accurate depiction of reality – to others, and, sometimes, to ourselves – is not high on natural selection's list of priorities."[86] No, but our accurate *perception* of reality at the deepest level is a different matter, at least when the reality in question lies outside ourselves. As we explore science, theology, or any other intellectual realm, that accuracy of perception (and potentially, depiction) is one thing on which we must and can rely.

4.15   The Theory of Evolution Has No Need of God; and If There is No God, There is No Basis for Morality, and Our Lives Have No Meaning or Purpose

This is the ultimate objection to the evolutionary account of our origins – the most profound objection, the most complex one, and the one that truly motivates most of the sincere theists who reject evolution or the Darwinian account of it. As discussed at some length by Pennock,[87] some of whose points I draw on here, the attraction of special creationism or "intelligent design theory" for many Christians really has nothing to do with what the scientific data do or do not show. The real issue for them is the existential crisis arising from their perception that Darwinian evolution undermines the very meaningfulness of human existence. Although I hold that this perception is a false one and that their fears are groundless, I take very seriously the concern of these sincere believers; indeed, my desire as a fellow believer to allay this concern is one of my main reasons for writing this book. Certainly, no defender of evolution should underestimate the persuasive power of this existential objection to an evolutionary worldview, or belittle those who raise such a deeply human concern.

So complex, in fact, is this issue that it might take another book the size of this one to explain in full why evolution does not exclude meaning for human life. Since the present work is intended to address the different (though related) topic of original sin and evil in the light of evolution, space is lacking here to do more than outline some of the main points.

First, even if God's existence is denied, a moral and meaningful life is still possible. As empirical proof of this, we have the personal testimonies of atheists themselves, many of whom profess to find life very meaningful indeed. The goodness of many things, after all – love of family, beauties of art and nature, work well done – can be appreciated in themselves, and even atheists can live moral lives in which they find value and pursue good purposes of their own choosing.[88]

In fact, as noted above in section 4.12, the supposedly "godless" evolutionary viewpoint can even give us, theists and atheists alike, a more honest understanding of ourselves. It reveals that what we are pleased to call our "morality" is far from being a single faculty, exalted in its spiritual purity. Instead it cobbles together high-minded philosophy and religious ideals with lowly self-interest, social conventions, and canny politics, the joints between these being all whitewashed over with hypocrisy. Realizing how mixed this bag of motives is, and how it (like all our other adaptations) has been assembled piecemeal over the course of our evolution, aids the examination we all need to make of our lives, regardless of our religious views or lack thereof.

Second, it is an error in any case to say that evolution makes God unnecessary, despite the emphatic assertions of this metaphysical (not scientific) view by such prominent evolutionists as Richard Dawkins, Daniel Dennett, William Provine, E. O. Wilson, and others (some of whom even claim that evolution is their "religion"). It is true that evolutionary biology, like all other natural sciences, seeks to explain the workings of nature without invoking supernatural causes; but this is emphatically not a denial that the supernatural exists. In technical terms, the naturalism of science is merely methodological and not metaphysical.

If evolutionary science's naturalistic methodology is a problem for creationists, then they should be equally scandalized by such technical fields as automobile repair or computer design, which also assume that God does not intervene in the workings of the machine. But surely no one thinks that engineering, chemistry, or other sciences imply that God does not exist; indeed, no one ever seems even to notice that these sciences too, just like evolutionary biology, "have no need of God." The fact that some individual evolutionists, chemists, and car mechanics are atheists is simply irrelevant; there is nothing in any natural science that *requires* atheism. This point is emphasized even by the atheistically-inclined agnostic Michael Ruse.[89]

When the atheist asserts that science disproves the existence of God, he or she is misrepresenting science and substituting it with a personal philosophy.[90] Furthermore, since science cannot address the philosophical question of why anything at all exists, the theist remains free to postulate a creator for the universe within which science operates. When the theist asserts that God is necessary to explain the very existence of a physical world, legitimate natural science is simply unable to comment one way or the other.

The issue of purpose usually arises in the form of the question: What purpose or goal does the evolutionary process (or the evolutionist's universe) itself have? Believers understandably fear that the answer must be "None." But here we must choose our words carefully.

As was indicated in section 4.11 above, if we take the word "purpose" to be equivalent to "goal" (or "intention" or "desired result"), then substitution of any of these terms makes it clearer that such a thing implies some sort of consciousness, even if only a very rudimentary one, in which the intention or desire resides.[91] (Biologists do sometimes use expressions like "the purpose of an evolutionary adaptation"; but this means only that the existence of the feature in question is accounted for by its having been selected to perform a certain desirable function, and it does not literally refer to a mind that does the desiring.[92] Here I am using "purpose" in a more restricted sense.)

At this point, of course, a lengthy debate could ensue over whether just any "living" thing – for example, the first self-replicating molecule – would qualify as "conscious"; and if so, whether other complex physical and chemical systems, or even the simplest physical entities, and the universe itself, would also have to be credited with conscious "purpose" in this sense. This latter argument might be made on the grounds that, if mind has its basis in the material brain as many modern thinkers accept, mind or "inwardness" of some sort must be at least incipiently present in all matter (as P. Teilhard de Chardin, A. N. Whitehead, and others have in fact argued[93]). I agree that intention (like mind, life, and other evolutionary novelties) has indeed emerged gradually over the course of an evolutionary history in which sharp boundaries can seldom be drawn, and that this may well point to an "inwardness" in all matter. However, it is perhaps most useful in the present context to use terms like "intention," "goal," and "purpose" only in connection with an emergent form or degree of this "inwardness" that is not manifest below the level of what we call life.[94]

Given this understanding of the terms, it follows that an impersonal, lifeless process of nature cannot be said to have a "goal" of its own choosing; it can only have *effects*, which are more or less predictable, or uses to which it can be put. Individual organisms, in contrast, can and do have at least one goal, toward which they universally and actively (even if unreflectively) strive, namely survival; whereas unconscious natural selection *in itself* has only the effects of constantly maintaining and maximizing their short-term ability to survive, and, in the longer term, of predictably generating by-products that include novelty, diversity, and ultimately (in isolated cases) intelligence.

To the atheist, this is all there is to the story; but the theist will see at once that any overarching purpose (function) there may be for the evolutionary process and its products *as a whole* can properly be said to reside only in the mind of the Creator who uses this process as an instrument. In other words, what we might call the "normative" purpose of evolution, or The Purpose Of The World As A Whole (as distinct from the purposes or goals we conceive for our own little selves), is that purpose or function (whatever it might be) which the Creator conceives for it. The absence of a "purpose" *within the evolutionary process itself* need not mean, therefore, that purpose is absent from the totality of all that is; we must simply be careful not to look for that purpose in the wrong places.

One of the wrong places in which theists are prone to look, however, is the idea that God has a plan or design that evolution is carrying out in detail. Theologian John Haught, following French philosopher Henri Bergson, argues instead that such a specific divine design "would close off the future and render our own lives essentially pointless, since all outcomes would already have been laid out in advance."[95] Ironically, it is creationism and "intelligent design" theory that fail to leave room for us creatures to play a meaningful role in history; whereas evolution can be seen as allowing the creation to become truly autonomous and able to enjoy a mature relationship with its Creator. (See also sections 8.2.4, 12.3, and subsequent sections below.)

Another dead end to be avoided is a too-limited idea of the world's purpose. Usually this takes the form of identifying this purpose simply with ourselves. "Thinking of ourselves as the final end of cosmic creation, we may no longer feel the need to participate as one species among others in a complex earth-community."[96] This prideful alienation from the rest of nature has caused untold ecological havoc. Although intelligent forms of life such as us (or superior to us) may indeed be the highest aim the Creator had in mind, it is dangerous hubris on our part to assume that God does not also place great value on our evolutionary "inferiors." As shown in section 4.13 above, a sense of our evolutionary connections to our fellow creatures provides a healthy corrective to this kind of pride. Philosopher Beatrice Bruteau even interprets the commandment "Honor your father and mother" in this context: "Do not despise your ancestors and antecedents; remember your predecessors in the universe-process, the way by which you have come to this point."[97]

Finally, whatever self-chosen values the atheist may find meaningful, there is no need for the theist to be satisfied with these, because (as explained above) evolution does not do away with God. There is still freedom for the theist to accept revealed religion as a more explicit guide to what is good and what is willed by God. In particular, this book testifies that acceptance of the essential tenets of the Judeo-Christian revelation is not precluded (in fact, is facilitated) by an evolutionary understanding of creation; the conflict perceived by some arises from a misunderstanding of the nature of Scripture. But the only plausible purpose of a communication as out-of-the-ordinary as divine revelation is to guide us out of our otherwise insoluble existential problems, not to satisfy our idle curiosity about matters in nature that we can discover for ourselves.

Above all, the believer who looks forward to the fulfillment of God's promises will find an evolutionary outlook to be as congenial to his or her faith as could be desired. "Evolution, … instead of banishing meaning from our lives and the cosmos, as many have interpreted Darwin's 'dangerous idea,' now allows us to experience our lives and the whole cosmic process as a purposeful struggle to realize the promise of new being."[98] Being products of evolution means being parts – *active* parts – of something vastly bigger than ourselves: an ongoing creation, a continuous chain of life on Earth stretching over more than three and a half billion years without an instant's interruption, and embraced in a still vaster universe some ten billion years older. Would any lesser world befit an all-powerful God? Can any believer's awe of the Creator be diminished, rather than deepened, by such a vision of the creation? Can such a display of divine patience and faithfulness, extended over such eons of unbroken continuity, fail to inspire confidence in the plans and promises of such a God?

If, then, the purpose and proper conduct of life are the real issues in the creation–evolution debate, we may ask the creationist: What do you believe the purpose of human life is, and why would an evolutionary origin for our species keep us from fulfilling it? If we have been made, by *whatever* process, in God's image, then what will separate us from the love of God? (Romans 8:29–39)

To summarize the scientific understanding thus far: the vast extent of the universe, the great age of the Earth, and the reality of cosmic and organic evolution have been established beyond reasonable doubt; and Darwinian natural selection remains unshaken as the cornerstone of modern biology despite a century and a half of skeptical critique and meticulous test. This breathtakingly powerful yet simple – and fundamentally selfish – process still appears both necessary and sufficient to solve what was once among the greatest puzzles of nature: how living things came to be so well adapted to their environments. Paradoxically, selection's relentless maximization of individual advantage even seems able to explain the origins of altruism and the first steps toward true moral consciousness. As we shall see further on, its inherent selfishness is also the key to one of the greatest puzzles of Christian theology and anthropology: original sin.

Notes

1. For detailed responses to a wider variety of arguments and critiques raised by anti-evolutionists, see any of numerous recent works and resources including Kitcher 1982, Godfrey 1983, Gastaldo and Tanner 1984, Strahler 1987, Berra 1990, Price 1990, Hughes 1992, Futuyma 1995, Shermer 1997, Schopf 1998, Kelley et al. 1999, Miller 1999, Pennock 1999, Skehan and Nelson 2000, Pennock 2001, and Rennie 2002; the *Reports of the National Center for Science Education* (Berkeley, CA) and its website <www.ncseweb.org>; and the Talk.Origins archive <www.talkorigins.org>. Alters and Alters 2001 is particularly designed for use by teachers at the secondary and postsecondary levels, and Kelley et al. 1999 specifically addresses the question of "How does one teach evolution with integrity and meet the challenges posed by creationism while being sensitive to the religious beliefs of students?."
2. Schmitz-Moormann 1997, 84.
3. Johnson 1996, 15. Johnson also documents at length the compatibility of this view with Thomas Aquinas' ideas about God's action in the world.
4. Haught 2000, 1, 86–87.
5. This was also pointed out by Monod 1971.
6. *National Catholic Reporter*, Aug. 10, 2001, p. 5.
7. Ayala 2001, 235.
8. De Duve 1996.
9. See, for example, Hopson 1987 and section 8.3 below.
10. Shanks and Joplin 2000, 28, 29; emphasis in original.
11. Cf. Behe 1996, reviewed by Blackstone 1997; see also critiques by Miller 1999, Pennock 1999, Shanks and Joplin 2000, and in Miller 2001. Haught (2000, 3–5, 45–46, 54) explains why arguments like Behe's for "intelligent design" are "both apologetically ineffective and theologically inconsequential."
12. Shanks and Joplin 2000, 30; emphasis in original.
13. Copley 2000.
14. Meléndez-Hevia et al. 1996; emphasis in original.
15. See, for example, Steele et al. 1998.
16. "Recognizing that the laws of heredity were so ill-understood as to be almost useless in theoretical application, [Darwin] shifted to the developmental aspects of the problem. Like a military strategist obtaining victory by choosing the right battlefield, he elaborated [his] theory along lines which would eliminate heredity from relevance to the questions at issue" (Ghiselin 1984, 164–165).
17. Ridley 2001, 58–59.
18. Sherwin 2004.
19. Morris 2004; emphasis added.
20. This evolution of an unbranching lineage is technically spoken of as "anagenetic" change.
21. Such evolutionary branching is termed "cladogenesis."
22. Ronshaugen et al. 2002.

23. Reznick et al. 1997.
24. Cf. Barton 2000.
25. Gould 1998.
26. A recent reassessment reaffirms that industrial melanism "is a product of selection," although the selective force(s) involved have not been completely clarified; Sargent et al. 2000.
27. Gingerich 2001 analyzes this phenomenon in detail, concluding (p. 142) that "[w]e can speak of microevolutionary and macroevolutionary change, of microevolutionary and macroevolutionary patterns, and of history on microevolutionary and macroevolutionary scales, but it is not clear that there are any separate microevolutionary or macroevolutionary processes. Generational change is so rapid that stability [in the morphological form of organisms] comes soon, but the stability is often perturbed [by environmental change] and then new microevolutionary and macroevolutionary patterns begin."
28. Some imaginable outcomes, however, like animals with wheels, are ruled out by physiological laws, or simply by the limitations – resulting from past history – of the material that selection has to work with in a particular case.
29. See Barlow 2000; Carson and Clague 1995. Carroll (1997) also has a good discussion of the East African cichlids.
30. Johnson et al. 1996; Barlow 2000; Sturmbauer et al. 2001.
31. Barton 2000.
32. Anderson and Handley 2001.
33. Byrne and Nichols 1999.
34. Cf. Barnes et al. 1985.
35. Domning 1978, 1987; Domning and Furusawa 1995.
36. Domning 1999, 2000, 2001, 2002a.
37. Thewissen 1998, Thewissen et al. 2001, Wong 2002.
38. Berta et al. 1989.
39. Koretsky and Holec 2002.
40. For a recent review of the present state of knowledge of the evolution of secondarily-marine vertebrates, including marine reptiles and birds, see Mazin and Buffrénil 2001.
41. Zimmer 1998.
42. Ackerman 1998.
43. Hopson 1987, 1994.
44. Creationists seized with glee on a recent announcement of one specimen from China that was initially considered transitional between dinosaurs and birds but was soon revealed (by evolutionists) to have been in part faked by an unscrupulous fossil dealer who pieced together parts of two different animals (*Acts & Facts* 29(3), March 2000). The creationist versions of the story conveniently omitted mention of the numerous other, unfaked fossils from the same area in China, reported by Ackerman (1998) and others, which make the same point: that the former "gap" between reptiles and birds is rapidly being filled by a host of intermediate forms.
45. See, among many fine recent treatments of human evolution, Tattersall 1993, 1995, Tattersall and Schwartz 2000, Campbell and Loy 1996, and Klein 1999; also the Institute of Human Origins website, <www.becominghuman.org>.
46. Darwin 1959, Chapter VI, sentence 223.
47. Packer and Pusey 1997.
48. Sigmund 1993, Nowak et al. 1995, Sigmund et al. 2002. Also falling into this category would be "the more ancient cooperative structure of homeostasis" among chemicals in protocells that Freeman Dyson (2001, 151) thinks preceded even the beginnings of replication in the origins of life. Dyson emphasizes the inherent tension between replication and error-tolerance, sees the former as having been introduced later, and portrays the "replicators" as the locus of all "selfishness." But if the first cells, as mere "error-tolerant tangles of nonreplicating molecules" (Dyson 2001, 149), managed even to survive (= maintain their homeostasis) long enough to contribute to evolution, then the internal cooperation among their constituent molecules must be

seen as contributing to their survival; and, as noted above, promotion of one's own survival is just as appropriately termed "selfish" as promoting one's own reproduction.

49. Pope 2001.
50. De Waal 1989, 231.
51. De Waal, in Floyd 2000.
52. Masani 1985, 308.
53. Packer 1994, 277.
54. Lott 2002, 48.
55. Haught 2001, 59; emphasis in original.
56. Perhaps this helps explain why many fundamentalist Christians who do believe in special creation seem little concerned about damage to our environment, and even argue that the imminence of the end of the world and the Last Judgment makes our planet expendable. They view our Earth, in fact, as something alien to themselves, hence little to be cherished – much as the Gnostic heretics viewed the world (see section 4.13 below).
57. Moore 2002.
58. Huxley 1894. Also theologian Gerd Theissen 1985; see note to section 9.2.2. below.
59. For example, Nitecki and Nitecki 1993, Bradie 1994, Farber 1994, Rottschaefer 1997, Ellis 1998, Murphy 1998.
60. For example, J. Huxley 1931, 1953, 1957; Wright 1994.
61. Jeeves 1998. See also Murphy 1998 on this "nonreductive physicalism."
62. This Christian doctrine does not necessarily rule out the possibility that "a God-given, soul-like aspect has characterized all forms of life from the beginning and that this aspect has been becoming more profound with evolutionary increases in complexity" (Wiseman 2002, 95). See also section 4.13 below.
63. Ayala 1998, 570.
64. Dewey 1910.
65. Bradie 1994, Farber 1994.
66. For interesting explorations of this subject, see Wright 1994 and Pope 1994.
67. Wright 1994, 338–339.
68. Wright 1994, 375–376.
69. Sober 1993.
70. Haught 2001, 29.
71. Wiseman 2002, 92; referring to John Paul II 1996, 415. Regarding the diversity of ways in which creatures image their Creator, St. Thomas Aquinas says that "because [God's] goodness could not be adequately represented by one creature alone, He produced many and diverse creatures, that what was wanting to one in the representation of the divine goodness might be supplied by another." (*Summa Theologiae*, I, q. 47, a. 1)
72. Smuts 2000 provides a concise, accessible essay summarizing these discoveries. See also section 8.1 here.
73. Whiten et al. 1999, Whiten and Boesch 2001, van Schaik et al. 2003. Some species of whales and dolphins have also evolved cultural faculties, in the sense of social learning; Rendell and Whitehead 2001.
74. Bradie 1994, 158; discussing Rachels 1990.
75. Marshall 2001, 81.
76. Whiten and Boesch 2001, 66–67.
77. Kuhl 1998, 93.
78. Cf. Ong 1960, Clarke 1996.
79. Ruse 1986, 206.
80. As pointed out by Tudge 2002, 43.
81. Packer and Pusey 1997.
82. Of course, biblical literalists have always honored this doctrine more in theory than in practice. "Ironically, despite his conviction that Scripture provides a bulwark against human error, in the

end Calvin depends more on his private reason than on a careful exposition of Genesis 2 and 3" (Williams 2001, 52).

83.   See, for example, the extensive discussion of this topic by Wright 1994, 263–379.

84.   Bradie 1994, 120. Cf. Niebuhr 1941–43, 2: 108–109: "The self never follows its 'natural' self-interest without pretending to be obedient to obligations beyond itself. It transcends its own interests too much to be able to serve them without disguising them in loftier pretensions. This is the covert dishonesty and spiritual confusion which is always involved in the self's undue devotion to itself."

85.   Cf. the passage from Wright quoted in section 4.12 above.

86.   Wright 1994, 265.

87.   Pennock 1997.

88.   Cf. J. Huxley 1957.

89.   Ruse 1986, 191.

90.   A common argument for atheism is that a good God would not permit evil and suffering. Though touted as an example of scientific logic, this ironically involves an elementary mistake in experimental design, which requires that all the variables in an experiment be controlled except for the one being studied. It also involves an illicit shift in the underlying premises. The God whose existence is ostensibly being tested by observations of evil is, ordinarily, the Judeo-Christian God, who is postulated to be (among other things) all-knowing and all-powerful. But the "experiment" ignores this and substitutes a straw God, one who knows no more than the experimenter does about what compelling reasons there may be for tolerating evil. Furthermore, since God is not under the experimenter's control and has not agreed to cooperate with the experiment (and may have good reasons not to), it cannot be shown that all the relevant variables have been controlled. The atheist's flawed "experiment" is therefore inconclusive.

91.   Cf. Murphy 1998, 487: "The shift from Aristotelian to modern biology can be described as the recognition that *intentional purpose* is not a category that applies at the purely biological level at all, but only begins to apply in the natural order at the psychological level." As noted below, some would say that it is now time for the pendulum to swing back some distance on this point.

92.   See Ayala 2001, 238–245.

93.   Cf. Haught 2000, Chap. 10.

94.   Ayala 2001 discusses in detail the applicability of terms such as "teleology" and "purpose" in biology, and comes to similar conclusions.

95.   Haught 2001, 112.

96.   Haught 2001, 141.

97.   Bruteau 1997, 175. She goes on to say, neatly summarizing the same argument I make here, "Nevertheless, you are now going to transcend that self-centered path, and the way by which you have come is no longer the way by which you will go. This is a phase transition. There will be new rules in a new world. Although stealing, deceiving, killing, and raping worked well in the natural selection world, it is no longer necessary for you to do these things. You are released (redeemed) from them. As the Talmud says, 'Under the sun there is nothing new, but over the sun there is something new.'"(Leviticus Rabbah 28:1).

98.   Haught 2000, 142.

No more Adam and Eve:
science refutes monogenism

A further point of past conflict between evolutionary science and theology is the concept of monogenism (descent of all humans from a single couple), upon which the Catholic magisterium has in the past found it necessary to insist, as noted in the Introduction. Biologically, of course, it is not impossible that a human population of the present size might have descended from a single couple. The process of evolution, however, normally takes place in breeding populations much larger than two, and there is no reason to suppose that humans were exceptional in this regard. And even if our ancestry could somehow be traced to a single pair, that pair would certainly have been members of a species or population from which they did not outwardly differ. On the whole, monogenism finds no positive support in biology or paleontology, and it has long been fair to say that it seems less than probable *a priori*.

Indeed, the magisterium, by its very acceptance of the possible evolutionary origin of "Adam," has already opened the door to polygenism, at least in the case of one couple. As Jesuit theologian Karl Rahner[1] pointed out, we have to accept that "Eve" came about in the same way as "Adam"; if one of these first parents evolved, it is untenable to deny that both did. It is then difficult to see how the mutually independent evolution of two human beings from lower forms could have been limited to these two only.

Advances in molecular genetics, however, have now made possible a much stronger statement than these. It turns out that, while a hypothetical human population of the present size might have descended from a single pair, the particular human population that now exists could not have. Our present population includes far more genetic variety of a very ancient sort than could possibly have been transmitted to us by way of a single human couple.

The evidence for this has been summarized by the geneticist Francisco Ayala,[2] and has to do particularly with a segment of human DNA known as the *DRB1* gene. This gene, part of a large and important set of genes whose functions are involved in tissue compatibility and defense against pathogens and parasites, exists in many alternate forms among humans as well as other primates. These alternate forms of the same gene evidently arose as modifications of a single ancestral form of the gene, and thus have a genealogy of their own. In fact, some of the forms of *DRB1* found in humans are more closely related to forms found in monkeys and apes than they are to other versions of the same gene found in humans! What this means is that these different versions of the gene originated in populations of primates that lived long before the first humans. Those early primates passed along some of the versions to us, and other versions to other species of primates living today. Based on the times (estimated from the fossil record) when different lineages of primates diverged, Ayala and his coworkers have calculated that the human *DRB1* genes started diversifying some 60 million years ago (very early in primate history, not long after the extinction of the dinosaurs), and that 32 out of the 59 human versions of *DRB1* were already in existence around 6 million years ago, at the time our ancestry diverged from that of chimpanzees and gorillas.

Now we come to the crucial point: as Ayala[3] explains,

> If 32 *DRB1* gene lineages have persisted since 6 [million years ago], it follows that no fewer than 16 individuals could have lived at any given time over that long span. The minimum number of individuals must have been much larger, because the probability is effectively zero that all 16 individuals in a population would be heterozygotes (that is, carrying two different genes), each for two genes different from all others.

In fact, the number must have been very much larger indeed. After taking into account a variety of relevant factors and using several different approaches (including computer simulations) to estimate the population size at any given time that would have been needed over the long haul to preserve those 59 different genes, Ayala concludes that "human ancestral populations must have consisted of 100,000 or more individuals over their long history."

But could there not have been even one, very brief time in all the history of *Homo sapiens* when our population was much smaller than that? As Ayala indeed notes, "[i]t has been suggested that a population bottleneck occurred at the transition from archaic to modern *H. sapiens*, some 100,000 to 200,000 years ago." He then goes on to calculate the smallest size of this bottleneck that could be consistent with the genetic data, and concludes that "the minimum possible number of individuals at a bottleneck is at least 4000...." However, this number (like the population estimates above) refers only to the approximate number of *synchronously reproducing* individuals, which was probably no more than about two-ninths of the actual "census" population. Hence, to maintain a long-term reproductive population of 100,000 we must reckon with an actual population size of 400,000 to 500,000, and even a "bottleneck population" of 4000 would correspond to 15,000 to 20,000 actual individuals. Given the present genetic makeup of humanity, therefore, a bottleneck population as small as two people (or even eight, in the case of Noah's Ark) was clearly a mathematical impossibility. (The same, by the way, is likely true of most living species, blowing out of the water the notion that each descended from a single pair on the Ark.)

What, then, of the studies of a different kind of DNA (mitochondrial DNA or mtDNA, which we inherit only from our mothers), which have indicated that all people living today may have in common a single female ancestor?[4] In fact, despite some erroneous interpretations in the media, this evidence does not mean that this so-called "mitochondrial Eve" was either the first human female, the only one living in her time, or the mother of all humans who lived after her. Rather, the fact that we may all share such an ancestor is merely a quirk of the genetic laws of inheritance.

Suppose that several females are alive at a particular time, each with a different version of mtDNA. Whenever one of these females or her direct female descendants fail to leave a daughter, her mtDNA lineage dies out (even though she may have male descendants). Eventually the original number of mtDNA lineages is reduced to only one, which is possessed by all the females in the descendant popu-lation.[5] Ayala[6] also explains why the "mitochondrial Eve"

> is not the one mother from whom all humans descend, but rather a mtDNA molecule (or the woman carrier of that molecule) from which all modern mtDNA molecules descend. The inference that all humans descend from only one or a very few women ... is based on a confusion between gene genealogies and individual genealogies. Gene genealogies gradually coalesce toward a single DNA ancestral sequence ..., whereas individual genealogies increase by a factor of 2 each generation: An individual has two parents, four grandpar-ents, and so on.... Coalescence to one ancestral gene originally present in one individual does not disallow the contemporary existence of many other ances-tors from whom we have inherited the other genes.
>
> The conclusion warranted by the mtDNA analysis is that the mitochondrial Eve is the ancestor of modern humans in the maternal line. Any person has a single ancestor in the maternal line in any given generation. Thus, a person inherits the mtDNA from the great-grandmother in the maternal line, but also inherits other genes from the three other great-grandmothers and the four great-grandfathers (about one-eighth of the total DNA from each great-grandparent). The mtDNA that we have inherited from the mitochondrial Eve represents a four-hundred-thousandth part of the DNA present in any modern human. The rest of the DNA, 400,000 times the amount of mtDNA, was inher-ited from other contemporaries of the mitochondrial Eve.

Ayala next calculates the number of these ancestors who were contemporaries of the mitochondrial Eve: given certain assumptions, there would have been some 10,000 individuals in the reproductive population alone, "which is almost certainly an underestimate." Taking this together with estimates by other researchers, and "despite considerable uncertainty, the mtDNA results yield a mean [reproductive] population size that ranges between 10,000 and [more than] 50,000 individuals throughout the Pleistocene [that is, roughly the last 1.9 million years]. This finding is consistent with the estimate based on the *DRB1* [evidence] of a population size on the order of 100,000 individuals over the last 60 [million years]."

The maternally-transmitted mtDNA has a male counterpart in the Y chromo-some, which is passed from fathers to sons. Studies have been done of a section of the Y chromosome called the *ZFY* gene, which is thought to be involved in the maturation of testes or sperm. This gene is identical in all men examined so far, and indicates that all modern humans share a single ancestor in the paternal line. As Ayala emphasizes, however, "this '*ZFY* Adam' is the individual from which all humans have inherited the *ZFY* gene, but he is not our only ancestor in his gener-ation. We have inherited the other thousands of genes from many other contem-poraries of this Adam."

A crude analogy may make this clearer. Genes, or different versions of genes, can be thought of as inventions (mutations) that originated with specific individu-als. Today's airplanes, for example, are all historically derived from the one first flown by the Wright brothers in 1903. But this does not mean that the Wrights invented all of our present technology, or that they were the only humans (or inventors) alive in 1903 – let alone that Orville and Wilbur were the parents of the present human race!

The foregoing evidence makes clear that monogenism – the hypothesis of a single pair of parents for the entire human race – is not scientifically tenable, and it should no longer be relied on as a presupposition for theology, or accepted as a valid inference from other theological propositions.[7]

Notes

1.   Rahner 1967.
2.   Ayala 1995.
3.   Ayala 1995.
4.   Cann et al. 1987.
5.   See de Duve 1995 and Laden 1998 for readable discussions of this point.
6.   Ayala 1995.
7.   Cf. Haag 1969, 107: "Whether mankind originated in monogenism or polygenism is a question which only science can answer; it is not a theological question. The thesis of polygenism cannot be rejected on the basis of original sin."

CHAPTER SIX

How suffering and death fit into evolution

Science has made yet a further departure from a literal reading of Genesis 1–3. Whereas much interpretation of the biblical account has attributed all physical suffering and death to the sin of Adam, the fossil record clearly shows that living creatures not only died but killed and ate each other, and even competed in evolutionary "arms races," for many millions of years before the first human sin.[1]

(Lest anyone try to argue, by the way, that all fossil animals interpreted as predators were merely feeding on the carcasses of the already-dead, conclusive and elegant proof to the contrary is provided by countless fossil clamshells that are found pierced by neat little holes. As can be observed happening today, these holes were laboriously drilled by predatory snails, which need not have bothered if their prey were already dead: clamshells automatically spring open when the clam dies.)

This pervasive suffering of animals has proven to be the toughest problem of theodicy – more problematic even than human suffering, which as a rule can be plausibly blamed on human sinfulness. Darwin himself was appalled by the scale and intensity of suffering in nature, as epitomized by the larvae of parasitic ichneumonid wasps:

> I had no intention to write atheistically. But I own that I cannot see as plainly as others do, and as I should wish to do, evidence of design and beneficence on all sides of us. There seems to me too much misery in the world. I cannot persuade myself that a beneficent and omnipotent God would have designedly created the Ichneumonidae with the express intention of their feeding within the living bodies of Caterpillars, or that a cat should play with mice.[2]

Even though Darwin never saw the movie "Alien," he was as repelled as we are by the life cycles of parasites (technically called parasitoids) that kill their hosts in such nasty fashion. But in fact, there is a wide spectrum of ways to eat and be eaten, to kill and be killed – some quick, some agonizingly slow – and neither the parasitoids nor the cats lie at either end of the painfulness scale; they are well within the mainstream.

A frog snaps up a fly in an instant; it seems to us quick, clean, and painless (and we don't care much for flies anyway). A leopard may take minutes to down and dispatch an antelope. Sharks or killer whales may spend hours attacking a large whale, partly eating it while it is still alive. Especially virulent bacteria or viruses, such as the ebola virus, "flesh-eating" staphylococci, or bubonic plague, can kill within days. Other infectious agents and parasites, like those causing malaria and AIDS, can live off us, and inside us, for years or decades till we finally succumb (with more or less discomfort) to the chronic and cumulative damage they inflict.

Other species find it more profitable to exploit their victims without killing them. The cookie-cutter shark makes its living by sneaking up on larger sea creatures and taking neat round bites out of their sides. Many parasites are careful not to lose their happy homes by killing their hosts. Some of these may even evolve into symbionts, working out détentes from which both parties benefit.

These are all consequences of the general requirement that living things consume something to keep on living. Green plants have found a way to get by on just minerals, water, and sunlight; but those of us more complex creatures not content with vegetating have no choice but to eat other living things. And, except in our own case, into this choice compassion cannot enter. The spider or snake may need to paralyze or kill its larger prey with venom before eating them, so as not to be injured by their struggles; but if the end is mercifully quick for the victims, evolution provides this not for their sake but only for the killer's own safety and convenience.

The cat gives a good example. Well-fed pet cats (but usually not wild ones) "play" with birds and rodents, perhaps because they are out of practice at killing, and/or unsure of their skill when faced with a possibly dangerous opponent like a large rat (and not good at judging whether a given opponent, such as a small mouse, is dangerous). In such cases the play-like hesitation in killing reflects, not enjoyment, but ineptitude or insecurity on the part of the cat. They may also prolong the chase because they have been starved of the hunting activity they instinctively seek, and overreact when given the chance. Alternatively, females may "play" with prey as a byproduct of their instinct to bring it back alive to their kittens and teach them how to kill.[3] Whatever the explanation, they have no reason *not* to inflict what strikes us as torment. Natural selection offers no reproductive payoff (to either predator or prey) for anesthetizing prey animals, or killing them quickly, simply in order to spare them from suffering: neither party will live longer or have more offspring as a result. Hence prey often suffer.

Mostly, we are no different from other predators in this regard. Suppose you are hungry and see something good to eat, but it happens to be bigger than you – say, a whale. You have a pointed stick; but a wounded whale, or even one mildly annoyed, can easily put an end to your hunger in a way you'd rather avoid. What do you do? The solutions humans have tried have ranged from taking their chances with the pointed stick, to poisoning the stick, to shooting the whale with firearms, to injecting it with compressed gas, to wiring a harpoon so as to electrocute the whale, to using a cannon-fired harpoon with an explosive warhead (the currently preferred method).[4] All these techniques typically cause slow and painful deaths (not devoid of risk to the whalers), and no more humane method has been devised (even though some hoped that the latter two techniques would minimize the whales' distress). A lot of animals are just plain hard to kill – not surprising, since evolution has engineered them to resist being killed. The larger the prey is relative to the predator, the more it is likely to suffer, simply because the predator has a harder, hence longer and messier, job to do. So, if the ingenuity of (at least somewhat) compassionate humans has failed to banish pain from whaling, is it any wonder that evolution itself has done no better in other cases of predation?

The issue then becomes: Why wouldn't a good God employ a means of creation that *could* do better? My answer, expanded on below, is that there *is* no such means permitted by natural laws in any material universe; and God has opted to create a material universe.

The result has been the billions of years of "nature red in tooth and claw" that scandalize many thinking people. Unlike most of the violence in our TV shows, however, these eons of bloodshed were not gratuitous, but absolutely unavoidable given the ground rules of natural laws in general and competitive Darwinian evolution in particular. Nor are pain and death merely unfortunate byproducts of the process: they play essential, *constructive* roles in the evolution of life.

Physical suffering is a necessary consequence of animals' ability to feel pain. This ability is in itself a good thing, with important survival value: in fact, an adaptation. It is a safety device that warns animals of the presence of danger (often in time to prevent serious injury, by recoiling from sharp objects or fire, or by vomiting up some nauseating toxic substance), and it conditions them to avoid similar occasions of danger in the future. Whenever we are tempted to imagine that life would be better if we could not feel pain, we need only reflect on the plight of those who actually are in this situation, such as victims of leprosy (Hansen's disease). The disfigurements that result from some forms of this terrible malady, such as the loss of fingers and toes, occur because the disease attacks the sensory nerves of the extremities. Unable to feel pain from fire, cuts, or other injuries, the victim fails to react to them immediately, and thus suffers serious wounds which can subsequently become infected. In time, the cumulative damage results in deformity or loss of the injured members, which could have been avoided had the body's natural defense – its sensitivity to pain – not been disabled.

Physical suffering in general is caused by the unwelcome stimulation of pain receptors or other sense organs (often for no such good reason as the above) through accident, disease, or environmental conditions. Much of the resulting discomfort (pain, heat, cold, fever, diarrhea, nausea, even anxiety) may serve no apparent purpose; but even this is deceiving. For example, we may indeed vomit even when no really dangerous poison is in our stomachs, but this is erring on the safe side.

> The cost of a false alarm – vomiting when no toxin is truly present – is only a few calories. But the penalty for a single missed authentic alarm – failure to vomit when confronted with a toxin – may be death.
>
> Natural selection therefore tends to shape regulation mechanisms with hair triggers, following what we call the smoke-detector principle. A smoke alarm that will reliably wake a sleeping family in the event of any fire will necessarily give a false alarm every time the toast burns. The price of the human body's numerous "smoke alarms" is much suffering that is completely normal but in most instances unnecessary.[5]

Like physical false alarms, proneness to anxiety also serves the protective function of promoting the avoidance of danger. The price (given the natural variation around a population's mean) is a certain percentage of the population who suffer excessively from anxiety and phobias. On the other hand, anxiety can also impel individuals to seek companionship and safety in numbers, thereby enhancing their survival. Selection could then have set up a positive feedback, intensifying the tendency to feel this emotion during times of stress. This could have been a powerful stimulus to the evolution of our strong social bonds – an unexpected dividend from the fear and anxiety we tend to list among life's liabilities.[6]

Psychological suffering is pain in a more than metaphorical sense: physical pain, and emotional distress such as the pain of social exclusion, both seem to be experienced and regulated by the same parts of the brain and hence share a common neuroanatomical basis. This perception of social pain has the smoke-alarm value of "alerting us when we have sustained injury to our social connections, allowing restorative measures to be taken."[7]

Suffering may also occur as an unavoidable byproduct of normal and vital biological functions. A classic, and evolutionarily interesting, example of such a function is human childbirth, which is painful and risky to a degree unique among mammals (cf. Genesis 3:16). This came about in human evolution because of conflicting selective pressures for efficient bipedal locomotion in adults (which calls for a narrow pelvis) and for a larger brain in their offspring (which requires a wider pelvis for the child's head to pass through). The anatomy of human females today represents an evolutionary compromise that is uncomfortable, to put it mildly.[8] But the payoffs (hands free for toolmaking, and a human brain to guide them) surpass even this painful price.

Suffering, then, may have been intrinsic to both our physical and our social evolution – which is to say, to the origins of our very humanity. What better testimony to its value could there be? More fundamentally, the ability to feel pain, and the surprising advantages that sometimes go with it, are in general so important to our survival that natural selection could not have failed to endow us with it, despite the fact that it makes possible (indeed, unavoidable) what we call suffering. The latter is perhaps easier to bear when we understand it as part of the price we pay for being human and, ultimately, for staying alive.

And as for death: given that any species would soon overrun the planet if all its offspring survived (and we have all seen calculations of how soon the progeny of one pair of houseflies would fill the known universe!), it is obvious that crowding and exhaustion of resources would have brought evolution to a halt billions of years ago if literally nothing ever died. Moreover, it seems doubtful whether complex forms of life could evolve on a finite planet in the absence of death to provide turnover in their gene pools. Natural selection would lose much of its force if no undesirable genes could ever be eliminated. (Likewise for our cultural evolution, where old ways and old ideas seem to pass away only with the deaths of those who hold them! As a scientist once commented, "Science progresses one funeral at a time.") Even if older individuals eventually stopped reproducing, the lack of recycling of the materials tied up in their bodies would soon choke off evolution, by simple sequestration of critical resources.

But benefits that survivors derive from the deaths of their contemporaries would not, under Darwinian rules, seem to explain how death itself (and the eventual deaths of the survivors) could have evolved through natural selection. Is it conceivable that death could somehow be of adaptive value to those that die? Seemingly not, if survival is the ultimate goal of adaptation; but recall that the survival promoted by natural selection is not necessarily that of the individual, but rather of the information embodied in that individual and in copies of its genes. Thus, after giving its offspring a good start in life, an individual may in some circumstances best help them (and hence promote the representation of its own genes in future generations) by dying and getting out of their way. If it belongs to a tightly-knit collective of close kin (like the ant colonies discussed in section 8.1 below), the individual's genetic self-interest may even be best served by sacrificing its own reproduction, or even its life, to benefit its siblings and their offspring. This logic is carried to its extreme when the collective is a multicellular organism like each of us – made up of countless genetically-identical cells which are themselves each liable to death, a death distinct from (yet connected to) that of the organism as a whole.

This brings us to the idea of programmed cell death, or *apoptosis*, which performs numerous functions in multicellular organisms. In the course of tissue and organ differentiation inside a developing embryo or young animal, certain cells are programmed by so-called "death genes" to self-destruct according to a precise timetable. The deletion of a tadpole's tail during its transformation into a frog is a familiar example. Likewise, the cells of a woman's uterine lining die and are shed on a monthly schedule, while deciduous trees annually inundate us with dead leaves. Flowers fade quickly once they are pollinated, so that the plant's energy can be channeled into producing fruit and seeds. ("Apoptosis" literally means "dropping off," as with flower petals or autumn leaves.) All these deaths of cells are essential to the normal living and functioning of the entire organism.

Cell death is even necessary to create important parts of the body that are permanent or constantly renewed, such as the corneas and lenses of our eyes and our outermost layer of skin, which all consist in whole or in part of the remains of dead or nearly-dead cells.[9] Cells of the immune system, which destroy invading microbes or the body's own mutated, possibly cancerous cells (often by inducing them to self-destruct), also destroy themselves if they fail to find a suitable target. "These are all deaths programmed into the overall life plan of individual animals; they are carried out to give the individual a chance to stay alive longer and to produce more offspring. The suicide of cells turns out to be almost commonplace, a perfectly normal – and essential – part of the rhythms of animal life."[10]

This business of programmed death, however, is not (as we might like to think) merely something that occurs within the confines of an individual body and is therefore irrelevant to death of the individual as a whole. As lucidly explained by cell biologist William R. Clark,[11] there is an inescapable continuity between the death of a single cell and the death of the entire body. The latter begins with the former, and in most organisms there is not even a distinction to be made: after all, most of them, namely bacteria and protists, consist of only a single cell to begin with.

Death itself, however, does come in different forms. In particular, we must distinguish between *accidental death* – caused by external factors such as environmental extremes, physical destruction, chemical or radiation damage, or starvation – and the *programmed death* referred to above, in which a cell literally commits suicide by carrying out a self-destruct program already encoded in its own DNA. A major reason why cells destroy themselves in this way is because they have suffered damage, especially damage to their DNA, that exceeds their capacity for self-repair. Because such DNA damage tends to accumulate over time as the DNA is copied and recopied in the course of cell division and metabolism, it is not surprising that programmed cell death turns out to be intimately involved in the process of senescence, or aging.

Why not just provide an unlimited capacity for self-repair? Because, in the real world, there are always limits. Repair has costs in the form of materials and energy (parts and labor, in the case of my increasingly creaky 1978 Chevrolet), and in every species it must compete with the demands of reproduction for a limited budget of both. Add to this equation the ever-present finite probability of accidental death, and you get a range of possible tradeoffs and resulting life strategies among which evolution can choose.[12] For example, a small, relatively fragile animal like a mouse, which is inherently likely to have a short lifespan due to accident or predation, should invest in rapid reproduction rather than in upkeep of its body; whereas an elephant, which is likely to live long because few things can kill it, should opt for slow reproduction and put more resources into repair of its body, which will probably have to last for decades. At least for complex creatures like us multicellular animals, however, life completely without death or aging seems not to be one of the options.

Now some remarkable facts emerge. Aging is not always, and has not always been, an inevitable part of life. The earliest single-celled organisms, like modern bacteria, reproduced asexually, by simple fission of one cell into two clones of itself. In this mode of reproduction, then, the organism – the single cell – never truly dies as long as it keeps dividing; and barring accidental death, it is in effect immortal.

> ... [A]ll [multicellular] animals eventually die. Many single-cell organisms *may* die, as the result of accident or starvation; in fact the vast majority do. But there is nothing programmed into them that says they *must* die. Death did not appear simultaneously with life. This is one of the most important and profound statements in all of biology. At the very least, it deserves repetition: *Death is not inextricably intertwined with the definition of life.* Where, then, did death that cannot be avoided come from? Almost certainly, it did not arrive on the scene until a billion or so years after life first appeared.[13]
>
> With only a handful of exceptions, single-cell organisms reproducing exclusively by simple fission lack one feature that ultimately brings death to all single cells that have sex, and to all multicellular organisms, including human beings: *senescence*, the gradual, programmed aging of cells and the organisms they make up, independently of events in the environment. Accidental cell death was around from the very first appearance of anything we would call life. Death of the organism through senescence – programmed death – makes its appearance in evolution at about the same time that sexual reproduction appears. Both sex and programmed death began when the vast majority of organisms were still single cells.[14]

Was this coincidence, or is there some inherent connection between sex and programmed death? For that matter, what is sex itself good for anyway, in the evolutionary sense? This is still hotly debated among biologists, but at least two important functions of sex are clear: (1) by mixing and exchanging genetic information from the parents (that is, recombination), it very rapidly generates new and potentially adaptive genetic variety in the offspring, and (2) in organisms that are diploid (that is, have two copies of every gene, as do most sexually-reproducing organisms), it provides redundancy to compensate for genetic mistakes resulting from mutations (at least one of the two copies is likely to be good).

Furthermore, we find that sexually-reproducing organisms take an additional precaution against DNA damage: at least one copy of their DNA is sequestered and used only for reproduction (that is, for making germ cells or gametes to be passed on to the next generation), leaving the majority of their DNA (which is not passed on to offspring) to be used in the construction, operation, and repair of their bodies. Because this latter DNA is constantly consulted and "read" by the cell's machinery, it is more subject to damage – rather like a library book that is read and photocopied by generations of students. By keeping pristine copies of their DNA "blueprint" or "instruction manual" carefully locked away as germ cells in the gonads or their equivalent – the "rare book room" of the body's library, where the "first editions" are kept while the cheap paperback editions circulate – sexual organisms avoid the risk of passing on to their descendants the everyday-use copies which have more likely been corrupted.

Another metaphor may be helpful. If you buy new software for your computer, you may receive it on a diskette which you are advised to copy immediately. The original distribution diskette from the manufacturer is to be kept in a safe place; the copy is for actual use. The copy is thus subject to damage, and considered expendable; the seldom-used original is available for restoring the software to your computer's memory in case of accident to the copy. Obviously, if one wishes to make an additional copy, the original diskette is preferable as a source over a much-handled copy that may have been corrupted. Indeed, if new copies are to be made and there is doubt about the integrity of the existing copies, it might be safest to first destroy all of the latter lest one of them, instead of the original, be inadvertently used to generate the new ones.

The parallel to our own situation is now apparent. The cells of our germ lines carry the "manufacturer's copies" of the DNA to our offspring, who make multiple copies in the course of their embryonic development. Some of these copies are sequestered in their own germ cells for future reproductive use; the others reside in the cells of the rest of the body (called somatic cells) for "everyday" use in growth and metabolism. These somatic copies of the DNA are not only at greater risk of damage, but are reproductively irrelevant; they are never passed on to offspring. From the viewpoint of the "selfish genes," the bodies these somatic copies construct serve only to protect and pass on the DNA in the germ cells: in the biologist's cliché, a chicken is just an egg's way of making more eggs. Besides, the offspring are usually to receive new gene combinations anyway, because of the genetic contribution of the other parent, rather than being clones of only one parent. Therefore, the somatic cells and their irrelevant, superfluous, possibly corrupt DNA are destined to be destroyed. *Unfortunately, these somatic cells are us.*

> The [evolutionary] drive toward ever-increasing size, and eventually multicellularity, led to the creation of extra-germinal (somatic) DNA. The advent of sex in reproduction made it necessary to destroy the somatic DNA at the end of each generation. We do not know which of these two events came first, but we do know that the creation and segregation of nonreproductive DNA never occurred in cells reproducing asexually. Death may not be necessary for life, but programmed death is apparently necessary to realize the full biological

advantage of sex as a part of reproduction. Not all cells that experimented with sex during evolution created somatic DNA, but the [ones] on the evolutionary path leading to humans and other animals did. In part this was a response to the need for more DNA to direct the operation of ever larger individuals. But once this tendency was combined with sex, death was the inevitable outcome.[15]

... For humans this means that once a reasonable number of our germ cells have been given a chance to impart their reproductive DNA to the next generation, the rest of us – our somatic selves – becomes so much excess baggage. That is the biological origin of senescence and death.[16]

In this view, then, the inevitability of individual death is the price we pay for having evolved to a certain level of bodily complexity. Whether our somatic selves, including our brains and consciousness, are really just "excess baggage" in the great scheme of things (as Clark seems pessimistically to conclude) is an issue to which I shall return later (section 8.3). But it cannot be denied that death of all sorts and at all levels has been unavoidable in evolution, and therefore inseparable from whatever outcomes of that evolution we hold to be of value. Cell biologist Ursula Goodenough sums it up neatly:

... Does death have any meaning?

Well, yes, it does. Sex without death gets you single-celled algae and fungi; sex with a mortal soma gets you the rest of the eukaryotic creatures. Death is the price paid to have trees and clams and birds and grasshoppers, and death is the price paid to have human consciousness, to be aware of all that shimmering awareness and all that love.

My somatic life is the wondrous gift wrought by my forthcoming death.[17]

Notes

1. See, for example, Vermeij 1987.
2. Charles Darwin, letter to Asa Gray, May 22, 1860; in F. Darwin 1887, vol. 2, 105.
3. Morris 1986, 70–71.
4. Mitchell et al. 1986.
5. Nesse and Williams 1998, 89.
6. Nesse and Williams 1998; Rosenberg and Trevathan 2001.
7. Eisenberger et al. 2003.
8. See Lovejoy 1988, Rosenberg and Trevathan 2001.
9. See Duke et al. 1996.
10. Clark 1996, 47.
11. Clark 1996.
12. Cf. Diamond 1993, 122–136.
13. Clark 1996, 54–55; emphasis in original.
14. Clark 1996, 62–63.
15. Clark 1996, 76–77.
16. Clark 1996, 103–104.
17. Goodenough 1998, 151.

CHAPTER SEVEN

Are we going anywhere?
A static or cyclic universe versus an evolutionary universe

A theology of evolution is not obliged to defend the emaciated notion of God that skeptics consider to be defunct after Darwin. It does not try to protect the remote "designing deity" that writers like Richard Dawkins and Daniel Dennett have in mind when they argue that evolution is inherently atheistic. A theology of evolution does not allow either creationists or scientific skeptics to define the meaning of "God," but instead takes as normative the sense of God given to us in the biblical experience.

John F. Haught[1]

7.1   The Bible as the Mother of Science – And of Evolutionary Thought

There is no more dramatic demonstration than the one just given – the essential role(s) of death in evolution – of how untenable a literal reading of Genesis becomes when its creation stories are viewed from an evolutionary perspective. The worldview of the authors of Genesis was, to our eyes, a "static" one in which the world, having been created in essentially its present form (apart from the sin of Adam), needed and possessed neither death nor any natural mechanisms for long-term change. But a physical world free of death was thinkable only when it was imagined to have lasted perhaps no more than a few days before Adam's sin. It becomes simply unthinkable if it is to have significant duration (as God supposedly intended), let alone if it is to incorporate any sort of organic evolution, or even familiar biological processes (such as recycling of materials that form the bodies of organisms, or embryonic development and immune response with their pervasive patterns of programmed cell death). This fact (among many others that could be cited) emphasizes likewise the untenability of any simple harmonization of the literal words of Genesis with a modern scientific cosmogony: they not only represent different paradigms, different modes of thought, but have entirely different purposes, as explained above in Chapter One.

For all the reasons given above, therefore, the still-persistent attempts of some believers to read Genesis 1–3 as an historical account of cosmic and human origins are hopelessly misguided, and from the scientific standpoint thoroughly discredited. But it would be equally wrong to conclude from this that the Bible and modern science are utterly unrelated or incompatible. Faulting the creation stories for their lack of modern scientific content distorts them as much as does the insistence of modern creationists on reading them literally, and obscures what science and Genesis do in fact have in common.

Though "static" in comparison to our concepts of evolution, the ancient worldview that colored the Genesis revelation (without being an integral part of it) was more complex than the word "static" implies. This was the worldview then (and still) largely prevalent outside the Judeo-Christian-Islamic tradition, according to which cyclic events (day and night, summer and winter, birth and death, even dissolution and regeneration of the universe itself) are endlessly repeated in a cosmos devoid of what we would call "progress." This dynamic but cyclic conception is, nonetheless, "static" in the sense that no *net* change, or only degeneration, occurs over the long haul, and history is only futility. There is all the difference in the world between this and an evolutionary universe, in which real, irreversible change along the axis of time draws the natural cycles out, metaphorically, into a spiral, and actually goes somewhere.

But the scriptures of the ancient Hebrews, though borrowing mythic and literary elements from the cyclic worldview of neighboring peoples, in fact represent that worldview's emphatic transcendence. It was precisely the biblical tradition that gave to human thought – and eventually to the scientific and evolutionary worldview – the notion of meaningful change through time and the valorization of history itself, springing from the idea of creation at a specific moment in time and other acts of God in history.[2] In anthropologist Mircea Eliade's words, the Hebrew prophets, by perceiving history as theophany, "for the first time ... placed a value on history, succeeded in transcending the traditional vision of the cycle (the conception that ensures all things will be repeated forever), and discovered a one-way time." They were the first who "affirmed ... the idea that historical events have a value in themselves, insofar as they are determined by the will of God."[3] This crucial conceptual shift, reflected in the mythical narratives of Genesis 1–3 and hammered home throughout the prophetic books, helped lay the groundwork for the origins of all of Western science, including the discovery of evolution.

Here it needs to be explained that the word *myth* in this context does not (as many believers might fear) have its popular meaning of fiction, fairytale, frivolity, or simple falsehood. In prescientific societies, and in the discipline of anthropology, myth has a much more serious and sophisticated meaning: a myth, as Monika Hellwig said above, "is a narrative which interprets the human situation in general by presenting a particular and very concrete event, image or story." *Myth* thus plays a role in prescientific or nonscientific human thought analogous to that of scientific *theory* (a word which also suffers under a popular connotation of low truth-value; cf. section 4.1 above): *both are serious attempts to explain why things are the way they are.*

Both kinds of explanations seek to understand *present* reality in terms of past and/or present events – the actions of gods, demons, heroes, ordinary creatures, and/or inanimate forces. Both can be deeply *true*; but the truth of myth is the truth of the poet, not that of the scientist or historian. The myth of the Garden of Eden, for example, contains truths that are particularly profound; but (as in the parables of Jesus, or other morality tales) its truth lies in its social and moral implications, not in the details of the story (the Good Samaritan and the Prodigal Son were fictional characters).

Both myth and scientific theory provide conceptual frameworks in which empirical data – individual "facts" of life – can be organized and made sense of. Myth does this by analogy – people and animals act in such and such a way because "in the beginning," indefinitely long ago, a creator, founder, or ancestor (real or imagined) set the pattern. Scientific theories, in contrast, have come to insist on tracing the actual sequences of physical events that connect origins with present realities. This involves an emphasis on literal history in place of mere formal resemblance, and on concrete causality in place of poetic imagination. (And obviously, it leads to trouble when modern "scientific creationists" – who have imbibed the modern spirit of rationality in their daily lives, and have ironically and mistakenly accepted that not even the Bible can be "true" unless it passes muster as "science" – overlook this difference and try to use myths as though they were scientific theories.)

Seen in this light, it is apparent how such a change in emphasis (from mere semblance to true causality) could cross the boundary between a myth (like that of Eden) and the scientific theories of today. People such as the Hebrews, who saw the providential action of God in the concrete events of their own history (such as the Exodus), could get used to the idea that history wasn't entirely a bad thing.[4] They expressed this growing confidence in their God when they came to make creation myths of their own, contrasting with those of their polytheistic neighbors. Following centuries of habitual belief that time and history were on humanity's (or at least Israel's) side, history and the changeable world of nature itself finally attracted the sustained interest of thinkers in the Abrahamic tradition, who began to sort through their traditional explanations of things, weeding out those that did not measure up to their rising standards of scientific proof. This task continues today.

Of equal importance to the meaningfulness of change-through-time in developing the scientific outlook were still other biblical insights: those concerning the rationality and benevolence of God and hence the constancy of God's creation, from which science was to infer the autonomy of nature and its laws. Describing the second and older of the two creation accounts in Genesis, historian of science Stanley Jaki writes:

> In all this there is a total lack of even a rudimentary piece of scientific detail. The account is, however, replete with a highly elevated mentality which constitutes the very climate of scientific thinking. Primitive as some details may appear in Genesis 2, it is animated by an uncompromising consistency of explanation which is the hallmark of scientific reasoning. In Genesis 2 there is only one effective cause, the power of God.... For all the primitiveness of the world picture of Genesis 2, it exudes a clear atmosphere undisturbed by what turns all other ancient cosmogonies into dark and dispirited confusion: the infighting among the gods and the lurking in the background of an irreconcilable antagonism between spirit and matter, good and evil.[5]

As for the later-written account in Genesis 1, despite its obvious use of structures and elements from Babylonian and other creation myths,

> ... the first chapter of Genesis is, in fact, a most lucid expression of that faith in the rationality of the universe without which the scientific quest in man could not turn itself into a self-sustaining enterprise.[6]
> ... For all the Mesopotamian flavour of Genesis 1, its author uses the common lore with unusual skill to drive home some very uncommon points. These are the absolute sovereignty and precedence of God over any and all parts of the world, the infinite power of God who brings things into existence

with sheer command, and his overflowing goodness which can only produce an intrinsically good world of matter, both in its entirety and in its parts.[7]

This tradition of strong faith in a reasonable Creator (displayed in Genesis, the Psalms, and elsewhere in the Hebrew Scriptures) engendered an attitude of trust, and in turn "this unconditional and firm trust in Yahweh produced a warm, confident, optimistic appraisal of nature" and ultimately of humanity's ability to understand nature.[8] Furthermore, as biblical scholar B. W. Anderson emphasizes, in contrast to the Greek notion of an impersonally rational cosmos, the regularity of the biblical universe is dependent on its covenant relationship with a personal God: "The covenant, rather than a rational principle, is the ground of the unity of creation."[9] This understanding of a divine covenant with the whole creation was a corollary and direct generalization of faith in a divine covenant with Israel. Thus (paradoxically to our way of thinking, which developed much later), the miracles in the Bible were not seen as violations of natural law, but as reassurances of the Lawmaker's unfailing concern.

In short, while the ahistorical-cyclic and historical-evolutionary worldviews are decidedly at odds, it is the biblical view that provides the bridge or, as it were, the "missing link" between them. The evolutionary outlook shares with the biblical view, and derives from it, a monumentally important trait: the emphasis on net change, indeed positive change, through time. In fact, the quantitative contrast between these two conceptions (creation over mere days as opposed to billions of years), and even the fact that the "history" in Genesis 1–3 is a mythical one, pale to insignificance beside their common perception that unique and important events have happened down through history – whether it be salvation history or evolutionary history.[10]

Indeed, it is the very notion of history, and evolution, that opens up space in our thinking for true salvation. This is the Bible's gift not only to science (as grounds for an expectation of progress) but, especially now in partnership with evolutionary science, to society in general (as grounds for hope of every sort). Haught notes that evolution helps eliminate from our theologies "the obsessive repetitiveness of expiation sanctioned by the longing for a lost paradise…" "Christian faith's revolutionary good news," he says, is "that the age of expiation is over and done with, once and for all." Furthermore: "Genuine hope for the future can survive only in a universe that forbids perpetually repeated reparations for the loss of a timeless primordial perfection. Perfection, evolution helps us to see, lies in the eschatological future, not in the indefinite temporal past, nor in an eternal present immune to the travails of becoming."[11] This evolutionary view of salvation, moreover, is specifically the one envisioned in theologies of the humility and kenosis (self-emptying) of God:

> I believe, along with many other theologians today, that only the notion of God as self-emptying love makes sense after Darwin. This is the God who suffers along with creation and saves the world by taking all of its evolutionary travail and triumph into the everlasting divine compassion. This is not a God that theology invented just to accommodate Darwin. This is the empathetic God revealed in the pages of the Bible. This is the God of Israel who felt the pain of the oppressed in Egypt. It is the God who identifies with the Crucified. This is

the God that Christian faith encountered long before we learned the story of
nature's evolutionary birth pangs.[12]

In particular, because the notion of an instantaneous creation "rob[s] suffering of
the possibility of being interpreted as part of the process of ongoing creation
itself,"[13] it is only evolutionary theology that offers hope of making sense of the
suffering in the world, and "justifying the ways of God to man" – perhaps the
greatest existential problem of them all.

These striking convergences of biblical ideas with the scientific and evolutionary
outlook of today are hardly coincidences. As Jaki[14] has shown in great detail, this
common trait of valuing history, shared by the Bible and science, is the result of
actual historical descent: the Western scientific mentality was a *direct and
conscious* outgrowth of the Judeo-Christian-Islamic tradition of thought which
took root in and shaped European culture. Thus, for all their superficial antagonism, the evolutionary worldview traces its own pedigree to the biblical account of
creation by a personal God and to the novel, positive view of history which that
account represented. Present-day creationists try to argue that evolution is instead
a "pagan" idea, derived somehow from the cyclic cosmic concepts of non-biblical
religions. On the contrary, the modern idea of evolution is both a product of the
Judeo-Christian-Islamic intellectual tradition, and profoundly at home within it.

It is worth noting, in fact, that where "pagan" ideas have had a major influence
in Western thought, that influence has not necessarily been congenial to evolution
or Darwinism. Biologists such as Ernst Mayr and Michael Ghiselin have emphasized that the essentialist metaphysics derived from Plato and Aristotle was a
major obstacle which Darwin and other evolutionists had to overcome in their
thinking, and which continues to cause conceptual problems even today.
Essentialists held that the reality of things, including living things, lay in the
unchanging "essences" that supposedly characterized whole classes of things, and
not in the "accidental" peculiarities of individuals. Essentialism consequently had
problems in dealing with change. Darwinism, in contrast, insists that change is the
rule, that species are fluid, and that individual variations are the key ingredient of
evolution. As Ghiselin puts it,

> An implication [of essentialism], of enormous historical importance, was that
> it became very difficult to classify things which change, or which grade into one
> another, and even to conceive of or to discuss them. Indeed, the very attempt
> to reason in terms of essences almost forces one to ignore everything dynamic
> or transitory. One could hardly design a philosophy better suited to predispose
> one toward dogmatic reasoning and static concepts. The Darwinian revolution
> thus depended upon the collapse of the Western intellectual tradition.[15]

Of course there was far more to the Western intellectual tradition than essentialism (in particular, there were the biblical elements, as already pointed out!), so
Ghiselin's last point here is rather a breathtaking overstatement. But it is true
that essentialism buttressed the idea of a static cosmos, and thereby formed a
stumbling block that had to be removed (largely through the work of Darwin
himself) before the biblical view of history could develop into a fully evolutionary
worldview.

Darwinism, therefore, did not by any means represent a total break with the intellectual past. On the contrary,

> the principle of natural selection represented the unexpected fulfillment of the promise of the theory of special creation ... in the sense that it accounted for the observed pattern of organic form and function with the aid of but a single overarching theoretical principle [analogous to the doctrine of divine creation].
> The idea that Darwin's theory of evolution by natural selection represents the fulfillment of the special-creationist tradition is still not widely acknowledged. This is a little surprising, for Darwin himself made it abundantly clear in his own writings. The frontispiece of the first edition of the *Origin of Species*, for example, contained two quotations, one from Francis Bacon on the "two books of divine revelation [nature and the Bible]," and the other from the Reverend William Whewell, an English natural theologian, who had observed that "with regard to the material world ... we can perceive that events are brought about not by insulated interpositions of Divine power, exerted in each particular case, but by the establishment of general laws." Together, these passages gave notice to Darwin's readers that his book fell squarely within the conventions of natural theology.... Thus, Darwin explicitly invited his readers to see evolution by natural selection as the means adopted by the creator to populate the earth with a diversity of well-adapted species.[16]

Darwin always insisted that there was nothing anti-religious or atheistic in his work. Only in later life did he gradually turn into an agnostic – out of a variety of motives shared by his Victorian contemporaries, not least among them the problem of animal and human suffering.[17] And although his theory in a sense "fulfilled the promise of the special creationist tradition,"

> it also destroyed that tradition by undermining the particular alliance of philosophy, theology, and natural science upon which it rested. In a Darwinian universe, there was no place for Platonic idealism or Aristotelian teleology; above all, there was no place for special creation. ... What is vitally important to notice, however, is that neither in aim nor in effect did he undermine the Christian doctrine of creation itself. Rather, by separating that doctrine from its two-centuries-long marriage of convenience with Greek philosophy and classical natural history, Darwin forced the radical re-examination of the relationship between theology and natural science.[18]

The outcome of this re-examination in the late nineteenth century included not only a variety of anti-Christian views like those of Thomas Henry Huxley, Ernst Haeckel, and Karl Marx, but "an equally wide range of pro-Christian reformulations of the science-theology relationship," including those of the Anglican Charles Kingsley, the Presbyterian Asa Gray, and the Anglo-Catholic Aubrey Moore. To the latter, "Darwinism was 'infinitely more Christian than the theory of special creation' because it implied 'the immanence of God in nature, and the omnipresence of his creative power.'"[19]

In its amenability to such widely differing, even opposing philosophical and religious interpretations (including the present one), Darwinian science, like other natural sciences, has thus shown itself to be essentially neutral on religious questions, rather than the embodiment of atheism that modern creationists and materialists both imagine it to be. Sprung from the same biblical roots as Christianity, Darwinism (like the rest of science) has grown to mature independence as an agnostic, disinterested, and objective observer of nature, ready to engage religion on an equal footing in constructive dialogue. The aim of this dialogue should be to construct a worldview consistent with all that we know – not to win the assent of scientists to some religious doctrine, nor to impose on religionists the anti-religious attitudes of some scientists, but to juxtapose scientific evidence shorn of theological biases with religious insights freed from outdated notions of nature. This juxtaposition, I believe, will be mutually enlightening and not mutually destructive.

Even today the development of a fully evolutionary worldview is not yet complete; and to retrieve the important truths contained in the mythical "history" of Genesis set in a static cosmos, we must continue to rethink our understanding of them from the bottom up in the vastly different, evolutionary framework which is the only one intelligible to us today. The shared origin of the Genesis story and the evolutionary story give us confidence that this can be done without discarding truly vital elements of either.

7.2 Is There "Progress" in Evolution?

Truth in advertising, however, requires us to admit that this rethinking will cause some discomfort, and to scientists as well as to biblical literalists. The biblical worldview is inescapably an optimistic, hopeful one: history is going somewhere, and God has promised that things will turn out right in the end. In other words, there is progress. Maybe this progress is only supposed to occur within human culture; but theologians who take evolution seriously, and who see creation as all of a piece, will also expect to find signs of it in the origins of humanity and in the entire sweep of evolutionary history that has brought us to our present state.

The trouble is that many evolutionists today deny there is any "progress" in evolution at all. This is an understandable reaction (though, I think, an overreaction) against certain errors of the past two or three centuries – in particular, the notion of the *scala naturae* or "ladder of nature" which all organisms were once thought to steadily ascend in the course of their evolution, and the philosophy of Social Darwinism, which equated social progress with (and thereby justified) the inexorable elimination of the "unfit" during humanity's struggle for existence.

These ideas, which are statements about individual evolving lineages, have, indeed, been thoroughly discredited. It is now clear, for example, that living things do not *automatically, necessarily* become bigger, more complex, more sociable, more intelligent, or in any absolute sense "better" with the passage of even eons of time. Instead, they simply do whatever they can to survive, each day, in each day's environment – to preserve the *status quo* of their own continued existence. If remaining as they are accomplishes that, then they remain much as they are, perhaps for millions of years – bacteria, coelacanths, opossums, or whatever. They may even become smaller or less complex, if natural selection so dictates. Not all kinds of fossil horses always got larger; some evolved to smaller sizes. The number of bones and teeth in the vertebrate skull has diminished from fish through amphibians and reptiles to mammals. Whales and sea cows went from four legs to two; snakes went from four to none. Tapeworms, in adapting to a parasitic lifestyle, lost most of their organ systems.

We have, in short, abandoned the old idea of orthogenesis – that lineages of organisms, driven by mysterious internal forces, evolve straight toward evident goals. (In practice, the "goals" were typically defined in retrospect as whatever quirky specializations were displayed by the last or latest members of the lineages.) And, as said above, there is no one particular evolved trait that all or most lineages display. But taking the record as a whole, it is fair to say that the *average* size, complexity, sociality, and intelligence (and other features) of organisms *in general* have shown a net increase, simply because the *maximum* size, complexity, sociality, and intelligence exhibited by *any* organism have increased. (Since life started close to zero on all these scales, the minimum can decrease little if at all.) Once there existed only single-celled life forms; now there exists an entire spectrum from single-celled life through all sorts of multicelled plants, fungi, and animals, including us.[20] Most of the single-celled creatures have not tended to become multicelled, nor have most of the vertebrates tended to become human-like (or turtle-like, or bird-like). But some have, and the whole envelope of diversity, size, complexity, sociality, and intelligence (and other traits) has been stretched as a result. If we insist on judging by some (any) single trait, the vast majority of organisms will doubtless be found far from the "progressive" maximum; but this can be seen to show merely that evolution is like a rocket: only a small percentage of its weight constitutes the payload.

Increase in the maximum for particular traits may level off with time or cease as inherent limits are approached (presumably, Earth-bound organisms like dinosaurs and whales can only get so big). There can even be temporary reversals (mass extinctions have periodically set back the clock on diversity). But the large-scale trend through time toward increase in the maximum (and net increase in the average) values of these traits is an obvious characteristic of earthly life *as a whole*; and it would, I predict, be seen wherever else in the universe life appeared and persisted for a similar length of time.

In a certain number of cases, in the course of keeping organisms adequately adapted relative to their actual competitors, selection has in fact brought about greater size, complexity, sociality, and/or intelligence within individual lineages. This is not surprising, since each of these things can clearly have adaptive value in many (not all) circumstances. Indeed, given the propensity of evolution to explore, sooner or later, every accessible corner of the universe of possible designs for organisms, almost any criterion of "progress" is likely to be met eventually by some creature or other – making evolution inevitably "progressive," but only in a rather trivial sense. Being large, complex, social, intelligent creatures ourselves, we humans naturally like to define these traits as progressive. This is our privilege; but we should acknowledge its subjectivity. Microbes inhabiting the hot springs of Yellowstone might prefer to equate evolutionary progress with the ability to live in near-boiling water, while tapeworms would presumably view their own elegantly simplified anatomy and freeloading lifestyle as the pinnacle of progress.

A more general criterion of progress, however, lies in the fact that selection favors *efficiency* in the use of energy and resources by all living things. For example:

> An impressive body of experimental research ... indicates that bacteria intro-
> duced to novel substrates initially metabolize those substrates with extremely
> low efficiency. Through time, accumulating mutations result in ever more
> efficient substrate utilization until populations reach a point where the prob-
> ability of further improvement with continued mutation effectively declines
> to zero.... Thus, the earliest organisms to use, say, sulfate in respiration
> undoubtedly did so with less efficiency than modern sulfate reducers and were
> eliminated over time.[21]

This "ratchet" effect, however sporadically it may operate, imposes a net directionality on the evolution of physiological efficiency: improvement, not stagnation
or decline. And, of even more significance: over geological time, this constant
competition for more efficient use of resources has led to greater ecological
specialization by species, hence greater diversity of species, hence more complex
interactions and networks among species.

Where the record shows the clearest evidence of progress, therefore, is in the
forest rather than the trees: not so much in the histories of individual lineages as in
evolution's overall net result. There is a clear directional trend through time in the
increase of *ecological complexity*, with the addition of new ways in which life uses
space, energy, and other resources. For example, living things now consume each
other in addition to just making food from inorganic ingredients; they live in
oxygen-rich as well as oxygenless environments; they occupy the land as well as the
sea; they climb, fly, and burrow in addition to swimming and crawling; and so
forth. Like water finding its way into every pore of a sponge, living things have
occupied almost every imaginable ecological niche (even, literally, inside the pore
spaces of rocks thousands of feet below the surface). They have truly multiplied
and filled the Earth (Genesis 1:22). Natural selection has driven them to do more
and more different things, and do them with greater and greater metabolic and
physiological efficiency; and most of these things have been achieved over and
over again by independent evolutionary lineages, demonstrating the consistency
and universality of the underlying drive.[22]

On the ecological level, then, it is obvious that selection has consistently and
reliably moved life as a whole toward more efficient function and more complex
interactions. Seen against this background, our own complexity and adaptive efficiency do not appear merely as the quirks of one minor branch of the evolutionary
tree, but instead finally emerge into view as the most marked expression of a truly
general trend. "Humans form but one of myriad branches of the Tree of Life, no
farther from its root than any other living organisms. Thus, the claim of special
status for human intelligence is fundamentally ecological, not genealogical."[23] No
other species survives in as many environments as we do; no other species interacts
among its own members and with other species in as many ways as we do; no other
species adapts to change as efficiently as we do, thanks to our strategy of cultural
evolution. We are biologically special not primarily because of things we do that no
other organism does; we are special because of the things all others try to do

(interact, adapt and survive) that we do better, more effectively, and more extravagantly than any of them.

And it is not without theological importance that our human uniqueness thus becomes fully manifest only in the context of *community* – both that of our fellow humans and that of other creatures. By community I do not mean something necessarily warm and nurturing; more usually it has been competitive and exploitative. But just as individual motives and actions have evolved in some cases in the direction of greater altruism, so have competitive and exploitative relationships been the starting point from which more nurturing ones have sometimes evolved, ultimately providing the context of our own evolution.

We are therefore on firm ground in saying that evolution intrinsically shows predictable trends, ones that can be objectively defined as "progress": an increase in the energetic efficiency of individual organisms, an increase in the complexity of ecosystems (communities of living things), and a consequent expansion of the universe of realized possibilities.

Given the conclusions of natural science outlined above, theology today has no alternative but to accept evolution as the method God used to create the wonderful diversity of living things on this planet – the world of nature that God finally pronounced "very good" (Genesis 1:31). As Pope John Paul II put it in 1985, "creation presents itself in the light of evolution as an event extended through time – as a *creatio continua* – in which God becomes visible to the eyes of the believer as 'creator of heaven and earth.'"[24] Catholic theologian Karl Schmitz-Moormann, in a 1997 textbook, was even more emphatic: "The debate over creation or evolution has ceased. Hence the task of theology is to read the evolving universe as creation. In this text we accept the fact of evolution as the way creation is."[25]

This view, however, leads at once to a major paradox, given the way this "method of creation" has been characterized above. Associating God in this fashion with "evolution red in tooth and claw" raises serious problems for theodicy in the minds of many people.[26] Are we to understand that physical suffering and death, which we have always labeled "evil," can not only be willed by God, but even be pronounced "good"? Even if they are unavoidable, indeed necessary to the evolutionary process, can they possibly be seen as having some positive value? Or must we reject as flawed and false any worldview that has such abhorrent logical consequences?

Here we encounter what philosophers call the problem of evil, and with it the traditional Christian explanation of evil: original sin. What possible form might these concepts take when transposed into an evolutionary worldview?

Notes

1. Haught 2001, 49.
2. See the classic treatments of these themes by Eliade 1954 and Jaki 1974.
3. Eliade 1954, 104.
4. Mendenhall (2001, 169) points out that King Josiah's death in battle falsified a prediction of the prophetess Huldah (2 Kings 22:20). "That Huldah's failed prophecy is retained in the biblical

record illustrates the Israelites' abiding respect for the historical facts, even the unpleasant and embarrassing ones."

5. Jaki 1974, 140.
6. Jaki 1974, 146.
7. Jaki 1974, 147.
8. Jaki 1974, 149.
9. Anderson 1984, 27–28.
10. Cf. Ong 1960.
11. Haught 2000, 141–142.
12. Haught 2001, 124.
13. Haught 2002, 547
14. Jaki 1974.
15. Ghiselin 1984, 52.
16. Durant 2001, 270–271.
17. Durant 2001, 272.
18. Durant 2001, 272–273.
19. Moore 1889, quoted in Durant 2001, 273.
20. For example, complexity in one sense – hierarchical structure, defined by McShea (2001) as "the number of levels of nesting of lower-level entities within higher-level individuals" – has clearly increased over the history of life. "For most senses of complexity – such as complexity as number of different part types or depth of causal chains in development – I have argued elsewhere that there are reasons for skepticism about the existence of a trend at the scale of life as a whole.... But for hierarchical complexity, a long-term trend – at least in the maximum – seems inescapable" (McShea 2001, 418). McShea points out that data are insufficient to establish a steady increase in mean or average hierarchical complexity; but this average has necessarily shown a *net* increase from the beginning to today, even if it may have fluctuated downward at times.
21. Knoll and Bambach 2000, 4–5.
22. Knoll and Bambach 2000.
23. Knoll and Bambach 2000, 10.
24. My translation.
25. Schmitz-Moormann 1997, xi.
26. For example Michael Ruse; see Ruse 1994 and accompanying articles. More recently, however, Ruse (1999) has come around to the explanation of physical evil espoused here.

Response to Part Two

Monika K. Hellwig

This section has really dealt with a range of objections to evolutionary theory. Not all of these are religious objections, and not all of them relate to original sin. A preliminary issue concerns the doctrine of creation. This doctrine is based on a number of stories in the Hebrew Scriptures, notably those in Chapters 1 and 2 of the Book of Genesis. The story in Chapter 1 is rather like a mural in seven panels, in which the creator orders the universe in six "days," resting and enjoying it on the seventh. Clearly, those believers who do not accept any literary or historical analysis of the context, literary genre, and purpose of the story, but read it as a strictly literal chronicle of the history of the cosmos, will need to reject all possible evolutionary theories in order to preserve their faith. Their problem, however, is not only with the natural sciences, but also with literary theory, comparative religious studies, history of ancient literature, and with biblical scholarship itself. Some of these believers have tried to ease the problem with evolutionary theory by suggesting that the "days" are really very long periods of cosmic time. However, this leaves the problem that the narrative of Genesis 1 has light created before the sun and moon, and that the stories of Genesis 1 and Genesis 2 contradict each other in important components.

The major religious denominations today are not committed to a literal interpretation of the Genesis narratives. Moreover, they have little objection to an evolutionary view of the universe as a whole. Their remaining problems have to do with the position of human beings within it. This concern began with the scientific assertion of the Copernican theory of the structure of the universe and the movements of the celestial bodies within it. Religious opposition at that time focused on the understanding that everything was Created for human beings and they for communion with the creator through obedience to the divine laws and ultimate bliss. If the earth were not the center of the universe, that seemed to contradict the divine order placing human beings at the apex of creation.

With the emergence of evolutionary theories in the nineteenth century, it was not only the centrality of human beings in creation that was threatened but the concept that the human person was ontologically different from the animal world – a difference not only in degree of intelligence, creativity, and conscious responsibility, but a difference in kind constituting an unbridgeable gap.

Thus as major Christian denominations came to reluctant acceptance of evolution, they employed various strategies. For example, prehuman evolution to the human may well have happened, but there must have been a special intervention of the Creator in a leap from the subhuman to the genuinely human. This was complicated for the Roman Catholic and some other churches by the fact that the philosophical base of the theological understanding of the human person separated the person into body growing from the parents and soul created specially and uniquely for each individual. Therefore, the bodies of prehuman creatures might have developed to the point that at the crucial moment the Creator intervened with the creation of souls.

The matter might have been left there quietly, were it not that a certain literalist assumption came into play, even with those churches and believers who were not committed to taking the Genesis story literally on principle. That assumption was that the human race must have been derived from a single couple, if all human beings were one in destiny. For the Catholic Church in particular, this arose in connection with missionaries to the Inuit who wrote to Rome in distress when they found Christian marauders hunting the Inuit to extinction because they did not consider them human. This, of course, could be related to what had happened and continued to happen to other Native American peoples, and to the whole phenomenon of slavery. The response to such behavior was a vigorous assertion that all human beings are within the protection of the one God because all are descended from the same first parents. Whatever the merit of this argument in defense of the weak, it reinforced the Church's commitment in the twentieth century to a monogenist understanding of the relationship of human beings to one another, even as it became clearer from scientific studies in genetics that this was hardly possible.

It is at this point that objections to evolutionary theory as applied to human becoming begin to be connected with the doctrine of original sin. Domning's main thesis is that human predatory and otherwise destructive behavior can be accounted for by evolutionary theory without resort to such religious explanations as the author finds in the doctrine of original sin.

Before engaging at any deeper level, the churches have resisted evidence of simultaneous break-through in many individuals to human levels of intelligence, creativity, and responsibility, because of continued insistence that all are equally involved in the human situation created by the "sin of Adam," because all are descended from the same couple, and are under the same corporate judgment.

On the part of the churches this may be a premature rejection of the scientific evidence, based on faulty argumentation. The unity of destiny of the human community and the responsibility of all human beings for one another and for their earth is not necessarily dependent on descent from a single couple. But the thesis of this book may be based on assumptions about the role and purpose of the doctrine in the synthetic worldview of Christian faith that are commonly enough held but would not satisfy contemporary theologians or students of comparative religion. As with the doctrine of creation, the following response will first describe how the doctrine has been composed, commenting along the way on difficulties believers have and have had with scientific findings. Second, this response will suggest how contemporary theology understands the form and function of the doctrine.

The doctrine of original sin is rooted in an ancient narrative, the story of a human couple set by their creator in a garden of perfect harmony in which there is a central condition for the maintenance of such a peaceful and wholly pleasant existence (Genesis 2 and 3). According to the narrative, temptation comes from a mysterious external source, and first the woman, then the man, yields. The peace and harmony are irrevocably lost in exile from the garden. Their children and later descendents will all be born into a world of tension, conflict, and bitter struggle, though a future rescue is promised to them.

Those who take this story literally will reject the thesis of this book out of hand because they understand that the word of God in Scripture declares that all evil is to be attributed, directly or indirectly, to the sin of a representative couple who failed the test. However, such believers also have a difficult task to explain how a good God can be so arbitrarily unjust in what seems to be a free and arbitrary determination that the innocent shall suffer retribution for the sins of the guilty. The official teachings of the major churches in our time rarely insist on literal interpretation of the story of the garden and the eating of the forbidden fruit, but they have been very reluctant to commit themselves explicitly to a more informed and nuanced explanation.

Theologians have not been so reluctant. As Chapter One indicates, there have been many attempts to provide a more coherent explanation. It should be noted, however, that the aim of such theological proposals is not to give a credible account of how evil may have originated in human history (which is Domning's concern). Rather the aim of the Scripture scholars, theological historians, and systematic theologians is to understand the meaning of the stories and the subsequent doctrinal formulations in terms of their role first in Hebrew and later in Christian faith. In this endeavor, these scholars have had to refer to comparative studies of ancient texts of various peoples, to literary analysis, and to contextual studies for the particular documents. For later formulations, where we have more historical records, they have had to consult what is known of the contexts, and to pay attention to the subject matter of the arguments that resulted in a particular formula.

In simplest terms it can be said that the Genesis 1–3 stories, like myths, fables, and parables, present in a narrative stretched through a time-line what is in fact an interpretation of the human situation at any time, in any "here and now." Adam is any one of us. The figure of Eve is more complex. Most narratives about women in both Testaments use these female figures as representative of a people, a city, a tradition, and so on. A credible reading of the story of the garden sees Eve, whose name is interpreted "mother of the living," as representing not only woman in conjugal relationship to man, but the mothering community or tradition in which individuals come to be. In this understanding, the story explains the human situation in which each individual is placed as tragic. The individual never begins, so to speak, simply in a supportive or even neutral context. The becoming of each individual is handicapped by the damage that has already distorted the society – damage caused by those who went before. Adam speaks truth to God when he says that the woman, the society, that was created to be support to the individual has become temptress and misleading. The Jewish tradition, which springs directly from the Torah or Pentateuch containing these narratives, has never had problems with this, in part because it does not cut off Genesis 1–3 as an isolated unit for interpretation, but continues with the narrative of evil deeds and their consequences in the following chapters. Moreover, the Jewish tradition does not speak only of the continuing consequences of past sins but speaks also of the "merits of the ancestors."

Thus far, then, the function of the story is to maintain that the world as we know it is not simply what the Creator intends. It is the outcome in part of human choices and actions, both good and bad. It should therefore not be taken for granted but subjected to prophetic critique.

Moreover, the Creator promises to intervene, because creation can be rescued. The story is one of hope and encouragement. Christian tradition has dealt with the ancient narrative in new ways. Paul in the Christian Scriptures (the New Testament) juxtaposes the figure of Adam, as comprehending all individuals in their state of disorientation, or sin, with the figure of the Risen Christ, as comprehending all individuals in a transformed state of reorientation, or grace (Romans 5). Adam becomes the counterfoil for everything associated with Christ, and incidentally in the early Christian tradition, Eve becomes the counterfoil to Mary (representing church, Christian community, as it ought to be).

From this arose the debate in the Western (that is, Latin-speaking) church of the fifth century concerning the "sin of Adam" which then came to be called original sin. The question was whether everyone was in need of redemption by Christ or whether there was the possibility of maintaining perfect innocence by virtue of the natural gifts with which human beings are endowed. Augustine of Hippo and others charged into the fray with the Pauline principle that in Adam all have sinned therefore all need to be justified in Christ. Augustine defended his position on the basis of the shared human heritage, and tried to relate it to what he saw as the flawed intentions of parents in begetting and conceiving. While the churches have not adopted that last position, both those of the Reform and the Catholic Church have accepted the basic argument that to be human is to be inevitably entrammeled in the state of original sin. Catholic teachings have emphasized that the problem is not only in the tainted environment but is inevitably within each person by the very fact of being a member of the human community.

Contemporary theologians have explored a number of ways of explaining this last claim. The most obvious is that a human person is not born with a capacity for critical judgment and discerning choices, but learns values and expectations through the relationships that build up such a capacity. If society is permeated with distortions, then the individual can only become free of them by meeting counter-cultural challenges and supports and by putting forth great efforts. With reference to this, contemporary theology, informed by insights of modern psychology and of the social sciences, can give very helpful explanations of the mediaeval claims about the then-called "preternatural gifts" lost with innocence and regained only with graced struggle, that is, the ability to live without fear of death, without distortion of perceptions and understanding, without disorder of goals in life, and without causing unnecessary suffering to oneself and others.

What, then, is the function of the doctrine of original sin in Christian doctrine and theology? In the first place it raises awareness that the evil and suffering in the world are not to be taken for granted as inevitable, but are to be vigorously critiqued as to their causes, and are to be staunchly resisted by prophetic action. In the second place, the evil is not to be seen simply as something outside of oneself; one needs to develop the capacity to look at one's own conduct, relationships, values, and expectations, and all that one takes for granted, to discern where these are shaped by disorientation in one's world. In the third place, the doctrine insists that the creator is greater than all creaturely actions, and therefore redemption from sin and suffering is really possible.

In answer to the scientist's objection that none of this really explains the historical, or prehistorical, beginning of sin and evil, the theologian can only answer that this is not the purpose of the doctrine of original sin. Faced with the question as to what then the theologian can say to explain that somewhere sometime there must have been a beginning of evil choices and destructive actions, the theologian is likely to give a simple philosophical answer as follows. The human capacity for creativity, that is, free will, inescapably carries risk. There is no way of enjoying freedom without risk. Human beings, who are by nature interdependent, are therefore at risk not only of their own freedom but of the way that others have used and do use their freedom. Hence all that has been done by human beings that is constructive and good benefits all of us. What has been done that is destructive and evil likewise hurts all of us. Necessarily a community of interdependent beings enjoying personal spontaneity or freedom will confer on its members both benefits and troubles stemming from all that has gone before. Religion is not needed to validate this logical necessity, and certainly cannot invalidate it either.

Asked by the scientist whether there is not an intrinsic systematic exigence in theology to trace this back to an actual, not a mythical, beginning, the theologian answers with a smile that the real systematic exigence is to clarify the situation of the here and now, any here and now, as a task for human living. As to reconstructing prehistoric events, a prudent Christian theologian is quite happy to let the scientist get on with it, because it does not have immediate relevance to the redemption.

Part Three
Towards a new understanding of original sin

Daryl P. Domning

CHAPTER EIGHT

Evolution and human behavior

It is easy to be both sentimental and theological over the more charming and agree-able aspects of Nature. It is very difficult to see its essential holiness beneath disconcerting and hostile appearances...

To stand alongside the generous Creative Love, maker of all things visible and invisible (including those we do not like) and see them with the eyes of the Artist-Lover is the secret of sanctity. St. Francis did this with a singular perfection.... So too that rapt and patient lover of all life, Charles Darwin, with his great, self-forgetful interest in the humblest and tiniest forms of life – not because they were useful to him, but for their own sakes – fulfilled one part of our Christian duty far better than many Christians do.

Evelyn Underhill[1]

We have seen above that the dominant force in Darwinian evolution – the force that accounts for the pervasive adaptedness of organisms to their environments, and thus for their ongoing evolution – is natural selection. In this process, what-ever heritable traits promote an individual's survival and reproduction will auto-matically tend to increase in the population by virtue of that individual's reproductive success compared to others. In the course of perpetuating and repro-ducing themselves, individuals compete for whatever resources are in short supply, and through this competition they are exposed to selection. Therefore, biological adaptation, biological diversity, and evolution itself are, and have always been, the results of individual characteristics or behavior that tend to preserve and perpetu-ate the individual's own genes – in other words, to put it crudely but not really anthropomorphically, the results of selfishness.[2]

Selfish behavior of some sort, whether in a literal or an abstract sense of "behav-ior" (and in the evolutionary but not necessarily the psychological sense of "selfish"), is the mainspring of Darwinian evolution, and not only on the individ-ual level but arguably on every biological level. This idea inspired, for example, the title of Richard Dawkins's book *The Selfish Gene*, which proposed that evolution is best viewed and explained from the perspective of the individual gene, wherein the whole individual organism is merely the gene's means of self-perpetuation. Many other writers have proposed that Darwinian selection also acts on larger biological units: groups, populations, and species.[3] The debates over these issues, however, need not detain us, because their outcome will not affect the present line of argument: selfishness is selfishness, regardless of the size or scope of the "self" that manifests it. It is therefore sufficient for us to think of selection simply as operating among individual organisms; and it is most relevant to consider in this regard the behavior of those "subhuman" creatures most similar to ourselves.

8.1   The Selfish Behavior of Primates and Other Animals

Modern studies of animal (especially primate) behavior offer the theologian much challenging food for thought, because they show that practically all of the overt acts regarded as "sinful" in humans are part of the normal, natural repertoire of behavior in other species. For example, Jane Goodall's pioneering studies of wild chimpanzees have revealed that these animals naturally engage in acts ranging from petty quarreling, bullying, and theft to deliberate deception, political intrigue, premeditated murder (even serial killings) of members of their own species, systematic infanticide and cannibalism, and organized, aggressive, lethal warfare against neighboring groups.[4] Even prideful behavior, proverbially the deadliest of all, is not absent: when seeking to make up after a fight, chimpanzees use not only third-party mediation but elaborate, mutually-agreed-upon public pretense simply to save face.[5] Nor is it necessarily even the case that their abilities in such regards are inferior to our own: "Deception seems to permeate all aspects of chimpanzee social life, and chimpanzee skills in deceit are a match for human lie-detecting abilities."[6]

If any of this language seems inappropriately anthropomorphic, I invite you to read the voluminous, carefully-documented technical reports of Goodall, Hrdy, de Waal, and others and draw your own conclusions. This is not to suggest that these animals are guilty of sin; they are simply doing things that would be sinful if morally reflective beings (humans) did them.

Whereas the aggressiveness of chimpanzees is by now well known, the habits of their close cousin the bonobo (or "pygmy chimpanzee") are much less familiar, but at the same time much more palatable to those who would prefer to have a more peaceable species than the chimpanzee as their closest primate relative. In reality, chimps are probably exactly as close to us genealogically as bonobos are, and at least as similar to us in their overall behavior and social systems (though all three species are divergently specialized); but bonobo behavior is of no less interest on that account.

In contrast to chimps, bonobos have relatively egalitarian, matriarchal societies which emphasize female–female bonding more than male-male contact, and there is a closer relationship between the sexes. Frequent and varied sexual behavior, in fact, is the "glue" that holds bonobo societies together and facilitates most forms of social interaction. It has been said that while chimpanzees use power to resolve issues of sex, bonobos use sex to resolve issues of power. As a result, the overt male aggression and intergroup warfare for which chimps are known is largely absent among bonobos, and infanticide has never been observed.[7]

It would be an error, however, to suppose that altruism always prevails and self-interest is absent from bonobo life. Apparently because they have adapted to ecological conditions different from those of chimps (viz., a greater abundance of food and consequently less occasion for competition), they are outwardly more pacific; but tensions exist below the surface. Neighboring groups do not seem to engage in murderous warfare, but do show hostility. Bonobos, especially males, are less inclined to share food than chimps; adult males compete for females, are involved in more fights than females (although fights between females can be more severe), and in the wild the males more often show deformed digits or missing hands or feet, very likely as a result of intraspecific violence. In particular, mother–son teams compete fiercely over dominance rank. On the whole, de Waal cautions against the tendency to romanticize bonobos:

> Even if strikingly pacific, they are not the long-lost noble savages. All animals are competitive by nature and cooperate only under specific circumstances and for specific reasons, not because of a desire to be nice to one another. The question of why bonobos are egalitarian and tolerant thus needs to be balanced with the question of in which areas they are most competitive....
>
> ... In other words, bonobo society is not all rosy. The species is no exception to the rule that cooperative tendencies are best understood in conjunction with competitive ones, even though I agree that in bonobos the emphasis seems to have shifted to the former.[8]

As we continue to learn the ways of our primate cousins, we are discovering that unattractive, self-centered traits are not confined to the higher apes; monkeys too are practiced in (albeit much less skilled at) deceit, status-seeking, and interfamily vendettas.[9] Physical abuse, exploitation, and outright murder of infants, to serve the interests of adults, are well documented.[10] Indeed, it is hard to think of any form of human misbehavior that is not somehow foreshadowed among other primates.

We are still far from knowing the true extent of such behavior in the animal kingdom as a whole, but all the evidence points to its being pervasive. This is conspicuously true of intraspecific killing, cannibalism, and infanticide.[11] For example, biologist Craig Packer[12] has documented the murderous habits of lions toward their own kind, such as the routine infanticide by adult males of cubs they have not sired, and females' ruthless killing of other lionesses who trespass on their territory. Infanticide in particular "is now known to occur in a wide range of [mammalian] species, from lions to prairie dogs, and from mice to gorillas. Current estimates of infanticide as a source of infant mortality (that is, the number of infants that succumb to attacks by conspecifics as a proportion of all infant deaths) are astonishing: 35 percent in grey langurs; 37 percent in mountain gorillas; 43 percent in red howler monkeys; and 29 percent in blue monkeys."[13] Spotted hyenas likewise kill and cannibalize their own kind, both cubs and adults.[14] Killing of conspecifics is also common among "lower" vertebrates and invertebrates. Female spiders and scorpions commonly kill and eat their mates after copulation, and the embryos of certain sharks even kill and cannibalize each other inside their mother's womb.[15]

One of the most zoologically prevalent forms of what humans regard as "misbehavior" is deception.[16] In the words of biologist Randy Thornhill:

> Natural selection theory predicts that intraspecific deception will be common between potential and actual mates, parents and offspring, relatives in general, and indeed between all socially interacting individuals of all animal species. According to theory, selection will favor individuals that can deceive other individuals because the deceiver may gain time or resources, both of which can be used for reproductive activities, or the deceived may be used to enhance directly the reproductive success of the deceiver.[17]

Thornhill goes on to list diverse examples of what he terms transvestism, or mimicry (behavioral or otherwise) of the opposite sex, which he says "may be a common form of deception in animals." He documents a striking case from the insect world: a male scorpionfly can win a mate only by presenting her with a gift of a dead insect; but some males, instead of catching their own nuptial gifts, steal insects by approaching other males who already have them and imitating the behavior of females. This "clearly enhances the copulatory success and probably the survival" of the deceptive males: "In hunting for prey, males expend time and are exposed to web-building spider predators. Transvestites rob males of their prey, reducing their own hunting time and risks. The reduction in hunting time allows transvestites to copulate more frequently.... [M]ales that steal rather than catch prey reduce inter-copulatory time by 42 percent, obtaining more copulations per unit of time ..."[18]

Examples could be multiplied. To offer just one more, the social insects (such as ants, bees, and termites) are renowned for their highly "cooperative" behavior. However, the two naturalists who probably know best the workings of ant societies paint a different picture: "The more carefully entomologists have examined the fine details of colony organization, the more extensive and complex have been the conflicts revealed. To pay close attention to the relationships of particular individuals is like moving into an outwardly peaceful city only to realize, after living there for a while, that the place is rife with family quarrels, theft, street muggings, and even murder. Dominance struggles occur even among ant workers of the same colony."[19] Even when ants do cooperate with their colony-mates, they often do so for ends that we would not exactly view as altruistic. Colonies of honeypot ants practice true slavery: they often overrun weaker colonies of the same species, killing their queens, capturing other colony members, and subjecting them to forced labor.[20] As for ants in general:

> The spectacle of the weaver ants, their colonies locked in chronic border skir-mishes like so many Italian city-states, exemplifies a condition found through-out the social insects. Ants in particular are arguably the most aggressive and warlike of all animals. They far exceed human beings in organized nastiness; our species is by comparison gentle and sweet-tempered. The foreign policy aim of ants can be summed up as follows: restless aggression, territorial conquest, and genocidal annihilation of neighboring colonies whenever possible. If ants had nuclear weapons, they would probably end the world in a week.[21]

8.2   Selfishness and Its Evolutionary Consequences

8.2.1   *Parsimony, Homology, and Primate Behavior*

This picture of nature painted by modern biology is a far cry indeed from the old tradition of popular natural theology, in which (as in Aesop's fables) anthropo-morphic tales of the supposed exemplary behavior of animals were commonly used to drive home moral lessons. Reality, unfortunately, has proven to be far less edifying. On the other hand, anthropomorphists of a different stripe have similarly used anecdotes of "criminal" behavior in animals to paint human criminality as an evolutionary atavism.[22] Social critics to this day are divided between those who describe human miscreants as "animalistic" and those who consider this insulting to the animals.

The resemblances between animal and human behavior now being documented by serious scientists and their video cameras have a rather firmer factual basis than these old collections of anecdotes, and cannot be so easily dismissed as ideologically-motivated anthropomorphism. For those seeking moral lessons, these new data cut both ways. While furnishing undoubted examples of cooperative, at least outwardly altruistic behavior, our fellow creatures just as surely continue to behave in other, quite appalling ways. The reason why is by no means mysterious. Such behavior has "selective value"; it tends to benefit them as individuals in terms of their own survival and reproduction. It is "selfish," it is effective, and it is consequently enforced by natural selection. This is no crude conjecture: in a growing number of careful field and laboratory studies combining genetic analyses with mathematical game theory,[23] it has been demonstrated that many animals, from ants to primates, employ remarkably sophisticated strategies to their own genetic advantage, despite lacking the degree of consciousness we would have thought necessary to play such complicated games so shrewdly. Selection, it seems, has programmed them well.

Whatever their inner workings, these acts of animals do bear an uncomfortable outward resemblance to our own worst efforts. What are we to make of this? If our methodology and mode of reasoning are to be consistent with those of the modern evolutionary biologist, we must apply to these data the principle of parsimony: barring evidence to the contrary, detailed resemblances between species are most plausibly and economically explained by inheritance from a common ancestor, rather than by independent acquisition of the similar traits. This simple but powerful principle underlies all attempts to infer genealogical relationships among entities by examining the patterns of changes that occur as they and their lineal descendants are reproduced through time (as demonstrated, for instance, in the textual criticism of ancient manuscripts, or modern chain letters, and the accumulated copyists' errors they contain[24]). In the last three decades, this well-tried, common-sense method has been elaborated by biologists into a sophisticated body of theory and technique (complete with computer algorithms) known as phylogenetic or cladistic analysis, which is now universally used to determine the evolutionary links among organisms.[25]

Applying this conceptual approach to the case before us, similar (good or bad) behavior among the living higher primates (including humans) is most logically and straightforwardly explained as a common legacy retained from an earlier stage of evolution, rather than as a set of traits separately evolved by different species subsequent to their genealogical divergence. Hence it is legitimate (parsimonious) to apply the term "selfish," in the evolutionary (non-psychological) sense, univocally to both humans and other organisms. Further, it is empirically apparent that the human behavior patterns denoted by our words "murder," "theft," "deceit," "possessiveness," etc., are not (as traditionally assumed) uniquely the property of humans; nor are these resemblances to other species likely to be coincidental (resulting from independent "invention" by different species). Instead, we may infer that these traits of ours are shared with other species precisely because the common ancestor of all these species possessed them. In biologists' jargon, we can say that the selfish acts of humans and other species are *homologous*; that is, similar because derived from a common source.

Lest we put all blame on our remote ancestors while claiming any available credit for ourselves, we must also admit that the same logic applies to our more amiable traits. For example, as Frans de Waal puts it:

> Forgiveness is not, as some people seem to believe, a mysterious and sublime idea that we owe to a few millennia of Judeo-Christianity. It did not originate in the minds of people and cannot therefore be appropriated by an ideology or a religion. The fact that monkeys, apes, and humans all engage in reconcilia-tion behavior means that it is probably over thirty million years old, preceding the evolutionary divergence of these primates.[26]
>
> ... [C]onscience is not some disembodied concept that can be understood only on the basis of culture and religion. Morality is as firmly grounded in neurobiology as anything else we do or are. Once thought of as purely spiritual matters, honesty, guilt, and the weighing of ethical dilemmas are traceable to specific areas of the brain. It should not surprise us, therefore, to find animal parallels. The human brain is a product of evolution. Despite its larger volume and greater complexity, it is fundamentally similar to the central nervous system of other mammals. ... The fact that the human moral sense goes so far back in evolutionary history that other species show signs of it plants morality firmly near the center of our much-maligned nature. It is neither a recent inno-vation nor a thin layer that covers a beastly and selfish makeup.[27]

This book, however, is concerned not with human behavior in general but with sin in particular. This (and not the "Calvinist sociobiology" castigated by de Waal[28]) explains my emphasis here on the darker side of our nature. I wholeheartedly agree with him that "[h]umans and other animals have been endowed with a capacity for genuine love, sympathy, and care – a fact that can and will one day be fully reconciled with the idea that genetic self-promotion drives the evolutionary process."[29] In a similar vein, Stephen Pope wrote that "love and care may go with rather than against the grain of essential aspects of our nature as human; rather than being simply transcended, suspended, or eliminated, natural human affective capacities can be developed, unfolded, and amplified in an ethic of love."[30] Yet the origins of these affective capacities paradoxically lie in a selfishness which does need to be transcended.

If morality, love, and care, after all, are so anciently rooted in our evolutionary history, why might not they, rather than selfishness, be described as the central (or at least an equal) driving force of evolution? The answer is that they are indeed ancient, but not so ancient as selfishness, and for a very compelling reason.

It was noted in section 4.10 that the origins of altruism can be explained in terms of selfishness, but not vice versa. Granted, the self-interest of organisms has repeat-edly led them to cooperate, even at the most primitive levels. For example, it is now accepted that primitive one-celled organisms (prokaryotes) joined symbiotically (that is, for mutual benefit), one living within another, to form the first nucleated (eukaryotic) cells, which gave rise to all higher forms of life. Hence "cooperation" of a sort played a key role at that evolutionary juncture, and probably at others;[31] and analogous forms of self-interested cooperation, we may presume, eventually gave rise to altruism (at least of a limited kind). But self-interested cooperation is still self-interested. It is thus a very long way from what we like to think of as true altruism: in Jesus' words, laying down one's life for one's friends (John 15:13). Even apoptosis, the programmed death of certain cells in the body described in Chapter Six above, can be explained in "selfish" terms analogous to the kin selection that produces sterile worker castes in colonies of bees, ants, and termites: self-sacrifice in such cases directly contributes to perpetuating copies of the sacrificial cell's (or worker's) own DNA.

Why could true altruism (as opposed to mere cooperation) not have been the primitive condition of life, with selfishness as its "degenerate" derivative? Routine self-sacrifice for non-kin, of course, is distinctly at odds with survival under natural selection. But more fundamentally, true altruism (if it exists in nature at all) requires the consciousness of another's existence and needs, empathy with that other's situation, and a decision to act despite the cost to oneself. True altruism therefore presupposes an intellect and will of a caliber that does not and cannot exist in the simplest life forms, and thus could not have been there at life's beginnings. Selfish behavior, even cooperative behavior, is compatible with unconscious, mechanical programming; true altruism is not. Our unconscious beginnings could only have been rooted in selfishness; we attained the sophistication of intellect required for altruism only after long ages of evolution that was, inevitably, driven by selfish urges.

(This makes clear one way in which solution of the problem of original sin and evil has long been prevented – by our insistence on turning an important piece of the jigsaw puzzle the wrong way around. The traditional interpretation of Genesis 1–3 has God's perfect creation later corrupted by human sin; but we now see instead that the root of sin – evolutionary selfishness, in Elliott Sober's terminology – was in the world's beginning, whereas perfection still lies in the future. The evolutionary perspective forces us to acknowledge that Scripture is, above all, not about the past but about the *present* in every age: about our existential problems, about our relationship with God, about our [present] hopes for the future, and even about creation itself – not as something *made* "very good" once upon a time, but as a *creatio continua*, something God *is making* "very good." As Jesus put it, "My Father is at work until now, and I am at work as well" [John 5:17].)

Darwin himself recoiled from "laying the foundation of the noblest part of our nature in the base principle of selfishness;"[32] yet that is precisely the conclusion to which we latter-day disciples of his have come – unapologetically, and indeed with satisfaction at the reconciliation of ideas this represents.[33]

8.2.2 The Roots of Sin

It should be clear from all this that the common source of our and other species' selfish acts cannot be any "sin of Adam," and that the (obviously nonhuman) common ancestor of humans and other creatures, with which such acts originated, cannot be identified with the biblical Adam and Eve. The heritage in question is in fact far more ancient than the earliest apes, or primates, or mammals, or ants, or even plants. The primate behaviors that are homologous with our human sins are no more than particular (albeit dramatic) instances of the "selfishness" that, in its broadest, evolutionary sense, is the common heritage of *all* life – animals, plants, even the lowliest microbes – and one supposes that Adam cannot meaningfully be interpreted as the first bacterium! Rather, we must conclude that the first humans were simply far too late on the scene to have originated the unpleasant overt behaviors that in our species alone, through our moral choices, took on the character of sins.

To avoid misunderstandings, it must be emphasized that this line of argument is not an assertion of genetic determinism for human misdeeds: our bad behavior is no more and no less "determined" under this view, either physically or metaphysically, than under the traditional doctrine of original sin.[34] Genetic *influences* on behavior do not (at least in beings with free will) amount to genetic *determinism* of behavior. Human free will can, in any given instance, override whatever genetic (or learned) leanings we possess; we are not, in any direct way, programmed by our genes to inevitably lie, kill, or steal. Our self-preservational instincts may point us in such directions, and the culture around us may reinforce those tendencies (or counteract them, as the case may be); but in the end, the DNA doesn't make us do it, any more than the Creator of the evolutionary process does (Sirach 15:11–20, James 1:12–15).

The contrary assumption poses what philosophers call the problem of intentionality, which has been the logical undoing of many systems of evolutionary ethics: truly ethical behavior requires freedom from genetic or any other kind of compulsion.[35] All the same, this ethically necessary freedom can put up with a certain amount of pressure, short of absolute compulsion. I could not have evolved in the absence of gravity, any more than in the absence of selfishness. This same gravity draws me powerfully toward the center of the Earth, but I can still choose to climb a ladder, even if it takes some effort.

There must be, in us as in other organisms, a genetic predisposition to act in self-serving ways, since such creatures as bacteria, plants, and "lower" animals have no cultural mode of information transmission on which we can blame their selfish behavior, nor is there evidence that any such predisposition has recently been deleted from our genetic code. It must still be there in us, no matter how deeply buried under the later accretions of culture and mental versatility which dominate our overt behavior (and which can, if we choose, keep those old instincts from surfacing). Chesterton, as usual, said it well: "a permanent possibility of selfishness arises from the mere fact of having a self, and not from any accidents of education or ill-treatment."[36] And Genesis, as usual, also said it well, though allegorically: although the serpent in the story played the part of Satan, it was itself just one of the animals God had made (Genesis 3:1). Our inclination to sin, in short, arose out of our animal nature itself.

8.2.3   Nature: The Good, the Bad, or the Ugly?

The theological implication of this argument seems at first paradoxical, but is in fact the key to the whole problem. How could "selfishness," with all its negative connotations, be not only a part of God's creative plan but a necessary part, the very driving force of the whole creative process, *all* of whose products (as of the sixth "day" of creation) were pronounced "very good"? How is it that Catholic theologian John Haught, putting the ultimate positive spin on this, can even describe divine providence itself as "the ultimate font of the power of self-affirmation manifested in all living beings"?[37] Evidently this purely biological, amoral selfishness (evolutionary selfishness) was not only not evil in itself, but was *a positive good* (in a natural, not moral, sense), since it was the means God employed to achieve a good result.

This point must be stressed, as it is central to my entire argument. Others have too readily passed over the fundamental role of selfishness in driving all of organic evolution, dismissing it as an unfortunate but unavoidable by-product of the process. Thus says physicist and theologian Jerry Korsmeyer:

> Our God of persuasive power calls into existence creatures who have some power of self-determination. Because these created, evolving entities are finite and what is good for one often means a bad result for others, and because these creatures resist the divine call and seek selfish ends, natural evil is produced.[38]

Korsmeyer is not speaking here just of human beings, but of all living things. He seems to imagine that evolution could (or at least should) occur without competition. But it cannot be true that creatures (especially subhuman ones) which seek selfish ends are in general "resisting the divine call." The divine does not call them to be, in their own lifetimes, other than what they are and must be, what evolution has made them: seekers of survival and self-perpetuation. The result may indeed be, in part, natural (physical) "evil;" that is, suffering and death. But just as certainly, it is also, in part, the natural good of evolution itself, which is the only thing that can bring any of their descendants eventually to the point of transcending selfishness. (Even that can probably occur in, at most, one species per planet, because the first species to evolve our level of intelligence would – by selfishly hogging all the space and resources – probably preclude any competitors from emerging.)

Here, however, we collide head-on with a deeply felt and passionately argued opposing view: "the universe is hostile to life in general and human life in particular; the evolutionary process and its products are contrary to human ethical standards; human survival and ethical advance can be achieved only in opposition to the cosmic process."[39] In short, says evolutionary biologist G. C. Williams, "Mother Nature is a wicked old witch." He here takes up T. H. Huxley's century-old argument to the same effect[40] and updates it, but the theme is older than either of them – the eternal hostility between humanity and nature. In section 4.11 above, I sought to rebut one aspect of this argument, the assertion that evolution is cruel and wasteful; but there is something more to be said.

Like every deeply persuasive view, that of Huxley and Williams surely has some truth to it. Moral striving is clearly a striving against something, and I myself argue that that something is a phenomenon of nature: the selfishness built into our biological makeup. But to brand the entire universe as our implacable enemy in consequence of this is going too far. Williams[41] himself skewers the same error made in the opposite direction by proponents of the "Gaia hypothesis," which claims that the Earth somehow regulates its own environment for the benefit of living things. Williams's own argument makes it sufficiently clear that, in fact, our earthly and cosmic environments are stacked neither in life's favor nor against it: the universe, though obviously such as to permit life, is otherwise neutral toward it. (Even proponents of the "strong anthropic principle," which holds that the physical constants of the universe were custom-tailored to support human existence, would not argue that the universe's intrinsic congeniality to life spares living things the need to struggle for their continued existence.) It is life that is active and has adapted to the conditions it has encountered.

Though life must struggle, the surrounding cosmos in no sense struggles back, and thus it cannot be called our enemy – any more than the golf course is hostile to the frustrated golfer, no matter what paranoid fantasies enter his head. Challenging, yes; hostile, no. How, after all, can one say that the blind, indifferent laws of the universe have brought forth life, and at the same time argue that this same blind, indifferent universe is fundamentally hostile to life? Even our inbred selfishness is morally neutral, aiding our survival even as it impedes our ethical advance. And as for evolution and its products being contrary to human ethical standards, since when is it sensible to apply human ethical standards to impersonal phenomena of nature?

It is time to put behind us the ancient notion, and even the thoughtless rhetoric, that nature is our foe, to be battled and subdued: the Gnostic and Manichaean idea that spirit must forever war against matter. Even (perhaps especially) the atheist should have no trouble seeing that the universe is no more malevolent than it is benevolent. And to the theistic evolutionist, the indifferent stuff of the universe is but the medium and instrument of the Creator; it is no more the author (or the adversary) of created order than are the canvas and brush of the painter, or the stone and chisel of the sculptor. In calling the entire creation "good," the Creator was not ascribing to it a moral quality that only moral agents can possess; its goodness is that of the admirable tool and the admirable work.

Particularly from a biblical perspective, we can see the physical world, with its blind, "purposeless" Darwinian processes, as simply the servant that does not know what its Master is doing. Through the service of these blind processes, however, the Master has brought into being intelligent creatures, capable at last of understanding their Master's purposes, and of being called no longer servants but friends (John 15:15).

8.2.4   Does God Need to "Guide" Evolution?

This last observation, however, necessitates one more theological caveat: detailed divine "guidance" of the evolutionary process was quite unnecessary, despite the instinctive belief of many theistic evolutionists to the contrary. This statement is in no way an acceptance of deism or of an "otiose God" no longer concerned with the world. On the contrary: the autonomy of the universe, and the self-sufficient laws governing its process of evolution, are necessary corollaries of a truly biblical theology, one that envisions a self-humbling, self-emptying God of selfless love.[42] The Creator "withdraws" from the world, inviting rather than commanding it, precisely because "love by its very nature cannot compel;"[43] and this withdrawal makes room for precisely the unpleasant (to us) Darwinian laws which are the only laws we know of by which life could assemble itself. The Darwinian "messiness" epitomized in the sufferings of all living creatures, and the humility of the Creator epitomized in the sufferings of Jesus, are two sides of the same coin.

The Jesuit theologian Antony Campbell makes the useful suggestion that we distinguish among "unguided," "guided," and "risked" evolution. In the first case, the Creator leaves the universe to its own devices; in the second, the universe is constrained to evolve only as God wills it. What evolutionary theologians of today (including myself) are advocating is the third alternative: "God took the risk of creating an evolutionary universe, is with it in its evolution (with joy and sorrow, happiness and pain), but without controlling the process itself."[44]

For most of human history this possibility was inconceivable, and even today it is hard for most people to swallow. Yet we are discovering that all sorts of seemingly complex patterns in the structure and activity of living organisms – a zebra's stripes, a flower's petals, the schooling and flocking of fish and birds, the construction of a beehive – are generated by surprisingly simple rules of cell growth and individual behavior. In these sorts of "self-organizing" processes, order in an entire system emerges spontaneously out of purely local interactions among the system's subunits, with no central control or influence from outside, let alone any preconceived blueprint of what patterns will emerge.

> Do ants or, for that matter, termite mounds, flocks of birds, or schools of fish have leaders that all the members of the group follow? The answer is, clearly, no. Imagine the kind of oversight that would be needed to build a termite mound. The mound may be thousands or millions of times larger than an individual termite, and the construction of the edifice may take longer than dozens of individual lifetimes. It is simply inconceivable that an overseer guides all those processes. The same holds true of the flock and the school: although their movements are as elegant as the finest choreography, there is no choreographer to direct each bird or fish. The natural world, it turns out, is replete with patterns and processes that exhibit organization without an organizer, coordination without a coordinator.[45]

Such processes have been extensively studied and modeled with computer programs known as "cellular automata," which allow patterns on a computer screen to evolve over time subject to any specified rules. The surprising result, says biologist Scott Camazine, is that "for some initial patterns, the only way to determine how they evolve under the rules is to watch them."[46]

This has profound implications, both scientific and theological. On the one hand, it vastly increases our appreciation for the power of natural selection: when the alternatives among which selection chooses can be not only simple "point mutations" that govern single traits like eye color, but *rules that generate entire patterns of form or behavior*, then these self-organizing processes can be quickly coded into the organisms' genomes, making evolution much faster and more efficient. (A computer programmer likewise works more efficiently by using a high-level programming language than by writing directly in the machine code of 0s and 1s.) And on the other hand: even very simple rules can generate patterns that are not merely complex, but *entirely unpredictable*, in practice and maybe even in principle. *The only way to determine how these patterns evolve under the rules is to watch them.* How much more true must this be when the "evolving" units are not just two-dimensional geometric patterns on a computer screen, but entire species and ecosystems? Perhaps not even God can know what will result, in other than the most general terms, except by watching (from a vantage point outside time and space) what comes out of the processes set in motion at the creation. But then, I would suggest, God (even if constrained by our notion of time) would not *need* to know this in other than the most general terms.

8.2.5   Is the Experiment of Life Repeatable?

As discussed in section 4.2 above, nature is a great dialogue between chance and necessity, between the creation of novelty and the workings of inflexible laws. As just seen, rules of development can sometimes generate unpredictable results, which are then subject to approval or veto by natural selection. Notwithstanding the essential, unavoidable role of random input, it is still true that an autonomous process, based on reliable laws, produces repeatable (indeed, inevitable) results, at least in broad outline.

For example, I agree with Christian de Duve and other scientists who think that the origin of life from nonliving matter, not just once but probably countless times, was inevitable given physical conditions that are common in our universe. As explained in section 7.2 above, life reliably tends to progress to higher levels of efficiency and of ecological and organismic complexity. Given the existence of life, therefore, I think the evolution of intelligence in some form was likewise bound to occur again and again, even if whatever intelligent creatures there are on other planets bear little resemblance to us.

> Whatever the reason(s) for the laws of physics being the way they are, there is no doubt that the Universe is set up in such a way that the production of carbon, oxygen, and nitrogen in profusion (by human standards) is an inevitable consequence of the life cycles of stars, and that it is inevitable that planets like the Earth will form around stars like the Sun and be laced with complex organic molecules, originally from interstellar clouds, by the arrival of comets. We are made of stardust because we are a natural consequence of the existence of stars, and from this perspective it is impossible to believe that we are alone in the Universe.[47]

Therefore, if God's purpose was to make versatile, intelligent creatures whom their Creator could engage in a personal relationship, there was no need to tinker with the evolutionary process along its way: any and every intelligent species would be acceptable, no matter what it looked like. If you want to give away money in a lottery, all you have to do is hold the lottery: as long as you don't care who wins, there is no need to rig the game, because sooner or later *someone* is guaranteed to win. And as St. Peter learned long ago, God does not play favorites (Acts 10:34).

Here, unfortunately, we stumble into yet another current argument, over the repeatability of the history of life. This recently erupted in a public spat between paleontologists Stephen Jay Gould and Simon Conway Morris.[48] Gould argued that the origin of life is "reasonably predictable on planets of earthlike composition," whereas our kind of self-consciousness is far from inevitable and maybe unique. Conway Morris took the diametrically opposed view: given the existence of life, "a creature with intelligence and self-awareness on a level with our own would surely have evolved – although perhaps not from a tailless, upright ape"; however, he entertained "the real possibility that life arose but once, and that we are alone and unique in the cosmos" because life itself is unique to our planet.

As shown above, this paleontologist agrees and disagrees with both protagonists: *both* life and intelligence, in my view, will predictably evolve wherever in the universe the physical conditions permit. (Creationists, of course, embrace the fourth possibility: that neither could evolve anywhere at all!) This seems to me the plain message of Earth's fossil record, wherein we see similar ecological niches evoking similar kinds of creatures again and again throughout the history of life: each time the tape is replayed, in Gould's metaphor, the story comes out pretty much the same in substance, if not in detail, though Gould might dispute it. Sometimes the hoofed stock walks and leaps on four legs, like a deer; sometimes it walks on five "legs" and leaps on two, like a kangaroo with its versatile tail. In other cases, the "wolves" on different continents (like Australia's thylacines or "Tasmanian wolves," versus South America's extinct borhyaenids) are so alike that they baffle even specialists who try to decide whether or not they are closely related. Either way, thanks to natural selection working on chance variations, similar jobs are being done in similar environments with bodies built in accord with the same physical laws, often with startlingly similar (though sometimes startlingly different) results.

Three paleontologists, three opinions: the reader will have to take his or her pick. This is not the place to pursue this scientific argument further; it is clear enough on all sides that we each bring our own presuppositions to judgment calls like this one. My own bias is that intelligence in itself has obvious adaptive value, even though the combination of traits that allows maximum development of intelligence (including stereoscopic color vision, a jointed skeleton which facilitates measurement of distances and precise repetition of movements, prehensile organs like hands that are free from a locomotor role, the limbic system of the brain which makes possible our rich array of emotions, and a complex social organization) may come together in only the rarest of circumstances and species. Such purely biological contingencies as these – generated by a "selfish" evolutionary process, and without need for divine micromanagement – suffice, in my view, to produce the moral equivalent of us, reliably and repeatedly throughout the universe.

8.3 The Challenge of Reductionism: Self, Soma, and Culture

Let us return for a moment to the issue raised above at the end of our discussion of death (Chapter Six). It was demonstrated there that, in a strictly Darwinian sense, our somatic selves (including our consciousness) can be said to exist only to perpetuate our "selfish" DNA. In his concluding passage, William R. Clark poses the resulting dilemma in particularly stark terms:

> We want so desperately to be more than just a vehicle for DNA, and at least transiently we are. Yet somatic cells will die at the end of each generation, whether they are part of an insect wing or a human brain. We may come to understand death, but we cannot change this single, simple fact: in the larger scheme of things, it matters not a whit that some of these somatic cells contain all that we hold most dear about ourselves; our ability to think, to feel, to love – to write and read these very words. In terms of the basic process of life itself,

which is the transmission of DNA from one generation to the next, all of this is just so much sound and fury, signifying certainly very little, and quite possibly nothing.[49]

This was a glum note indeed on which to end a book; and one might well think that this represents all science can say on such a subject without trespassing on the realm of the spiritual. I wish to suggest, however, that even the agnostic or atheistic scientist is justified in slightly more optimism than this.

If we are to reduce ourselves to mere vehicles for DNA, we might as well pursue reductionism to its limit. After all, DNA itself is only a means to an end, only a storage medium like a computer disk – a storage medium that cells themselves invented to preserve their most useful evolutionary innovations. What is truly fundamental, and potentially immortal, is the *information* (laboriously compiled by natural selection) that DNA encodes. As we have learned from the rise of computer viruses, which (unlike DNA molecules or real viruses) are not material objects, pure information is capable of using matter and energy to propagate itself under the right circumstances. DNA is just one of information's ways of making more information – that is, more copies of itself.

If this is the case, then what is to prevent evolution from pioneering new ways to create and preserve information – new operating systems and storage media, in other words, like those that make our computers obsolete every few years? It has done so in the past; for example, the evolution of sex provided a quantum leap in the amount of new and potentially adaptive genetic variety that organisms could generate per unit of time. Similarly, the evolution of culture in our more immediate past accomplished much the same sort of breakthrough, allowing invention and exchange of adaptive information to occur faster by many orders of magnitude than was possible by genetic means. *And culture is an artifact of precisely those brains which seemed a moment ago to be no more than collections of expendable somatic cells.*

There is ample evolutionary precedent for radical flipflops in the functions and relative adaptive values of physical traits. Indeed (as was said in section 4.7 above), this seems to be the usual way in which evolutionary novelties arise. A set of gill supports which aids in breathing and filter-feeding in a primitive jawless fish takes on a subsidiary function in supporting the margins of the nearby mouth, and eventually is transformed into jaws, setting subsequent vertebrate evolution onto an entirely different, predatory track. Eons later, the bones forming a reptile's jaw joint happen to lie so close to the eardrum that they fortuitously help conduct sound waves to the ear; when an overhaul of the chewing mechanism renders these bones superfluous as parts of the jaws, they are opportunistically drafted into full-time service as components of the new, improved mammalian hearing system.[50] And so on. What began as a minor, subsidiary structure or function, almost an epiphenomenon, regularly ends up as the dominant feature of a new flowering of evolutionary success, with the most far-reaching consequences.

One such example, perhaps worthy of comparison with our primate ancestors' invention of culture, was our fishy ancestors' "invasion" of the land. Invasion, however, is too teleological a term: at the outset, staking a claim to terrestrial real estate was surely the farthest thing from their rudimentary minds. Air-breathing lungs and legs with digits (both of which seem to have evolved originally for use in water) were probably first of use to them when they still lived in shallow lagoons, marshes, and other wetlands, and had to wriggle through wet vegetation and survive in temporarily stagnant water. Their legs and lungs, in other words, started out as means of preserving their basically aquatic status quo, and only later proved useful for life on truly dry land.[51] For millions of years thereafter, their amphibian descendants remained tentative in their commitment to land, always returning to water to lay their eggs. In effect, an amphibian was a fish egg's way of producing more fish eggs, while in the meantime exploiting the resources of more or less terrestrial environments. Only with the evolution of a type of egg capable of surviving on completely dry land – the defining characteristic of a reptile – was the ancestral tie to aquatic habitats broken completely. The reptile and its desiccation-resistant "amniote" egg were DNA's, and information's, new way of propagating itself into habitats drier than any previously accessible to vertebrates.

What, then, is so strange in supposing that somatic cells themselves might stumble on a way to reproduce information that is even more efficient than that of the germ cells? And that this new, somatic-based, "cultural" adaptive mechanism might quickly come to overshadow in importance the genetic mechanisms of evolution? And that, as a result, the somatic (brain) cells responsible for this new, non-DNA-based mechanism of information storage and transmission might therefore be entitled to recognition as more than mere "vehicles of DNA" – and that their cultural products might signify, even in a purely Darwinian sense, much more than mere sound and fury?

Notes

1. Underhill 1991, 14–15.
2. Bruteau (1997, 50–53, 166–173) steps the reader lucidly through the logic of how living things had to evolve such characteristics and concepts as selfhood, competition, cooperation, predation, pain, self-reference, deception, judgment, value, inequality, intelligence, knowledge of the other, sensitivity, memory, choice, consciousness, self-consciousness, creativity, imagination, rights, morality, cruelty, sin, justice, sympathy, friendship, and altruism. "All this," she notes (elaborating on an insight of Teilhard discussed in section 13.1 below), "comes from the very nature of finitude itself."
3. See Sober and Wilson 1998 for a recent discussion.
4. Goodall 1986; see also Hrdy 1977, Fossey 1983, de Waal 1982, 1989, 1996 regarding other primates.
5. De Waal 1989, 238–239.
6. De Waal 1986, 240.
7. De Waal and Lanting 1997.
8. De Waal, in de Waal and Lanting 1997, 84–85.
9. Cheney and Seyfarth 1990a, 1990b; de Waal 1989.
10. Hrdy 1977.
11. Hausfater and Hrdy 1984.
12. Packer 1994; Packer and Pusey 1997.
13. De Waal and Lanting 1997, 118; see also Hrdy 1977, Hausfater and Hrdy 1984.
14. Kruuk 1972, 246, 256.
15. Grzimek et al. 1973, Dominey and Blumer 1984, Polis 1984.

16. For a wide-ranging study of this topic, see Mitchell and Thompson 1986. Hauser 1997 provides a methodological analysis and critique of studies of deceptive behavior.
17. Thornhill 1979, 412.
18. Thornhill 1979, 412, 413.
19. Hölldobler and Wilson 1994, 88–90.
20. Hölldobler and Wilson 1994, 73, 126.
21. Hölldobler and Wilson 1994, 59.
22. For example, Lombroso 1887.
23. See Dugatkin and Reeve 1998.
24. Platnick and Cameron 1977, Bennett et al. 2003.
25. For a full exposition see, for example, Wiley 1981.
26. De Waal 1989, 270.
27. De Waal 1996, 217–218.
28. De Waal 1996, 17.
29. De Waal 1996, 16–17.
30. Pope 1994, 154. Pope 2001, 421 argues that conscious motives cannot be conflated with unconscious or biological drives; unconscious selfish motives on the genetic level are compatible with genuine moral altruism on the level of the conscious individual.
31. Cf. Margulis and Sagan 2001.
32. Darwin 1871, 1:98.
33. It has even been argued that Darwinian principles are functionally equivalent to important features in the moral theology of St. Thomas Aquinas (Pope 1994).
34. Cf. the view of St. Augustine; Duffy 1993, 94.
35. See Gewirth 1993.
36. Chesterton 1905, 79.
37. Haught 2001, 107.
38. Korsmeyer 1998, 123.
39. Williams 1993, 229.
40. Huxley 1894.
41. Williams 1993.
42. See Haught 2000.
43. Haught 2000, 112.
44. Campbell 2000, 99n.
45. Camazine 2003, 35.
46. Camazine 2003, 38.
47. Gribbin and Gribbin 2000, 225.
48. See *Natural History* 107(10), Dec. 1998–Jan. 1999.
49. Clark 1996, 178–179.
50. See Hopson 1987.
51. See Thomson 1980, 1994; Coates and Clack 1991; Daeschler and Shubin 1998.

CHAPTER NINE

Evolution and human ethics

[T]he human animal is no longer innocent in its quest for survival. Because now there exists the additional possibility of recognizing the other as a self with a claim to survival equal to one's own. ... Selfishness now presents itself as an acute problem, for in asserting my self-interest, I am aware of my violating not only your self-interest but your very integrity as a self with a consciousness which I know to be parallel to my own. Animal innocence gives way to human guilt.

Craig L. Nessan[1]

9.1   The Moral Divide

Section 8.2.3 above concluded that the amoral "selfishness" of the evolutionary process was not only not evil, but was a positive good in that it was the means of bringing about God's good creation of living things – including the intelligent ones who in turn would create what we know as culture. What, then, went wrong? How did "the mainspring of evolution" end up as "original sin"?

The step was actually a very short one. The appearance in history of creatures capable of self-conscious reflection (whether or not one attributes their attainment of such consciousness to direct divine intervention) gave a moral dimension to acts that previously had lacked such a dimension. The acts themselves did not change; what was new was the actors' consciousness that they were free to choose among alternatives that would differ in their harmful or beneficial effects on others, and were even free to make their own self-interest the measure of morality – to claim for themselves, in the biblical allegory, the godlike Knowledge of (that is, sovereignty over) Good and Evil.

We can see, moreover, that this freedom of choice need not have come out of nowhere, or by way of a *deus ex machina*; its origins too, like all the other steps in this story, are intelligible in terms of evolution. In the contemporary view of our evolved intelligence as a composite of diverse faculties, "our nature is many-faceted and internally contradictory, and ... political behavior often involves a trade-off between dispositions that work in opposition in certain contexts. The result is psychological ambivalence and flexible behavioral compromise in specifiable directions."[2] Such psychological ambivalence in the face of choices is just the prerequisite needed for the appearance and exercise of free will.

Here we may note a clarification by philosopher Elliott Sober: "Morality does not rule out selfishness. What it rules out is *selfishness come what may*. It rules out a kind of selfishness that is totally insensitive to the situations of self and other."[3] (Note how our discourse, and our thinking, are hobbled by our lacking so much as a non-pejorative word for a "selfishness" that is not immoral!) Evolutionary selfishness, in Sober's terms, is one thing; psychological (conscious) selfishness is another; and psychological selfishness that disregards the needs of others is yet a third. Only the last, I would argue, is sinful; in many situations I can see to my own needs (act selfishly) without sinning against others. (For example, I might choose to get some needed extra sleep after an exhausting day, instead of doing some voluntary charitable work for which no one is depending on me.) What I wish to emphasize is the historical, ontological *continuity* among these three distinct kinds or degrees of selfishness: each in turn has arisen out of, and built upon, its predecessor.

The "stain of original sin," therefore, is no more nor less than the first of these kinds: that innate tendency to act selfishly which drove our entire evolution right up to and beyond the moment we became human – evolutionary "business as usual." This tendency is so ingrained in all living things that it would be practically inconceivable for our first human ancestors not to have acted on it, in ways both harmful and not harmful to others. The harmful acts themselves, however, only acquired a moral dimension (became "actual sin") when committed deliberately by self-conscious creatures aware that they were harming others; and the evolution or infusion of this freedom of moral choice is what made us human in the theological sense. Like a spent booster rocket lifting astronauts into orbit, the creative selfishness of evolution carried us as far as the plane of humanity; but to continue our upward journey, we must become detached from it.

Therefore, although the inherently selfish yet "good" behavior of other living things is a "law of nature," this law is in no sense normative or prescriptive for human behavior – contrary to the view, or the fear, of some evolutionary philosophers. Instead, as discussed below, humans are called to follow a higher law than the creative selfishness of evolution: what John Haught has called the "creative selflessness" of God.[4] We might read this meaning into the words of St. Paul: "while we were not yet of age we were like slaves subordinated to the elements of the world; but when the designated time had come, God sent forth his Son ... to deliver from the law [here, the law of nature] those who were subjected to it, so that we might receive our status as adopted sons." (Galatians 4:3–5)

This point is worth dwelling on a moment longer, since it is consistently misconstrued by special creationists and perhaps even by some evolutionary biologists. As a recent creationist tract put it,

> ... evolution holds that suffering and death are 'good,' and have been on earth for hundreds of millions of years, long before man. In fact, it was the death of the 'unfit' which was paralleled by 'survival of the fittest' and allowed man to evolve from the animals. In evolution, our ancestors possessed animal desires fueled by animal instincts; thus, evolution is specifically used to justify sinful behavior.[5]

But explaining is not justifying. We are beings with free will, responsible for our moral choices and no longer limited to acting on our instincts. Any evolutionist who actually argued as above would be ignoring the crucial moral divide that we crossed when we became self-conscious moral agents.

This new overlay of moral consciousness subtracted nothing from the cerebral hardware and behavioral software with which organic evolution had endowed us. It did, however, permanently change the rules of the evolutionary game. It came on the heels of the evolutionary increase in intelligence that allowed our higher-primate ancestors to invent "culture," the systems of thought and material technology that are now our primary means of adaptation to our physical and biological environments. Human evolution has long since all but abandoned genetic change and its glacial pace; henceforth our evolution is mainly cultural, is incomparably faster – and is directed by our own moral (or immoral) choices. Cultural evolution too, of course, can be driven by selfishness, and it usually has been. But we now have an alternative. Will we stick to the selfish behavior without which our ancestors never would have survived, let alone evolved? Or will we incorporate into our cultural adaptations the kind of altruism that Christianity and other ethical systems urge on us, as our best guide for our future evolution? Having eaten the fruit, we can go on doing what comes naturally; or (as Satan said, truly for once) we can become like God: unselfish.[6]

9.2   The Evolution of Ethics

9.2.1   Ethics Among Animals

In my earlier discussion of one of the objections to evolution (section 4.12), I argued against attempts to derive human ethics explicitly from evolutionary theory. This, however, is not to deny the historical origin of human ethics, in part at least, from our evolutionary background; nor more generally, to deny the historical importance or value of ethics arrived at purely by natural means, including human reason uninformed by supernatural revelation. Attempts to construct systems of "evolutionary ethics" have sometimes suffered from simplistic and overly narrow notions of what counts as "evolutionary" (or "biological"[7]). Specifically, competition of the crudest kind is merely the most basic, not the most refined, form of behavior through which natural selection can act. Until quite recently, however, biologists (and ethicists) were unaware of the sophistication of many animals' social behavior; and consequently they imagined that many kinds of cooperation were human monopolies and hence had to be explained as human inventions rather than legacies of Darwinian evolution.

On the contrary, the pervasive occurrence, diversity, and biological importance of both cooperation and competition in a wide range of species are now recognized. In combination, cooperation and competition, by leading to social behavior, may even have made possible intelligence itself, and consequently ethics. Many biologists today argue persuasively that primate and human intelligence, or at least important aspects of it, evolved in response to selective pressure for social sophistication, including cooperation together with competition and exploitation of others. On this view, our intelligence was molded less by the demands of physical survival, such as tool-making and cooperative hunting, than by the psychological demands of social interaction and political gamesmanship.[8]

Like all games, social and political life has rules, including those we call ethics. Because social living among primates is very ancient, I would guess that the overwhelming majority of human ethical principles – taboos against killing, stealing, deceit, and the like, at least within one's own social group, and in general a sense of fairness – have deep evolutionary roots, regardless of whether they are handed down through our genes or through our learned social customs. Such ethical principles, and ones even more subtle, can in fact be seen at work in many nonhuman animals today.

De Waal,[9] for instance, has documented at length the primate origins of reconciliation, consolation, succor, and other behaviors (even high-level "diplomacy" and peacemaking between leaders of warring groups) that we would consider desirable, ethical, or virtuous in a human context, just as we would consider many of these same animals' selfish behaviors sinful in a human context. Elements of what we call morality are found in other species. And this should not be surprising, since ethics of some sort, including what de Waal[10] calls community concern, are essential to the functioning of any society, animal or human. As ethologist Marc Bekoff[11] puts it, "morality evolved because it is adaptive." The Golden Rule, in the form of reciprocal altruism, is followed by many of our fellow creatures.

Indeed, it would not even be surprising if, as de Waal[12] argues, some animals (like some humans) occasionally performed altruistic acts in the absence of any tangible payoff: sympathy for one's associates had to start somewhere. For it to have evolved, some payoff must once have been present, but the actor need not have been conscious of this or consciously motivated by it. If it was sometimes adaptive to internalize and facilitate deceitfulness by means of self-deception, perhaps a similar adaptive mechanism promoted the service of others. On the conscious level, there may be only the satisfaction of helping another – a feeling from which our species has abstracted a moral principle, and then, by free will, internalized it as a duty. This would explain how genetic selfishness could become compatible with genuine altruism on the part of the conscious individual, as argued by Pope.[13] "To this day the sincerity of human feelings continues to be a topic of debate," notes de Waal,[14] but I agree with him that "people can be altruistic and honest without on every occasion thinking of the advantages." This blurring of category boundaries – this gradation between "pure" extremes, like selfishness and altruism, yielding intermediate states in which matters and motives are decidedly mixed – is what one naturally expects to see in the course of evolution.

Considering ethics among "higher" animals as at least partly cultural artifacts, we might say that (learned) ethical behavior is a mental analogue of tool-using behavior: it serves to facilitate the individual's success in society, and incidentally makes social life more safe, tolerable, and pleasant for all. Moreover:

> Not satisfied with a society fashioned by uncoordinated individual efforts, one of humanity's chief accomplishments is to translate egocentric community concerns into collective values. The desire for a modus vivendi fair to everyone may be regarded as an evolutionary outgrowth of the need to get along and cooperate, adding an ever-greater insight into the actions that contribute to or interfere with this objective. Our ancestors began to understand how to preserve peace and order – hence how to keep their group united against external threats – without sacrificing legitimate individual interests. They came to judge behavior that systematically undermined the social fabric as "wrong," and behavior that made a community worthwhile to live in as "right." Increasingly, they began to keep an eye on each other to make sure that their society functioned in the way they wanted it to function.[15]

This conscious enforcement of social norms – *any* norms, "objectively" good, bad, or indifferent, that a society chooses – provides a powerful evolutionary explanation not only of pragmatic ethics but also of quirky customs that in themselves may have no adaptive value. The adaptive advantage may lie instead in the social cohesion resulting from the social control itself:

> The seemingly nonfunctional nature of human behavioral diversity is one of the main reasons that many people remain skeptical about evolutionary approaches to human behavior. Unfortunately, the critics cannot explain the behavioral diversity themselves, beyond vague appeals to "culture." When strong rewards and punishments that can be imposed at low cost are incorporated into evolutionary game theory, the concept of behaviors that are nonfunctional and even dysfunctional outside of the context of the social norms becomes quite reasonable. The effect of social norms on the evolution of arbitrary behaviors is much like the effect of female preference on the evolution of arbitrary ornaments in males, such as the peacock's tail. Not only does this unite the seemingly opposed adaptationist and nonadaptationist camps, but it provides an explanation of behavioral diversity that is more specific than vague appeals to culture. If we could eliminate the ability to impose powerful social norms at low cost, but retain all other aspects of human cultural processes, we might witness a dramatic collapse of behavioral diversity.[16]

9.2.2 Human Ethics Before and After Jesus

The evolution of human intelligence, then, led naturally to the elaboration of diverse ethical systems, at the same time it was producing more complex political, economic, military, and other communal expressions of selfishness. Greater intelligence likewise enabled us to build houses, while our chimpanzee cousins (with exactly as long an evolutionary history as ours) continued to shiver miserably in the rain. Ethics were understood as no less integral to the definition of civilization than living in houses; "civilized behavior" is today a synonym for "ethical behavior." So we find that ethical precepts, in the form of collections of wise sayings, are among the earliest known forms of human literature. From the *Instruction of Ptah-hotep* in the Egypt of 2450 BCE, to Confucius, Buddha, and the Greek philosophers of over two millennia later, the world of "pagan" antiquity enjoyed an abundance of edifying advice – not to mention codes of enforceable law, from Hammurabi to the empires of China, Rome, and elsewhere. (A frequently stated purpose of these law codes was to protect the weak from oppression by the strong[17] – an arguably altruistic aim on the part of a ruler, though one paying that ruler tangible dividends in the form of good order and good repute among his or her subjects. Belying crude notions of "survival of the fittest," the identical technique of leadership is also used by chimpanzees.[18])

What, then, was left for the revealed religions to contribute? Apart from radical monotheism, this is not so obvious as one might think. The Ten Commandments and the wisdom literature of the Bible contain little that is not found in the ethics of other traditions: lying, stealing, killing, offenses against filial piety and marital fidelity, neglecting the cult of the gods – all these are universally reviled. At first glance, it would seem that the God of the Hebrew Scriptures sought to accomplish little more at the outset than weaning the Hebrew children away from polytheism, human sacrifice, and temple prostitution, and getting them to practice the elementary ethics that the civilized peoples around them already preached.

However, there is a novelty in the biblical commandments: they reveal a God whose *fundamental* concern is with ethics, rather than with power or social control. Indeed, as Bible scholar George Mendenhall[19] explains, they are not really "commandments" at all (grammatically, they are not even stated in imperative or prohibitive form!), but are better thought of as ten "commitments" – plain statements describing the religious values and ethical obligations that are freely embraced by those who choose to follow Yahweh. Through them, Yahweh was *inviting* those who entered the Covenant to acknowledge the universal cross-cultural validity of a *divinely-endorsed value system.*[20] Departures from these commitments were therefore seen as offenses against God (to whom the Israelites were *individually* bound by the Covenant) and not just against one's fellow humans. This reflects the more basic revelation, noted above in section 4.12, of God's passionate concern for humanity and for the creation in general. And significantly for our purposes here, what people were challenged in the Decalogue to take on were commitments "all of which restrict self-interest."[21]

Beginning with the monarchic period, however, the Israelites gradually lost sight of this initially ethical focus of Yahwism. Mendenhall[22] shows that although their society had started out radically distinct from those around them (as discussed in section 9.3 below), they allowed it to become just another nation among the nations, themselves just another ethnic group, and their God just another religious figurehead for a ruling elite. The Law of Moses itself was eventually elaborated into numerous precepts that served mainly to demarcate the people of Israel from other cultures and to provide them with concrete ways in which to show their devotion to their God – but amid all these ritual precepts, the ethical essentials easily got lost. In response, for centuries thereafter, prophets such as Amos, Hosea, Isaiah, and Jeremiah strove to raise the moral standard above the merely legalistic and ritualistic, and to get back to the ethical ideals that were the original essence of the Law. Their success was mixed, however, and ritual and legalism remained central concerns.

Thus, over the ensuing centuries, the complexities of the Jewish Law occasioned much learned debate about the relative importance of what had become a host of distinct commandments. At length, a lawyer put the question to a rabbi named Jesus of Nazareth, whose reply (Matthew 22:37–40) is a milestone in our ethical evolution.[23] The greatest law, said Jesus, is to love God (no surprise there); but the second-greatest is to love one's neighbor as oneself. Though not in itself original with Jesus (it is found in Leviticus 19:18, 33–34), that latter provision of the Law had up till then been considered no more important than many others. Even though "neighbor" was usually construed narrowly in his culture to mean fellow-countryman, for Jesus to give such prominence to this idea – putting the interests of others on the same level as one's own self-interest, and not just from sporadic generosity but as a consistent rule – was downright novel from the Darwinian viewpoint.

But then (as told in Luke 10:25–37) Jesus went on to drive home just how novel he meant it to be. The lawyer, ever alert for loopholes, pressed him further: "And who is my neighbor?" The reply was the parable of the Good Samaritan. Today we may fail to appreciate that the title this parable came to bear is an oxymoron – as much so as a "good Indian" would have been in the nineteenth-century American West, or a "good Palestinian" in Israel today. Samaritans were despised enemies of the Jews. What Jesus meant was: "Who is your neighbor? Your enemy is your neighbor. Even the one you despise most is your neighbor. It is *that neighbor's* interest that you are to set equal to your own." And throughout his teaching, Jesus made clear that this pertained especially to the despised poor: in short, to those who not only would not but could not repay.

Here was something new. Here was altruism stripped of the very possibility of reciprocity. Like many of his predecessors, Jesus approved of the Golden Rule, but it would be a serious mistake to reduce his teaching to this minimal principle alone. If, as he (and Rabbi Hillel before him) said, the rule of reciprocal altruism really sums up the Law and the Prophets (Matthew 7:12), that only goes to show how small an advance the Law of Moses had made beyond the law of the jungle. For it is one thing to say (or imply, as in Leviticus 19:33–34), "Treat others as you would have *them* treat *you*;" this implies at least the possibility of reciprocity. But it is subtly different for Jesus to say, "Treat your neighbor as *you* treat *yourself*." Of course, when your "neighbor" is your kinsman, even this latter injunction involves no more than classic kin selection: genetically, to a certain degree, your neighbor *is* yourself. But with his parable of the Good Samaritan, Jesus explicitly ruled out this sense of the word "neighbor": for him, "self" (on this concrete, biological level) is as different from neighbor as may be. And between you and your literal self, no question of reciprocity can arise.

(Of course, Jesus makes this distinction between self and neighbor – negating a primitive concept of kinship based on genetic affinity – in order to raise our consciousness to a higher view of kinship with *all* people, based on our common parentage in God [and now reinforced by discovery of our common evolutionary parentage]. However, this does not mean that we may not give priority to serving our closest relatives or associates when we are responsible for them – following the "order of love" as Aquinas, Calvin, and others have traditionally taught.[24] Jesus acknowledges that duty to our dependents comes first [Matthew 15:4–6].)

Another significant aspect of Jesus' command, easily overlooked,[25] is its clear premise that one should treat oneself *well*. Obviously, we are not being told here to model our treatment of others on self-hatred, nor to uncritically tender the self-sacrifice demanded by oppressors.[26] Jesus and the Law of Moses both take it for granted that there is nothing tainted about proper esteem of oneself. Seen today from a Darwinian vantage point, this implies a reaffirmation of the basic goodness of human nature – indeed of the whole living creation – in which selfishness plays a central, creative role. Once noticed, this reaffirmation seems all the more striking for the offhand way it is slipped in: *of course* it is good and healthy and in accord with God's plan to love yourself! How could the world be otherwise? And yet, at the very moment in history when Jesus implicitly reaffirmed the goodness of the self-love that had gotten us to our present stage of evolution, he also explicitly called on us to leave behind that limited good in favor of something greater.

St. Paul, who wrestled at length[27] with the Mosaic Law's inability to offer salvation, was acutely conscious that Jesus had somehow changed radically the rules of the game: "if anyone is in Christ, he is a new creation. The old order has passed away; now all is new!" (2 Corinthians 5:17). And he knew where the change had been made: "The whole law has found its fulfillment in this *one* saying: 'You shall love your neighbor as yourself'" (Galatians 5:14; emphasis added). Just how fundamental this change was, though, perhaps not even St. Paul could see as clearly as can a modern evolutionist; because, in fact, Jesus plainly told his followers to do nothing less than defy the ancient law of natural selection.[28]

"You have heard the commandment, 'You shall love your countryman but hate your enemy.' My command to you is: love your enemies.... If you love those who love you, what merit is there in that?" (Matthew 5:43–48)

"Love your enemy and do good; lend without expecting repayment. Then will your recompense be great. You will rightly be called sons of the Most High, since he himself is good to the ungrateful and the wicked." (Luke 6:35)

"Whoever wishes to be my follower must deny his very self, take up his cross each day, and follow in my steps. Whoever would save his life will lose it, and whoever loses his life for my sake will save it." (Luke 9:23–24)

"If anyone comes to me without turning his back on his father and mother, his wife and his children, his brothers and sisters, indeed his very self, he cannot be my follower." (Luke 14:26)

The crowd seated around him told him, "Your mother and your brothers and sisters are outside asking for you." He said in reply, "Who are my mother and my brothers?" And gazing around him at those seated in the circle he continued, "These are my mother and my brothers. Whoever does the will of God is brother and sister and mother to me." (Mark 3:32–35)

"Do not suppose that my mission on earth is to spread peace. My mission is to spread, not peace, but division. I have come to set a man at odds with his father, a daughter with her mother, a daughter-in-law with her mother-in-law: in short, to make a man's enemies those of his own household. Whoever loves father or mother, son or daughter, more than me is not worthy of me. He who will not take up his cross and come after me is not worthy of me. He who seeks only himself brings himself to ruin, whereas he who brings himself to nought for me discovers who he is." (Matthew 10:34–39)

Jesus told [a young man], "If you seek perfection, go, sell your possessions, and give to the poor...." Hearing these words, the young man went away sad, for his possessions were many. Jesus said to his disciples, "... It is easier for a camel to pass through a needle's eye than for a rich man to enter the kingdom of God." When the disciples heard this they were completely overwhelmed, and exclaimed, "Then who can be saved?" Jesus looked at them and said, "For man it is impossible; but for God all things are possible." (Matthew 19:21–26)

"Whenever you give a lunch or dinner, do not invite your friends or brothers or relatives or wealthy neighbors. They might invite you in return and thus repay you. No, when you have a reception, invite beggars and the crippled, the lame and the blind. You should be pleased that they cannot repay you, for you will be repaid in the resurrection of the just." (Luke 14:12–14)

Though a reward is promised, its spiritual nature – approval by God, though quite likely ingratitude, even persecution, from humans – is as far removed from Darwinian rewards as is possible to imagine. In fact, the latter rewards are to be consciously avoided! While evolutionary ethicists sometimes seek to explain altruism in terms of the value to the altruist of a good reputation, Jesus warned against even this subtle ploy:

> "Be on guard against performing religious acts for people to see. Otherwise expect no recompense from your heavenly Father. When you give alms, for example, do not blow a horn before you in synagogues and streets like hypocrites looking for applause. You can be sure of this much, they are already repaid. … Keep your deeds of mercy secret, and your Father who sees in secret will repay you." (Matthew 6:1–4)

And just to underline the fact that this philosophy runs flatly contrary to the (Darwinian) way of the world:

> "[Father,] I gave [my disciples] your word, and the world has hated them for it; they do not belong to the world any more than I belong to the world." (John 17:14)

To follow Jesus, in short, is to obey his most basic command: "Reform your lives" – that is, change your whole way of thinking and acting and your whole approach to life (Mark 1:15; cf. Jeremiah 7:3ff.).[29] It means rejecting much behavior that is genetically programmed as well as much that is culturally prescribed – rejecting self-advancement in favor of advancing the Reign of God.[30] It means defying the system of rules that John's Gospel personifies as "the Prince of this world." It means finally facing up to the implications of Isaiah 55:8: "For my thoughts are not your thoughts, nor are your ways my ways, says the Lord."

Nor did Jesus stop at giving advice. He lived his life selflessly (few celebrities today would renounce the copyright to their own names; Mark 9:38–40). But beyond that, he even modeled this new ethic in his own death, which he knowingly incurred by publicly shaming the powerful who neglected the needs of the powerless. (Transcending the misdirected arguments over whether to blame Jews or Romans for his death, we can see here why *all* of us are truly implicated in killing him and all other martyrs to truth and justice: to quote Monika Hellwig in Chapter One, we all contribute to that "force for evil that … tends to crush out of existence any who persist in acting in critical opposition.") Furthermore, Jesus consciously and explicitly cast his death in the pattern of, and as a renewal of, the sacrifice that concluded the Covenant: the rapprochement or (re)conciliation between God and Israel (Matthew 26:28; cf. Exodus 24:4–8, Colossians 1:19–20). As he did, so are we to do.

> "I give you a new commandment: love one another. Such as my love has been for you, so must your love be for each other." (John 13:34)

Thus the final step: from "Treat others as you would have *them* treat you" to "Treat others as *you* treat yourself" to "Treat others as *I* treat you" – which is to say, with a totally disinterested altruism, with the same lack of expectation of repayment that he urged in Luke 14:12–14.

To disciples such as Paul, what was most astonishing in Jesus' self-sacrifice was his willingness to die for sinful humans:

> It is rare that anyone should lay down his life for a just man, though it is barely possible that for a good man someone may have the courage to die. It is precisely in this that God proves his love for us: that while we were still sinners, Christ died for us. (Romans 5:7–8)

God/Christ, divine and in need of nothing, is not conceivably motivated even by the heavenly reward offered to us; his willingness to die in our service thus represents perfect altruism.[31] And this self-sacrificial altruism is incomprehensible to the "wisdom" of the world, because it is directly at odds with the way of the world (which mandates, among other things, Darwinian behavior).[32]

> The message of the cross is complete absurdity to those who are headed for ruin, but to us who are experiencing salvation, it is the power of God. ... Has not God turned the wisdom of this world into folly? (1 Corinthians 1:18–20)

Not surprisingly, this world is perennially puzzled by un-Darwinian, un-self-centered behavior, especially when encountered in its most pronounced forms, such as monastic vows of poverty, chastity, and obedience.

Let's dwell for a moment longer on this contrast between God and God's creatures. Theists are often accused of creating God, or gods, in their own image; and clearly this has been true of most of the gods humanity has worshipped. But the God of Abraham, Isaac, and Jacob is different. Yahweh – the "I AM" of the burning bush, the Pure Act of Scholastic philosophy – is in fact the most radically alien being that the human mind has ever tried to grasp. No extraterrestrial dreamed up by science-fiction writers rivals in "otherness" the eternal, immaterial, self-existent, all-knowing, all-powerful, infinitely loving and compassionate deity of the Abrahamic tradition. What would a god *not* made in our image look like, if not this? This God seems more the antithesis than the mirror image of what we are; and mystics agree that whatever statement we make about the divine must immediately be qualified by its negation – so inadequate are our human concepts to encompass or exhaust the mystery of God.

Furthermore – as if this notion of divinity were not already alien enough to our own nature – Christianity has added the mind-bending assertions that this God who is absolutely One is at the same time a *community* of three "persons"; and (the ultimate scandal to all other religions) that one of these "persons" has stepped into our history by taking on a real human nature, complete with a human body! So familiar to us Christians have these doctrines become, however, that we usually fail to appreciate how strange they have seemed to the rest of the ancient and modern world. Writers of fiction, or recruiting brochures, could scarcely have concocted a set of theological propositions with *less* immediate appeal to the rational human mind (cf. the reaction of the Capernaum congregation in John

6:41–66!), or more at odds with the rest of our religious, and even our evolution-ary, history.

The case in point is this matter of perfect altruism. Just how original and unique was the total transcendence of self-interest in the life and teaching of Jesus? It is hard for us Christians to judge clearly through two thousand years of hindsight. Perhaps it was only a small step from the limited, conditional altruism of previous ethical systems to the pure altruism of Jesus. Perhaps the idea of pure altruism can also be found in Buddhism or other faiths. I will leave that question to students of comparative religion. I think the relevant measure of its "otherness" is that no matter where or how often this divine altruism has been revealed to us, even despite two millennia of "Christian" civilization it is still utterly foreign to our human nature (cf. John 8:23). The culture of Wall Street, the mentality of the downsizing corporation, the politics of indifference to the poor and minorities, the readiness to exploit those lacking the power to protect themselves – these are what come naturally to us.[33] Even the atheistic evolutionist Richard Dawkins agrees that "pure, disinterested altruism" is "something that has no place in nature, something that has never existed before in the whole history of the world."[34] This is why the precepts of Jesus seem, and are, so terribly challenging; and why, more broadly, the idea of God as a "suffering servant" is still so shocking.[35] What Jesus calls us to is nothing less than the subversion (or better, the *conversion*) of evolution itself.

From reciprocal altruism to pure altruism may be a small extrapolation in pure logic, but Darwin was right in sensing what an impossible leap it is in the concrete world of biology. Darwinian evolution was both necessary and sufficient to raise us to the jumping-off point for such a leap, by making us the conditionally-altruistic creatures that we are; but it can carry us no further. Even when (as envisioned by Stephen Pope[36]) we are conscious of none but altruistic motives, and thus deserve some credit for our morally good acts, we can never be quite sure of our total freedom from genetic selfishness, and can never in any case be equally altruistic toward all people everywhere. The divine, universal altruism of Christ, even the very idea of it, is therefore something that we, by our own power, can scarcely even approach asymptotically, never perfectly achieving it. As the farmer told the lost traveler in the old joke, it really seems in practice that "You can't get there from here."

At least one prophet before Jesus had an inkling that God would need to inter-vene in person to get us over this hump, by changing, in a sense, our very hearts:

> The days are coming, says the Lord, when I will make a new covenant with the house of Israel and the house of Judah. It will not be like the covenant I made with their fathers ... I will place my law within them, and write it upon their hearts ... (Jeremiah 31:31–33)

Why, after all, would a God who was content to let physical, biological, and cultural evolution take their course for billions of years suddenly step in with something as meddlesome as a direct revelation of the divine will? Surely not for lack of patience. If we believe that such explicit revelation has actually occurred (especially in the person of Jesus), then we can only understand it as necessitated by our own constitutional inability ever to figure out that divine will on our own. "What? Put my own interests on the same level with those of somebody whom I don't need and who can't do anything for me in return? Nah, God would never expect me to do that. What ivory-tower philosopher dreamed that one up? It's not even possible. Show me someone who ever did that!"

9.3   The Theme of Adoption in Scripture

We Christians see Christ as the culmination and fulfillment of a coherent development, a "history of salvation," chronicled throughout the Hebrew Scriptures as well as the New Testament. If this is true, and if Jesus really taught a way of living that was at variance with the rules of Darwinian evolution, and if Jesus' teaching truly reveals to us the mind of God the Father, then we should find evidence throughout the Scriptures[37] that God is not at heart a Darwinian – however much use the Creator may have made of Darwinian processes in the act of creating. We shall not be disappointed in our search.

We have seen that the essence of evolution is genetic change; that this change occurs in populations of genetically-related organisms; that survival of genes like one's own (in numerous direct or indirect offspring) is the ultimate good that natural selection promotes; and that, as a result, it's kinship that counts. If, therefore, an individual has a friend or ally in all this ruthless Darwinian world, that friend is most apt to be found among its closest kin. There are apparent exceptions, where the ally is entirely unrelated; but if the crocodile welcomes in peace the small bird that cleans its teeth, it is because they have worked out a mutually advantageous exchange of benefits. Most of the time, when the lion lies down with the lamb, only one of them gets up again.

We saw in the previous section that the God of the Bible, as revealed in the original Covenant, is not concerned with political power or social control, but with ethical behavior for its own sake. This God, moreover, seems oddly unconcerned with the ties of blood that make evolution go. This is an eclectic God, whose choices show a cheerful disregard of the protocol of kinship in which we naturally put such stock. With this God, biological kinship and number of biological progeny ultimately count for as little as political rank or social status, and anyone is apt to be adopted (not to say drafted) to serve God's purposes. As we are pointedly reminded, "God can raise up children to Abraham from these very stones" (Matthew 3:9).

This theme of adoption and, more broadly, approval bestowed on the seemingly unworthy runs prominently throughout the Bible. The Creator, who obviously shares no genes in common with us mortals, gratuitously made a covenant with the sinful human race, and repeatedly renewed it. The initial covenant with all of humanity (symbolized by Adam and Noah) was supplemented by a particular covenant with a single group, made first through Abraham. Within this extended family, however, at turn after crucial turn, blood relationships were set aside, often in favor of adoptive ties. The fulfillment of God's promises also frequently involved taking lightly human laws of status, marriage, and inheritance – laws that, in the view of sociobiologists, might have had some Darwinian basis.[38]

Abraham, told by God to leave his native place and family and wander in strange lands, was promised many descendants; but when his wife Sarah remained barren, he sought fulfillment of God's promise in a biologically natural fashion – through surrogate motherhood – and sired Ishmael. He was told, however, that God had another way, and the aged Sarah gave birth to Isaac. But then Abraham was ordered to kill this very son, in whom his hope of posterity rested: challenging him, in the starkest terms, to choose between his own Darwinian fitness and God's mysterious will – between fidelity to the One who made the promise, and idolatry of the promise itself.

Although his trust in God was finally vindicated, and the promised descendants materialized, still the promise's fulfillment continued to run through channels that were irregular by human standards. Women who bore only one or a few children and those late in life, whose earlier barrenness seemed self-evidently a curse from God, were ultimately seen as favored above those who achieved the human and Darwinian ideal of many offspring (Sarah, Rebekah, Rachel, Manoah's wife, Hannah, Elizabeth). Younger sons were routinely preferred over their elders (Abel, Isaac, Jacob, Joseph, Judah, Samuel, David, Solomon). Moses gained his advantages of position and education through adoption as an infant – adoption, in fact, by foreigners. God did not even seem to insist on compliance with moral precepts, whether these were of Darwinian or divine origin – choosing instead to work with and through flagrant transgressors. Jacob gained his older brother's inheritance by fraud, and notorious public sinners were not even barred from the highest positions of divinely-appointed leadership: Moses was wanted for murder, and David was guilty of murder compounded with adultery.

Out of loyalty to her mother-in-law, Ruth forsook her native Moab for her adoptive nation of Israel. But the Messiah's lineage was also traced (in Matthew 1) through an assortment of irregular unions with women of less exemplary virtue (Tamar, Rahab, Bathsheba); and Ruth's own people, the Moabites, were considered offspring of the incest of Lot's daughter. The circumstances of the Messiah's own conception were reportedly such that public scandal was barely avoided, and he became the son of Joseph and a member of the House of David only by adoption.

As the worldly-wise would predict, this habitual and subversive divine disregard of natural (nature-derived) social norms could lead to nothing good: in shocking defiance of sociobiological convention, Jesus (who had no wife or offspring of his own) disparaged family values and patriotic ties (for example, Matthew 5:43–44, Mark 3:31–35, Luke 14:26); praised celibacy (Matthew 19:12); forgave adultery (John 7:53–8:11); accepted as disciples women of dubious reputation; consorted with traitors, apostates, and Gentiles; and ended up even asserting (Matthew 19:21–24) that wealth is not *prima facie* proof of God's favor! "Within the gospels," notes Jesuit theologian William Reiser, "Jesus appears as a boundary breaker. That is, Jesus is constantly challenging group assumptions about who belongs and who does not."[39]

Did all these departures from the usual (or at least the "proper") way of the world really happen as reported? Admittedly, extraordinary circumstances of origin including divine conception, virgin birth, being cast adrift in a basket, and/or adoption by mortals were commonly added to the résumés of ancient rulers and heroes.[40] Hebrew folklore was probably no exception where such embellishments were concerned; or it may simply be that instances of adoption were unusual enough to be noteworthy, given that "adoption was not a widely practiced institution among the Jews."[41] But the God of the Hebrews seems to have fostered these sorts of occurrences more than any contemporary deities; and the best example of all is the origin of the Hebrews themselves.

Yahweh's loyalty to a single "chosen people" might seem to contradict my assertion that this god cares little for ties of kinship. Appearances, however, can be deceiving. It turns out that the makeup of this people was more heterogeneous than was traditionally acknowledged – even before honorary membership was extended (under the Christian dispensation) to Gentiles. The Exodus from Egypt, the formative event of Jewish history, was the divine act of adoption *par excellence* – an act by which (through the people's voluntary acceptance of God's covenant) God not only chose a human community, but simultaneously *created* one where there was none before. (The same word *bara'* used in Genesis 1 for God's creation of the world is also used, for example in Isaiah 43:1, for God's creation of Israel.[42]) God thus "chose" this people like a leader individually choosing picked men for a new mission, creating a new unit that had no previous existence. "The oldest biblical sources say nothing at all about Israel being Yahweh's *'chosen'* people; instead, as in Exodus 15 and Deuteronomy 32, they refer to it as Yahweh's *'created'* people."[43] As Isaiah 43:19–21 has it, "See, I am doing something new! Now it springs forth, do you not perceive it? ... For I put water in the desert ... for my chosen people ... the people whom I formed for myself...." Enlistment in this new outfit, furthermore, was open to volunteers: as was the case much later (John 1:12), "Any who did accept him he empowered to become children of God."

In the biblical account, the Hebrews enslaved in Egypt were the descendants of Jacob (= Israel), whose family had found refuge there during a famine. However, it is scarcely plausible that only one clan out of all those living in the drought-stricken lands east of Egypt would have sought and obtained relief in the valley of the Nile. More likely, the Hebrews living in Egypt at the time of the Exodus were derived from a motley assortment of Semitic tribes and bands that had straggled into Egypt as refugees or for other reasons (not least the invasion of the Semitic Hyksos). Indeed, the Bible admits that when the Israelites left Egypt, "a crowd of mixed ancestry also went up with them" (Exodus 12:38; cf. Numbers 11:4). This mixture reflects in part the intermarriage of Israelites and Egyptians (cf. Leviticus 24:10), but perhaps also a more deep-seated diversity.

This picture also squares well with the derivation of the name "Hebrew," which many scholars equate with the word *habiru* or *'apiru*, known from many contemporary records. But whereas "Hebrew" has come to refer to a specific ethnic group, *habiru* seems to have originally meant something like "transgressor," and denoted a socioeconomic or politicolegal category, made up variously of semi-nomadic tribes, poor villagers, landless peasants, outlaws, bandits, guerillas in the hills – in general, marginalized and disaffected people living on the fringes of urban civilization, perhaps having renounced any allegiance to organized polities, and more or less regarded (by urbanites) as the dregs of society. Although these people, like the Palestinian city-dwellers from whom they were distinguished, all shared a broadly Semitic ethnic identity, the term *habiru* was apparently not in itself an ethnic label.[44] Our own word "hobo" might somewhat resemble it in connotation as well as in sound.

It follows (at least in the view of some scholars) that the Hebrews in Egypt were originally united only by their identity as Semitic foreigners and refugees who, as people of the lowest status, were eventually put to forced labor by the Egyptians. This insight lends enormous significance to the statement of God that "Israel is my first-born son" (Exodus 4:22; cf. Isaiah 1:2, Jeremiah 31:9, Hosea 11:1, Romans 9:4). Far from choosing any of the existing superpowers such as Egypt or Babylonia (which would surely have felt worthy of the honor), this God dramatically showed a "preferential option for the poor" by literally making a new nation from scratch, from the least promising material available (lacking even title to any real estate), and then adopting it as God's own. No selection of the "fittest" here.[45]

However, the making of a nation as such – a political unit – probably was not really God's intent:

> From its very beginnings, the Yahwistic faith transcended tribal religion, for it was intended and actually functioned in a way to create a community above the tribal level. It is only a subsequent period of religious history which made out of the faith a tribal religion, in which the function of the deity was regarded by blind nationalism as merely the protection of tribal-national political and economic interests.
>
> ... Consequently, entire groups [in Palestine, after the Exodus] having a clan or "tribal" organization joined the newly-formed community, identified themselves with the oppressed in Egypt, and received deliverance from bondage....
>
> ... The subjection of individuals and groups to a non-human Overlord by covenant, and the solidarity of the newly formed community meant that they could and did reject the religious, economic, and political obligations to the existing network of political organizations. By this process, they became "Hebrews." The religious community of early Israel created a contrast between the religious and the political aspects of human culture which had been inseparable in the idea of the "divine state" or the "divine kingship," because a complete identification of religious with political authority and obedience, so characteristic of ancient and modern paganism, became impossible.[46]

> There can be nothing upon which the biblical traditions insist more strongly than the fact that "Israel" is specifically a *religious* community; the tradition that all the tribes were lineal descendants from a single ancestor is an attempt to give expression to a unity which was created by the religious factor, and is paralleled exactly by the attempt to express cultural relationships in ancient civilizations generally by the identical procedure.... Israel began as a specifically religious community; only in the course of time and historical calamity did the religious community come to rely largely upon biological continuity based upon endogamy and considerable resistance to the access of ethnic outsiders.... Early Israel was an ecumenical faith, a catholic religion in the best sense of the term, the very purpose of which was to create unity among a divided and warring humanity.... From a source of unity it became, like Islam and Christianity, a source of division and hostility.
>
> ... But the prophets, and ultimately Christianity kept the older tradition alive.[47]

In this view, the God of Abraham, Isaac, and Jacob rejected Darwinian social organization even more radically than we have suspected – certainly more than the phrase "chosen people" would lead us to believe. In this pre-Christian version of liberation theology, the "chosen" of God were precisely those rejected by the humanly powerful; God indeed "singled out the weak of this world to shame the strong" (1 Corinthians 1:27). The descendants of those whom Moses led out of Egypt were probably joined by disaffected masses of people already resident in Canaan, who overthrew their unpopular rulers to claim the Promised Land for the traditionally weak (cf. Matthew 5:5: "Blest are the lowly; they shall inherit the land") – all in the name of a God who sought to turn upside down a social order (indeed, a natural order) based on triumph of the strongest and the traditionally privileged. It is this same God whom we follow today:

> All who are led by the Spirit of God are sons of God. You did not receive a spirit
> of slavery leading you back into fear, but a spirit of adoption through which we
> cry out, "Abba!" (that is, "Father"). (Romans 8:14–15; cf. Galatians 4:3–7)

When God's people relapsed into Darwinian ways, made themselves instead into a nation based, like all the others, on ethnicity, and conducted themselves according to the letter rather than the spirit of the Law, the prophets repeatedly called on them to reform; and from one such episode of (attempted) reform grew what we know as Christianity. Thus did Paul speak of those who followed the Sinai covenant in his time as "begotten in the course of nature" like Ishmael, and of those who followed Christ as being "children of the promise, as Isaac was" and as ones "whose birth was in the realm of spirit" (Galatians 4:22–31). The Spirit of God leads us to break with the norms of "nature" and set out upon a new course of evolution, one in which Darwinian ways have no longer any place.

Notes

1. Nessan 1995, 112.
2. Boehm 1997, 359.
3. Sober 1993, 214; emphasis in original.
4. Haught 2001, 117. As even Michael Ruse acknowledges, "Christianity calls upon us to rise above our brute natures" (Ruse 1994, 23n).
5. Morris 1996.
6. Since writing the above, I have discovered several other authors who present similar views of evolution and sin. The first of these, Donald T. Campbell, outlined very nearly the same idea as long ago as 1975. However, he did not make fully explicit its implications for the theology of original sin, and (if I understand him correctly) he confused the issue somewhat by attributing a genetic basis to much of human social and cultural evolution. This sort of "sociobiological" premise is viewed more skeptically today, and in any case it is not essential to the argument as I have developed it here.

    Gabriel Daly (1989, Chap. 7) also comes to many of my conclusions, albeit in a very brief treatment. At one point (p. 138) he mischaracterizes our evolutionary heritage as "a genetically produced nostalgia" for the lost innocence of our animal past, and he does not see in the evolutionary view a solution to the problem of evil. In other respects, however, his discussion of these issues is very stimulating and insightful.

    Holmes Rolston III (1999, 299–302), while emphatically rejecting sociobiology, also seems to share many of the views I espouse here, though he expends inordinate effort on the semantic argument that the word "selfish" should not be applied to subhuman entities. I think he unduly minimizes the biological precursors of human sin.

More recently, Patricia A. Williams (2001) has written an excellent book that invokes sociobiology in its subtitle but actually takes a moderate stance on genetic determinism, quite in line with my position. Proceeding by a very different route, she arrives at many of the same conclusions I do. However, instead of understanding original sin broadly enough to reinterpret it in evolutionary terms, she construes it rather narrowly as inextricably tied to the myth of Adam and Eve, rejects it as unsalvageable for this reason, and substitutes for it what she calls the "sociobiological" model of human nature (essentially the same model presented here). Furthermore, as mentioned again in a note to section 12.3 below, in proposing a solution to the problem of evil, she relies more than I would on the argument that good often comes out of evil. But on the whole, these differences between us are relatively slight and may be largely semantic.

Beatrice Bruteau (1997, especially Chap. 9) has synthesized a most compelling and comprehensive picture of cosmic and organic evolution as the incarnation of the Divine. Practically all of the points I have made here are at least implicit in her exposition, including the essential role of selfishness in evolution, though she does not particularly stress this nor explicitly identify it as the explanation of "original sin."

7. Cf. Bradie 1994, 125.
8. See Whiten and Byrne 1997.
9. De Waal 1989, 1996.
10. De Waal 1996.
11. Bekoff 2002, 36.
12. De Waal 1996.
13. Pope 2001, 421.
14. De Waal 1996, 117.
15. De Waal 1996, 207–208. Cf. Sigmund et al. (2002) on the evolutionary benefits of instinctively going out of one's way, at direct cost to oneself, in order to punish group members who don't play fair. More generally, Boehm (1997) discusses the evolution of the moral community and of political intelligence.
16. Wilson 1998, 276.
17. Cf. Boadt 1984, 186–188.
18. De Waal 1996, 129–131.
19. Mendenhall 2001, 60–63.
20. Mendenhall 2001, Chap. 2.
21. Mendenhall 2001, 61.
22. Mendenhall 2001, Chaps. 4–7.
23. It continued, of course, the prophetic tradition of ethical reform; significantly, this passage from Matthew 22 is followed by the memorable excoriation of the religious establishment in Matthew 23.
24. See Pope 2001, 424–426.
25. I overlooked it myself until my pastor, Fr. Michael Tyson, OFM, stressed it in a sermon one Sunday.
26. Cf. Edwards 1999, 15–17.
27. In Romans 5–8, Galatians 3–6, and elsewhere; cf. John 1: 17.
28. More precisely, "Jesus asks us to minimize the dispositions evolution encourages us to augment, but not to reject them outright unless they interfere with our perception or acceptance of the present and coming reign of God" (Williams 2001, 187). Theissen (1985, 67–72) traces "protest against the principle of selection" back to the Jews exiled in Babylon. He sees culture generally as "a process which reduces selection"; religion as "the heart of human culture"; and biblical monotheism as the clearest expression of this religious "rebellion against the principle of selection" (Theissen 1985, 49). This, however, may be too sanguine a view of culture and religion. True, both ameliorate some of the grosser effects of selection, as in prolonging the lives of some who would otherwise be more quickly eliminated; but in most other ways, our cultures and even most of our religions are more comfortable with the corollaries and consequences of Darwinian selection than Jesus seemed to be. See also note 32 below.

29. See also Brown 1985, 141–142.
30. Domning 2002b expands on this point in the language of Ignatian spirituality.
31. For an excellent exposition of these and related themes and their implications, see Hellwig 1992.
32. These ideas have come up before. Thus Edwards (1998, 380), in criticizing Gerd Theissen's (1985) evolutionary interpretation of Scripture: "A critical theological question to be addressed to Theissen concerns the opposition he sets up between natural selection and the way of Jesus Christ. Does Theissen mean to suggest that natural selection is evil? What does this do to the biblical teaching of the goodness of creation? Is divine action only through opposition to natural selection? Is the way of Jesus really opposed to natural selection?" I have given here my own answers to these questions; in brief, God has used natural selection in bringing about the good creation, so selection is not "evil" except in the sense that it unavoidably entails physical suffering and death. But moral agents such as humans are called to conform their actions to a higher, more selfless standard, modeled by Jesus. The more problematical point is "Theissen's argument ... that culture is a process which 'reduces selection' and that religion is the heart of human culture. He sees religion as a protest against the principle of selection" (Edwards 1998, 379). Culture, however, is more equivocal than that, and is older and more inclusive than religion; it can promote and facilitate competition as well as moderate it. Even religion, in its many varieties, is not always a "protest against selection." The pertinent dichotomy is not between selection and culture, or selection and religion, but between selfish and unselfish forms of *behavior*. A similar oversimplified contrasting of the biological and the social or cultural can be found in Campbell (1975) and Hefner (1993). It is also important to keep in mind that the divide between biological (genetic) and cultural evolution does not coincide with the divide between the non-human and the human; apes have culture, and some human behavior is instinctual.
33. An outstanding example was the European institution of absolute monarchy as it culminated in the baroque period (but persisted into the twentieth century). Though ostensibly Christian, its hypocrisy, immorality, and the mutually corrupting nature of its connections with Christian Churches reached monumental proportions (a vivid survey is provided by Molesworth 1969; see especially pp. 25, 65). The deep congruence of absolutist customs with Darwinian principles is easy to see: "For the most part these people of the court and the nobility were, quite simply, obsessed by their social rank and honour. To the majority of them it deeply mattered whether they sat above or below a person at a meal or what someone's antecedents were, whether Majesty smiled or a prince of the blood was affable. This was the end aim of their lives. Even the most pious church-goer would fly into a passion if she or he was misplaced at a formal ceremony" (Molesworth 1969, 64–65).
34. Dawkins 1989, 215.
35. Cf. Haught 2000, Chap. 4. Edwards (1998, 387–388) adds the valid point that "[t]he Christian ideal of love is undeniably altruistic, modeled on the Cross of Jesus, but it is more than altruistic. It concerns self-possession as well as self-giving, love of self as well as love of the other. In Christian trinitarian theology altruism is understood within a vision of mutual and equal relations. So, while Philip Hefner sees altruistic love as holding the status of 'a cosmological and ontological principle,' I believe that it is Persons-in-Mutual-Relations that has this status." This is consistent with what I am saying here, though I stress altruism because it is a more immediate point of contact with Darwinian concerns.

   Another clarification: I do not go as far as some would in supposing that a "suffering God" necessarily forfeits omniscience, knowledge of the future, or other attributes traditionally ascribed to divinity. But these issues are irrelevant to my argument here.
36. Pope 2001, 421.
37. The well-supported idea that Jesus was not so much a religious innovator as a reformer who sought to restore the worship of Yahweh to its original purity (Mendenhall 2001, Chap. 8) implies just such a continuity in the Scriptures.
38. Cf. Pagels (1988, 11) regarding sexual customs of the ancient Jews and their emphasis on the importance of procreation and progeny, deriving from a formerly pastoral-nomadic lifestyle.

39. Reiser 1997, 204.
40. Cf. Gaster 1969, 224–230.
41. Fitzmyer 1968, 316.
42. Schmidt 1984. This word is used in the Hebrew Scriptures exclusively to describe the creative activity of God.
43. Mendenhall 2001, 90; emphasis in original.
44. Cf. Mendenhall 1970, 2001.
45. Cf. the biblical concept of God as the *go'el* (liberator, redeemer, protector, avenger) of Israel; Gutiérrez 1991, 20.
46. Mendenhall 1970, 108–109. It was into just this sort of paganism that the Israelite monarchy subsequently relapsed (Mendenhall 2001), as did the absolute monarchies (and more modern polities) of Christian Europe (Molesworth 1969; see also the note to section 9.2.2 above).
47. Mendenhall 1970, 118–119.

Response to Part Three

Monika K. Hellwig

The argument postulating an "intelligent designer" is proposed as encompassing the whole creation. Thus analysis of a specific process of mutation or selection is not relevant to the argument. There is no reason that an intelligent designer could not allow for random events within an evolutionary process. Beyond those questions already covered in the response to the first part, the main issue of theological interest in this part is not really whether evolutionary theory necessarily excludes acceptance that there is God. It clearly does not exclude God as an explanation of why there is anything rather than nothing, neither does it require God as an explanation of why there is anything rather than nothing.

What evolutionary theory does challenge in many interesting ways is how we who are believers understand God and the act of creation. For a believer to think in evolutionary terms means greater attention to creation as a continuing present reality. It also means, therefore, a challenge to discern where the process is going on without us and perhaps in spite of our efforts, and where on the other hand our human intervention is contributing for good or ill in what is in the process of becoming in our universe and in our own world.

The relevance of this to human morality is clear in principle though not always in the particulars of practice. The realization of our pervasive participation in ongoing creation exponentially increases human responsibility. Moreover, it casts this human responsibility in a more distinctively prophetic mode, because morality cannot then be seen as conforming to the status quo, but rather of discerning how things ought to change. It is not a responsibility with which most people are well equipped to cope. To conform to the status quo is fairly straightforward, because all the markers are in place. To discern how things ought to change requires clear understanding of the meaning and purpose of human life for individuals and for society. It requires criteria for what is a good human life and what is a good society. And it requires a great detachment from self-interest in a more inclusive grasp of the human situation as a whole.

An observant contemporary theologian cannot but agree with a significant point made by Domning in this part, namely that the boundary that marks the distinction between the human and other animals need not be sharp to be real and consequential. It comes into play not only in relation to evolutionary theory but also in such issues as rights of the unborn and claims of the severely retarded. In many situations in practice the theoretical construct of what constitutes a human being is not met in the particular, though we acknowledge that any individual born of a human mother is to be accepted as human. While the question of the break-through into the human in the remote past may have speculative interest, it is not of theological concern, whereas the claims of the severely retarded are of immediate theological concern.

Part Four
Original selfishness:
a contribution to evolutionary
theology

Daryl P. Domning

CHAPTER TEN

Adam and Eve reinterpreted

William Blake ... said that there is in every human being two limits: Satan and Adam. Satan, the vigorous individualist, the self-adoring, self-sufficing creature, is the limit of what we can become under the steady action of self-will. ... Adam, the unfinished, plastic creature, being made in the image of God, is slowly and tentatively producing under the steady action of the Divine Charity ... the Divine vision of perfect man: Christ our Brother. ... On the one hand there is the steady, secret pressure of the yeast of grace, ever at work creating Adam. ... On the other hand there is Satan, instinctive animal man, in command of all the lower centres of consciousness ... and holding on to his rights – the I, the Me, and the Mine. "All this will I give thee if thou wilt worship Me."

Evelyn Underhill[1]

10.1 A New Interpretation of Original Sin

But let us return to Adam. This much we know for certain, if cause precedes effect: whoever or whatever he is taken to be, the Adam of the Fall was not responsible for introducing physical suffering and death into the order of nature. Nor, as shown above, can poor Adam be blamed for all the forms of mayhem that we humans inflict on each other; those were well established among evolving organisms long before his and our advent. Thus far has Genesis (as it has been viewed through the lens of Romans 5:12–19) been decisively falsified by science. (In fairness to the authors of Genesis, it needs to be emphasized that the doctrine of original sin and a "Fall" of all humanity caused by one individual's sin is not to be found in Genesis 2–3, or elsewhere in the Hebrew Scriptures.[2] "Indeed, in Scripture in its entirety, the event of Genesis 3 is mentioned only in Romans 5, 1 Corinthians 15, and 1 Timothy. The idea that a fall occurs in Genesis 3 dates to the late first century [CE]."[3])

Nonetheless, important aspects of what became the Christian concept of original sin find their parallels, and possibly their roots, in Jewish sources. Rabbinical tradition has long acknowledged a conflict within us of two opposing inclinations or impulses (*yetzer ha-tov* and *yetzer ha-ra*), respectively good and evil – or perhaps not so much evil as just self-aggrandizing, and even necessary for survival, though needing restraint. The *yetzer ha-ra* has even been described as "essential to life in that it provides life with its driving power."[4] Also prominent in Jewish tradition is the concept of *galut* (exile) – not just physical exile from the Promised Land, but the spiritual alienation that "limits the human ability to be in free contact with God,"[5] which has clear affinities with the notion of original sin. These ideas are obviously congruent with what I am describing here (for example, the selfish impulse as the driving force of evolution). The figure of Adam (especially in the hands of St. Paul) put a face on such currents of thought as these; but Adam was a symbol, whereas the psychological and theological insights formed the enduring substance.

Likewise, the essential spiritual insight of the creation account – that humans and humans alone have a moral dimension to their actions, and have chosen to act immorally (that is, selfishly) from the very dawn of their existence – contradicts nothing that science knows of human origins. After all, this undeniable *fact* of universal human immorality was the original empirical datum that philosophers and theologians set out to explain – for example, by the doctrine of original sin. Far from contradicting science, this immorality is precisely the behavior that Darwinian theory would predict. This is true regardless of whether we are descended from a single Adam or not – in the words of Pope Pius XII,[6] whether "after Adam there existed on this earth [no] true men who did not take their origin through natural generation from him as from the first parent of all."

The reason why the Catholic Church has nonetheless felt obliged to insist on some form of monogenism is not based on any biological considerations, but rather on the simple need to explain why *all* human beings had to be saved from "original sin" by Christ's sacrifice.[7] Original sin, wrote Pius XII, is that "which proceeds from sin actually committed by an individual Adam, and which, passed on to all by way of generation, is in everyone as his own."[8] It is clear that the first part of this formulation is logically contingent on the second: the only compelling theological reason to postulate a literal Adam is in order to account for the *universality* of sin[9] – because, *in a static universe, there is no other way to account for it.* This is the source of the difficulty. As Teilhard put it, "if the dogma of original sin is constricting and debilitating it is simply because, as now expressed, it represents a survival of obsolete static views into our now evolutionary way of thinking. Fundamentally, in fact, the idea of a Fall is no more than an attempt to explain evil in a fixed universe."[10] Given what is written in Genesis 1–3, it was inevitable in the Western thought of earlier centuries (that is, prior to the discovery of evolution) that whatever was universal to the human race should have been ascribed to inheritance from Adam and Eve – at least that which stemmed from sin, since only humans among earthly creatures can commit sin.

However, has there not always been an unexamined assumption here: namely, that the *universality* and the *moral character* of original sin both necessarily stem from *one and the same* individual, act, and moment in time?

Let me state at this point a working definition of original sin that is uncontroversial and has been used in slightly different forms by various authors: it is simply *that need for salvation (by Christ) which is universal to all human beings and acquired through natural generation*. Now, as noted by Alszeghy and Flick, "[a]ny hypothesis capable of explaining these two dogmatic truths [the universality of sin, and participation in it through natural generation] is … to be considered tenable."[11]

What I have sought to show above (and in diagram form in Figure 10.1) is that the *overt selfish acts* which, in humans, demonstrate the reality of original sin (by manifesting it in the form of actual sin) do indeed owe their universality among humans to natural descent from a common ancestor. This ancestor, however, far from being identifiable with the biblical Adam, must be placed in the very remote past, indeed at the very origin of life itself. It was the common ancestor not only of all humans but of all other living things on Earth as well. However, it is not this ancestor itself that is of real interest, but the "natural descent" that proceeded from it: the very nature of physical life and the process of natural generation, which, we have seen, are governed by natural selection and the selfish behavior it requires. This requirement applied equally to the first living thing and to every one that followed it. (And not on this planet alone, but everywhere in the universe that life and intelligence may evolve: sin will predictably come to exist wherever natural selection brings moral agents into being.)

In other words, *the human acts themselves share a genealogical unity, but their sinfulness proceeds from a source that is logically and temporally separate from their common genealogical origin, much more recent, and not necessarily unitary* (since the necessary universality is already supplied by the genealogical inheritance of inclination to perform the acts). *This explicit logical differentiation, and radical historical decoupling, of the source of original sin's universality* (the common origin of life) *from the source of its moral character* (human free will) *is the essence of what I here propose as new.*

A remaining question is whether descent from a literal Adam is still necessary to account for the universality of the free will which makes possible the moral dimension of human actions. This will be left to theologians to debate; but it is hard to see the literal Adam in even this more limited role as a necessity – especially for a faith tradition that has insisted on the separate creation (not inheritance) of each individual soul, together with its qualities of intellect and free will. It would seem, then, that we can have (at most) special creation of souls or an at least outwardly plausible argument for monogenism, but not both. As for our putative first parent,

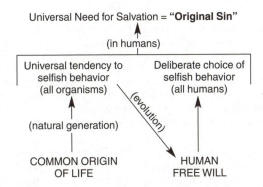

Figure 10.1   The composite origin of "original sin." Starting with the earliest living things on Earth, natural selection, acting *through natural generation*, enforced selfish behavior on *all the descendants* of those common ancestors (as it would also do on any living things that evolved independently on other planets). In the ensuing course of evolution, there arose creatures with free will, who affirmed their selfish genetic (and culturally-reinforced) tendencies by deliberate choice in committing actual sins. These two elements (*universality* of the tendency and decision to sin, and acquisition of that tendency through *natural generation*) combine in us to bring about our universal need for salvation (= "original sin").

once he is relieved of the responsibility for uniquely bequeathing to us our inherent biological selfishness, can he not play his role in salvation history equally well whether we call him (in Hebrew) Adam or (in English) Everyman?

10.2 Advantages Over the "Cultural-transmission" and Other Interpretations of Original Sin

This concept of original sin does not exclude that of Schoonenberg and most other post-Vatican II Catholic theologians, who (as outlined by Monika Hellwig in Chapter One) tend to equate it with the sinful situations or structures into which each person is born.[12] However, the concept proposed here significantly broadens and deepens this notion (which can be referred to as the "cultural-transmission" model of original sin) to include the environmental, social, and behavioral situation into which *humanity itself* was born – as it were, "the society before (human) society" which was molding our ancestors' behavior (both learned and genetically determined) for millions of years before they became human.[13]

This addresses what from my point of view is a central weakness in the "cultural-transmission" model: its failure to explain where the sinfulness of human society came from – or more precisely, the Schoonenberg school's lack of interest in even asking this, the first question that would occur to an evolutionary biologist. Denis Edwards provides a clear example of this individual-centered, basically ahistorical way of looking at the problem:

> It is not the structure of the human (as a fallible symbiosis of genes and culture) that constitutes original sin, but the inner impact on each human person's free situation of previous human rejection of God. As Karl Rahner has pointed out, original sin has to do with the fact that we actualize ourselves as free subjects in a situation that is always determined by other persons and by history. The sin of others is intrinsic to and partly constitutive of the situation of our human freedom. The sin of others is a universal and permanent part of the human condition from the beginning and is in this sense original.[14]

But "the beginning" has to include that of the human race as well as that of each individual. What previous human sins were there to condition the situation of the *first* human beings? The "cultural-transmission" school offers no answer to this obvious question, even though most of its proponents profess the harmony of their views with evolution.

It appears that Schoonenberg and his followers down to the present, lacking an explanation of how original sin and its transmission began, have walked away from that issue. Perhaps they were dissuaded from such investigations by *Humani Generis* and the prevailing climate of persecution of Teilhard and other progressive theologians. Or perhaps we see here an instance of a deeper, metaphysical problem that leads them to see origins as unimportant: "Nostalgia for this lost perfection [of a Platonically-inspired metaphysics of the 'eternal present'] persists deeply in the souls of all of us. It is not surprising, then, that evolution is still taken by many theologians as a relatively inconsequential process of becoming."[15]

In any case, the Schoonenberg school redefined the problem as one of how original sin is now transmitted to each of us. This is admittedly the more practically relevant question, and the one at the heart of the doctrine of original sin, properly understood; and on this point they have contributed valid and valuable insights. But it is obvious that without returning to the question of origins, no complete solution to the problem is possible.

The more thoroughly evolutionary concept proposed here explains the situation of the first humans, and also does away with the need to take seriously the various elements of biblical literalism (such as the pseudoproblems of monogenism and "preternatural gifts") which have hobbled attempts to reinterpret the doctrine by Schoonenberg[16] and many others. (Note that it is not necessary to specify exactly who, what, when, where, or how many the "first humans" were; nor to take a position that the boundary between nonhuman and human was either sharp or fuzzy; or that it was crossed by only one group, of whatever size; or if by more than one group then simultaneously by all. These things we do not know, and probably never will, especially if we define "humans" by such an intangible trait as moral responsibility. The essential point is that at one time there were no humans, however they may be defined, whereas at a later time there were; hence somewhere, in some sense there must have been "first humans.")

Just as importantly, my concept retains an ingredient that is central to the traditional understanding of original sin but is arguably missing from the cultural-transmission model: identification of original sin with some definite trait that is passed on by "propagation" or "generation" as part of our human nature, and not merely by imitation.[17] I have identified this trait as the biological "selfishness" (the instinct for self-perpetuation) that is literally programmed into the genes of all living things – "the instinct of unlimited self-assertion," our "inheritance from the ancestors who fought a good fight in the state of nature," in the words of T. H. Huxley.[18] In no way do I discount the importance of the factors emphasized by the cultural-transmission school (the insidious effects of a sinful social milieu on the young). But I give greater concreteness to the concept of original sin by connecting it with a known biological phenomenon, and incidentally bringing it back into agreement with the traditional understanding of original sin as something literally transmitted by human propagation. (This explanation does not, however, suffer from the misguided tendency, often attributed to St. Augustine, to place the blame on sexuality.[19] The "stain" lies not in the mode of propagation but in the genetically- as well as culturally-programmed, selfish behavioral tendencies that are propagated.) Our inclination to sin, or "concupiscence," is propagated *together with* all other aspects of our humanity: it is integral to and inseparable from our human nature itself, because of how our human nature was brought into being. In short, *evolutionary selfishness is a necessary and sufficient explanation of the sinful social structures on which the "cultural-transmission" school blames our individual sinfulness.* This inherited evolutionary selfishness is the biological phenomenon that accounts for our theological need of grace and salvation, which I have defined above as original sin in the formal sense.

Furthermore, this evolutionary concept of original sin may help bridge the gap between "situationalist" and "personalist" approaches to the topic, which G. Vandervelde considered so far apart as to be incapable of synthesis.[20] With the situationalists, such as P. Schoonenberg and K. Rahner (and with the Council of Trent in 1546), it affirms that something real is involuntarily transmitted to us prior to and conducive to our individual sins, and also that we (both as a species and as individuals) in a sense begin our existence alienated from God (in the absence or privation of that fullness of grace which is later made available to us), and indeed strongly inclined against unselfish behavior (though not yet in a state of personal guilt). With the personalists, such as A. Vanneste, it affirms that all will freely choose to sin, and it also explains why: our inborn selfishness powerfully inclines us toward sin, but without disabling our free will. The resolution of this paradox lies in the evolutionary necessity and hence inherent natural "goodness" of this selfish inclination, despite its inevitable eventual manifestation as sin.

As hinted above, a further question that can be put to the "cultural-transmission" school is that of whether they are not actually arguing for the transmission of original sin by "imitation, not propagation" – in other words, whether they are not flirting with Pelagianism.[21] I would not deny that culture can be thought of as integral to "human nature" and hence that its transmission can be considered integral to "human generation" in the broadest sense (cf. section 8.3 above). But

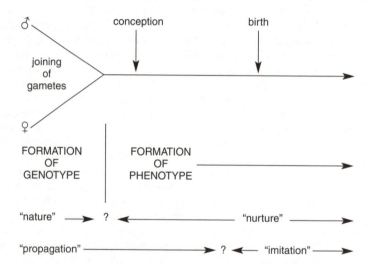

Figure 10.2   **Timelines of human ontogenetic development, showing distinctions relevant to whether different explanations of "original sin" depend on "propagation" or "imitation." Biologists conventionally understand the individual's genotype to be completed at conception; the phenotype then develops under the dual influence of the genotype and the environment ("nature" and "nurture," in common parlance). But propagation and imitation are not necessarily synonymous with nature and nurture, respectively. Does the theologian's concept of "propagation" include the period of gestation? Does it even include some postnatal acquisition of traits, thus overlapping in time with "imitation"? When does "imitation" begin, and what does it include?**

we Neo-Darwinian biologists normally draw the line between "nature" and "nurture" at the boundary of the genome: that which is not inherited in the strict genetic sense (the genotype) is, not necessarily consciously "imitated" or even "learned," but at least *acquired*, hence part of the phenotype (see Figure 10.2). Admittedly there is a gray zone bounded by these strict and broad senses of inheritance, and this is where Schoonenberg and others see the field of action of original sin. They argue that *all* humans (not just "crack babies" and other victims of individualized childhood trauma or abuse) acquire *from society* (hence *after* their genotypes are determined) the inclination to sin, even before being able to make any conscious decisions of their own.

Would the Fathers of Trent have agreed that an inclination thus acquired – universally, yet phenotypically – answers to their notion of communication by "propagation, not imitation"? Perhaps the question itself is too anachronistic, given the different context and concerns of Trent; and in any case we no longer need be restricted in our thinking by the language and categories of 1546. So I would not fault Schoonenberg *et al.* if they did depart from Tridentine strictures; nor would I object to their use of a more inclusive concept of inheritance than the genetic one – were it not that a more natural and elegant way of explaining original sin now presents itself. Unlike them, I use genetic "propagation" in explaining it, not because Trent did, but because that seems to me the obvious conclusion from the biological evidence. This explanation, fortunately, requires no hairsplitting over what does or does not qualify as "propagation."

With regard to "concupiscence," the Council of Trent, following Augustine, distinguished this from original sin on the grounds that concupiscence remains after justification by grace, and original sin does not.[22] However, what I have described above as original sin sounds very much like Trent's concupiscence (= "disordered," selfish desire, "the inclination to sin"), since we always have to struggle against our "original selfishness."[23] I think my decoupling of the universality of original sin from its moral character gets around this problem by offering a different way to distinguish between (1) that which is passed on by biological propagation (genetic as well as phenotypically-acquired) and can be predicated even of animals ("evolutionary selfishness," the inclination to act selfishly) and (2) that which can be predicated only of humans (the inherited inclination to commit *sin* in the strict sense: culpable choice by a moral agent to act on selfish desires that are harmful, resulting in actual sin and guilt). Only the combination of these two elements constitutes what I term "original sin" (or "original selfishness," below) and calls for grace and salvation.[24]

Both elements remain in us, however, even after Baptism, so we should not say that Baptism "removes" original sin; rather that Baptism and other sources of grace simply enable us to *transcend* our original selfishness. In Evelyn Underhill's words, Baptism "knocks off the fetters of our sub-human past."[25] Grace builds on and perfects nature, rather than removing it. Because our physical life is Darwinian in origin and nature, however, this baptism is aptly spoken of as a "dying" to this life so that we can take on a new life in Christ (Romans 6:3–11, Colossians 2:12). As Catholic theologian Herbert Haag expressed it, "baptism does not bring about the removal of 'original sin,' but rather rebirth as a child of God; it makes man [and woman] a member of Christ."[26]

This view thus preserves the traditional insight that our real individual situations are in some way different from the mythical Adam's – that we do not start our moral lives with a clean slate, as Pelagius taught, but are in some way handicapped by inheritance: the inheritance of a proneness to sin. The literal "Adam" himself, however, must be seen in retrospect as only a literary device to explain, in the context of the Genesis narrative and its static worldview, the ultimate source of this inheritance, for which a more concrete explanation now presents itself.

This more concrete explanation of the historical source of our sinfulness in fact relieves the biblical account of the burden so often and so wrongly imposed on it – the burden of satisfying our curiosity about the distant past, when in fact it was written to help us with the far more important task of living in the present. As Carmelite scripture scholar Carlos Mesters says of the Eden narrative:

> The precise aim of the narrative is to function as a mirror and to confront men with themselves and with their consciences. The one who limits himself to examining the material of the mirror, asking only if it is myth or reality, fable or history, unreal or real, and forgetting to look at himself in this mirror, is twisting the meaning of the narrative. Such a person has thwarted the principal aim of the narrative and will never perceive the errors that God wishes to denounce in one's life by means of the mirror.[27]

The great virtue of the "cultural-transmission" approach is to focus on just this aspect of the doctrine of original sin: its practical meaning for our everyday lives. The Schoonenberg school rightly recognizes Eden as an etiological myth (an ancient attempt to explain how we got into our present fix) that is secondary in importance to confronting the practical problems at hand. But we human creatures, embedded in history as we are, still need etiological myths, even in the twenty-first century – only now we demand of them not only mythic power but historical concreteness as well. Our era, the era of historical geology and evolutionary science, is the first in human existence to have acquired means of exploring deep time and of discovering something of our true origins; and nothing less will any longer do. We want not just etiological myths but literal etiology. We want a metaphysics that does not just promise us a hopeful future, or even just help us deal with the imperfections of the actual present, as opposed to a perfect "eternal present" in some timeless realm "above" creation.[28] Rather, our metaphysics must be adequate to embrace, and valorize, the actual past as well as the present and future.

For this reason, we must go beyond the Schoonenberg school's focus on our present, and add to that understanding a new account of our origins, this time based on actual scientific data. The great virtue of Christianity is that it can support and encompass this kind of etiology that is not only myth but fact.

Finally, what of Eden itself? Should we edit it out of future Bibles, as an outmoded myth that has outlived its usefulness? By no means. Its poetic power is still unrivalled; we must simply learn to sort out its elements of allegory from its essential truth. Perhaps a paraphrase like the following might do justice to our modern understanding while doing no violence to the Scripture itself, which, I think, really says to us: *If it were not for your sinfulness, you would be living in Paradise.*

- The story is about *our* sinfulness: *we* are each Adam and Eve.
- All that is now keeping us out of Eden (that is, the Kingdom of God) is our *present* sins, not some sin of the primordial past.
- When and to the extent that, with the help of God's grace, we put our sinfulness behind us, we will be living in that Kingdom/Kin-dom of God which is already among us (Luke 17:21).

I believe that the story of Eden means to teach us no more than this, and no less. This is truly a lesson for all times and all people, perhaps the most vital of all lessons we need to learn, and not one ever to be discounted simply because it is not couched in the language of contemporary science.

Notes

1. Underhill 1991, 25.
2. See Haag 1969; also Williams 2001.
3. Williams 2001, 38, citing Westermann 1984, 276.
4. Jacobs 1971, 1591.
5. Kepnes 2000, 295.
6. Pius XII, *Humani Generis*, 38.
7. Cf. Haag 1969, 74: "… the Catholic doctrine of original sin is nothing other than an attempt to describe theologically the situation of mankind outside of Christ."
8. *Humani Generis*, 38.
9. Alszeghy and Flick 1967, 201.
10. Teilhard 1971, 80.
11. Alszeghy and Flick 1967, 201. An example of a natural phenomenon that could not be the basis of such a tenable hypothesis, because it satisfies at most only the second condition and not the first, is the fact that the developing brain adapts to childhood trauma from violence or abuse in ways that lead the child to abuse others in later life, thereby perpetuating the antisocial, though adaptive, behaviors (Teicher 2002). This "inheritance" of an acquired characteristic cannot explain the universality of sin because not all humans suffer such abuse.
12. See, for example, Schoonenberg 1965, 1967, Alszeghy and Flick 1967, Connor 1968, McDermott 1977, Duquoc 1978, Duffy 1988, Jacquet 1989, Ratzinger 1990, Wiedenhofer 1991, Schmitz-Moormann 1997, Zimmerman 1998, Korsmeyer 1998, Edwards 1999, Haught 2000, and references therein cited.
13. Cf. Teilhard 1971, 40–41: "The specifically human Fall is no more than the (broadly speaking, collective and eternal) actualizing of this '*fomes peccati*' [stimulus to sin] which was infused, long before us, into the whole of the universe, from the lowest zones of matter to the angelic spheres."
14. Edwards 1999, 66–67.
15. Haught 2000, 85.
16. Schoonenberg 1965, 177–191.
17. Cf. Canon 3 of the Council of Trent's Decree on Original Sin. Granting that Trent's expression *propagatione* was "intended less as an explanation of the transmission of original sin than simply as a rejection of Pelagianism" and of its "bad example" theory of original sin (Connor 1968, 225), I nonetheless think that that council hit on something true here.
18. Huxley 1993, 49–50. See also Niebuhr 1960 regarding sin as selfishness.
19. Pagels (1988) and Duffy (1993) provide detailed accounts of Augustine's views and his controversies with Pelagius, Julian of Eclanum, and others. Daly (1989, Chap. 6) also gives a valuable perspective.

20. Vandervelde 1975; see also Korsmeyer 1998, 61–66.
21. I use this pejorative term with apologies to Pelagius himself, whose branding as a heretic is now increasingly acknowledged to have been less than fair!
22. Neuner and Dupuis 1975, 129–131. For an enlightening analysis of Trent's Decree on Original Sin, see Duffy 1993, Chap. 6.
23. Martin Luther likewise identified concupiscence with human selfishness. "Luther, seeking to reassert the essential goodness of creation, interpreted concupiscence as man's self will, his being 'incurvatus in se' [turned in on himself]. It is not primarily or essentially sensuality, but is man's selfish and evil will which seeks itself even in God's presence" (Bodensieck 1965, vol. 3, article on "Sin," p. 2176).
24. It may seem that I am wandering from my definition of original sin given above; that is, the universal human need for salvation. But there is ample precedent, going back to Trent and before, for distinguishing what have been called the "formal" and the "material" meanings of original sin. As Duffy (1993, 222) explains: "There were three different schools of thought in late Scholasticism concerning the interpretation of original sin. One school, followers of the Lombard and the Augustinians, identified original sin as ... identical with concupiscence.... The Thomist school distinguished: formally, original sin is the absence of the original righteousness effected by grace and materially, it is concupiscence.... For the Scotists and the nominalists, original sin is simply the lack of the grace of original justice, which humans ought to have. Concupiscence is not included in the concept. It was this third school that the Protestants attacked, taking it to mean that original sin is purely an external hindrance, leaving no trace in the person.... In the Protestant view, concupiscence was the third element in original sin, lack of fear of and faith in God being the other two. Concupiscence is not just an inclination to particular evils in the ethical sense; it is a religious aberration, the striving of humans to be as God, and it cannot be done away with in the single instant of baptism. It was this view that raised the hackles of Catholics, for it appeared to undermine the efficacy of baptism." Given this long and convoluted history of the term, I question the value of trying to restrict the meaning of "original sin" to just one of these elements; as many have recognized, it would be better to discard this hopelessly confused and confusing term altogether. My usage here is closest to that of the Thomists, in that it includes both senses of the term: formally, it is the need for grace, which finds its root cause and material manifestation in concupiscence.
25. Underhill 1991, 91.
26. Haag 1969, 107.
27. Mesters 1974, 75–76.
28. Cf. Haught 2000, 83–88.

CHAPTER ELEVEN

The meaning of salvation and the "Fall"

[T]he epic of evolution is the story of the emerging independence and autonomy of a world awakening in the presence of God's grace....
...[O]ne of the great gifts of post-Darwinian thought is that it makes the notion of ongoing creation much more immediate and understandable than at any other time in the history of Christianity.
John F. Haught[1]

11.1 Semantic Difficulties

The definition of original sin that I used above (section 10.1) called it a "need for salvation by Christ." What implications does this evolutionary concept of original sin have for our theology of salvation? I submit that it makes salvation history more coherent, and more consistent with the idea of a Creator who made the universe all of a piece and functioning as intended from the start, needing no ad-hoc adaptations or repairs along the way, but at most merely a planned-for mid-course correction.

The difficulty with original sin in this context is largely, I think, a semantic one, and arises from the connotations of the words "sin" and "fall." Theologians, of course, have always insisted that original "sin" does not in itself imply personal guilt on the part of Adam's descendants; yet this term, which Cardinal Ratzinger[2] has called "certainly misleading and imprecise," nonetheless continues in use. Would it not clarify things, and remove some difficulties, to speak of original "sin" as *original selfishness*? Infants, for example, are guiltless of sin, but undeniably self-centered. This self-centeredness is in them by natural generation and is necessary and good for their survival, yet it is an obstacle to an eventual relationship with God. Hence they have the same need for Christ's salvation as all other people (as the Church has always taught), even though they are as yet innocent of actual sin. (In traditional technical terms, they are born in a state of "passive original sin" or *peccatum originale originatum*, as distinct from Adam's personal sin or the "Fall," which was "active original sin" or *peccatum originale originans*.)

Related to this semantic problem is our habit of describing our sinfulness as "disordered" – as though it were in some sense chaotic, confused, and/or a distortion of some pre-existing moral order. (Similarly, Lonergan[3] sees sin as fundamentally irrational – which is true from the perspective of eternity, but often not true on the short-term timescale on which natural selection operates.) We are now in a position to be more precise: our sinfulness in fact is often very well ordered and shrewdly focused – on the attainment of our own selfish interests, just as was the behavior of all our evolutionary ancestors. When we do sin in confusion, our guilt is the less for it; our gravest sins are committed with clear

149

head and cool deliberation. Our internal moral order (such as it was and is) has not broken down; rather, with the dawn of human conscience, the rules of the evolutionary game have been changed, the bar has been raised. It is not that our behavioral gyrocompass has suddenly spun out of kilter; it is merely trying to keep us on the same old selfish course, when the time has come in our evolution for a radical course change.

Similar problems arise from the word "Fall," which inescapably connotes a downward movement. Sin is metaphorically a step downward from virtue; but is not the knowledge of good and evil (gained even, perhaps only, through sin) in another sense a step upward from moral unconsciousness? The Genesis story of the Garden of Eden, which parallels the ubiquitous ancient myth of the Golden Age, emphasizes the former metaphor, and its image of humanity's "fall" and consequent need for salvation pervades Christian thought. Yet this central theme of salvation history can be expressed in other terms that do not convey the same subliminal (and inappropriate) impression of a God whose original, idealistic plan for creation was doomed in practice to fail. As Teilhard wryly put it, "if we accept the hypothesis of a *single, perfect* [human] being put to the test *on only one occasion*, the likelihood of the Fall is so slight that one can only regard the Creator as having been extremely unlucky."[4]

My own belief is that God (who had decided to create by means of an evolutionary process driven by selfishness) was perfectly aware of the limitations of the first human beings who would emerge from that process. Only one step up from the apes, with no previous human history to guide them, they were surely the least likely of all people to avoid moral mistakes. Of all humans who would ever exist, they bore the least resemblance to the preternaturally-endowed, superhuman Adam of my childhood catechesis; and it is not credible that God could have considered their sins more momentous than those of any subsequent miscreants, or held them accountable for any special moral "headship" of the entire human race. (To do so would be analogous to condemning infants because they need toilet-training!) On the contrary: the God who loved us when we were still sinners (Romans 5:8) surely viewed their moral blunders with forbearance (as we view the misdeeds of children), seeing them as a practically-necessary consequence of the process that had raised them to the human plane.

This may seem to conflict with the image of the violent and vengeful "Old Testament" God, intent on punishing sinners, that we find in many passages of the Hebrew Scriptures. However, these passages can be better understood from a different angle:

> In one sense, these "wrath of God" passages [e.g., Amos 9:1–4; Hosea 13:7–9, 16] are not even about God, much less God's temperament. A second reading shows that they are about the actual historical consequences of the collapse of social order. They are about refugees, about human violence, about humanity's unspeakable capacity for cruelty, and about a widespread disregard for human life. They concern not realities in heaven but those here on earth. Linking these terrible things to an angry God was merely the Hebrew way of saying that human beings inevitably pay a terribly high – and terribly real – price when they neglect their fundamental ethical commitments. In other words, the God who works through the processes of history simply does not

tolerate such persistent contempt for the principles that dignify human life: Yahweh "gets angry" when human beings "sin."

Under these circumstances, an uplifting and inspiring picture of a more benign Yahweh presents an ethical problem. Is the alternative to the picture of an angry God at war against human ruthlessness indeed the picture of a smiling God unaffected by it? Is the price for this picture of a good-tempered God to be paid by the innocent who must, as a result of this picture, continue to suffer at the hands of the wicked, whose ruthlessness now constitutes no offense against the sacred? From the perspective of the innocent – and it is their perspective to which the biblical prophets were especially attuned – there is nothing attractive about such a God. On the contrary, there is something cruel about such cosmic indifference. In the Bible, it is Yahweh's wrath that brings about salvation by finally destroying the source of injustice and suffering. A god who cannot get angry is a god who cannot "save" anyone.[5]

God, then, has very definite opinions about our wrongdoing, and no doubt feels anger as well as empathy. But this God *works through the processes of history*, both evolutionary history and human history; and "the historical process itself is the exercise of divine governance."[6] God, like a good parent, knows that the children must learn from the consequences of their own mistakes, and sees in how many ways we are still, indeed, childlike.

Even today our sins have "an aspect of immaturity."[7] Sin "is less lost innocence than incompleteness. Sin is the measure of a human being's distance from Christ and the authentic self."[8] God knew from the beginning that, in the fullness of time, like children needing moral training, humans would need divine help to transcend what selfish evolution by itself could do for them. ("Take note, the spiritual was not first; first came the natural and after that the spiritual." 1 Corinthians 15:46) They would need a divine example of altruism transcending mere reciprocal altruism, an example who, by his actions and by the relationships he formed with them, would make possible for them that personal relationship with God that God had intended all along.

> God did not send the Son into the world to condemn the world, but that the world might be saved through him. (John 3:17)

> The grace of God has appeared, offering salvation to all men. It trains us to reject godless ways and worldly desires, and live temperately, justly, and devoutly in this age as we await our blessed hope, the appearing of the glory of the great God and of our Savior Christ Jesus. It was he who sacrificed himself for us, to redeem us from all unrighteousness and to cleanse for himself a people of his own, eager to do what is right. (Titus 2:11–14)

> Father in heaven, creator of all, you ordered the earth to bring forth life and crowned its goodness by creating the family of man. In history's moment when all was ready, you sent your Son to dwell in time, obedient to the laws of life in our world. Teach us the sanctity of human love, show us the value of family life, and help us to live in peace with all men that we may share in your life forever. (Alternative opening prayer, liturgy of the Holy Family)

This personal relationship with God, in turn, would include collaboration with God as co-creators of the universe, putting the finishing touches on it by actually helping to build what archaic traditions imagined as the timeless Golden Age, what the author of Genesis 2–3 portrayed as the primeval Garden of Eden, what Isaiah 11:1–9 envisioned as a future paradise, and what Jesus described as the already-begun Kingdom (or better, "kin-dom") of God.

"Salvation," then, is not just something done "to" us, the benefits of which we receive passively. Salvation involves the presentation to us, in the life of Jesus, of a *pattern* for reform of our lives (the basic Gospel demand); and a pattern, by definition, is something to be actively *imitated*. Minimally, we are called upon to *believe*; but as opportunity and ability permit, we are also expected to *act*, in conformity with our divine example.

It should be noted that this view points us in the direction now being taken by many theologians,[9] who regard the life, teaching, example, and relationships of Jesus as salvific and not, strictly speaking, his death on the cross. The cross was simply the price, under "the laws of life in our world," that Jesus inevitably had to pay for his prophetic actions – the natural outcome and therefore the symbolic culmination of his mission. It was also the ultimate demonstration of how astonishingly far God is willing to go on our behalf. As Patricia Williams expresses it:

> This new interpretation of the atonement involves both revelation and transformation. The atonement as revelation is an old idea, articulated most clearly by Peter Abelard who extols Jesus as an example for humanity to emulate. Athanasius ... celebrates the atonement as transformation, believing it changes human nature. The ideas of these two venerable Christian theologians best capture how scientifically educated people can most plausibly interpret the atonement now.[10]
>
> ... God's response to our rejection is to seek unity – at-one-ment – with us. One way God does this is to show what the at-one-ment of God and humanity looks like through showing us Jesus. The atonement is not an action Jesus performs. It is the message Jesus incarnates and enacts.
>
> Jesus has power to transform our lives. Because he is human, he is like us, setting an example we can emulate. ... Building on our evolved altruism and our capacity to use symbols, with the help of the Holy Spirit, we can overcome our egocentricity and love God and neighbor as Jesus did.[11]

The evolutionary perspective, therefore,

> ... makes sense of God's readiness to accept and forgive, for it says the very capacities and talents that make us human are the capacities and talents that enable us to be evil. If God loves us, it cannot be merely our good part, because there is no good part. We are whole beings, good-and-evil beings, not good beings who became evil .... God loves the whole person and, so, forgives. The problem of sin is not so much whether God forgives us but whether we are too proud to accept unmerited pardon.[12]

In short, the "Fall" was inevitable; the old selfish behavior was freely chosen, predictably though not deterministically, by all our early human ancestors, as well as (more to the point) by ourselves today. Even the greatest saints do, like Paul, that which they wish not to do (Romans 7:15); and Paul's analysis of this situation could not be more congruent with what modern evolutionary science reveals: "My inner self agrees with the law of God, but I see in my body's members [read: in the biologically inherited sources of my behavior] another law at war with the law of my mind; this makes me the prisoner of the law of sin in my members" (Romans 7:22–23).

We all acquire, through natural generation, that need for salvation by Christ which by the above definition is (passive) original "sin"; but the cause of our being in this state lies in a natural, necessary evolutionary process, not in any single Adam's "active original sin," which is only a fiction. (At best, it could be read as an allegory of the collective selfish actions of our ancestors that were favored by natural selection, and thereby encoded into our genetic heritage.) Because our natural, selfish urges lead us to do injustice to others, the essence of the salvation we need lies in our responses to these urges being made more just, and is aptly spoken of as "justification." Rather than being God's "Plan B," the Incarnation and Redemption were part of the plan from the very outset,[13] as we acknowledge in the Easter liturgy when we paradoxically extol the "necessary sin of Adam, which gained for us so great a Redeemer." (The word "redemption," however, gives rise to further semantic problems. With Antony Campbell,[14] I prefer to speak of "salvation.") For this reason, the proper focus of the Christian doctrine of original "sin" is on Christ, the historically real "Second Adam," and not on his allegorical counterpart the "First" Adam.[15]

11.2 The World as a Work in Progress

God responded to this need, these limitations of ours by sending aid – freely given, unmerited on our part – in the form of the Son and the Spirit. What they will accomplish with our help, and what we could never accomplish on our own – namely, the building of the Reign of God or of "Eden" – is thus in essence a free gift of God.

> O Lord, you mete out peace to us, for it is you who have accomplished all we have done. … We conceived and writhed in pain, giving birth to wind; salvation we have not achieved for the earth, the inhabitants of the world cannot bring it forth. (Isaiah 26:12, 18)

> [Zechariah, father of John the Baptist, prophesied:] "… All this is the work of the kindness of our God; he, the Dayspring, shall visit us in his mercy to shine on those who sit in darkness and in the shadow of death, to guide our feet into the way of peace." (Luke 1:78–79)

> Jesus said to his disciples: "… It is easier for a camel to pass through a needle's eye than for a rich man to enter the kingdom of God." … "Then who can be saved?" Jesus looked at them and said, "For man it is impossible; but for God all things are possible." (Matthew 19:24–26)

As biblical scholar George Mendenhall says: "The biblical tradition insists that nothing short of an act of God can enable people to transcend (personal or corporate) self-interest, and even then, usually after everything else they rely on is destroyed (Isaiah 6:8–12)."[16]

At the same time, this indispensable gift of God purposefully left the building of God's Reign incomplete: it left something for us creatures to do in partnership with the Creator. We see this even in the (second) biblical account of creation, where, as Carlos Mesters[17] points out, humankind was not born into Eden but was created before it and then placed in it – as a gift of God, but also "to cultivate and care for it" (Genesis 2:7–8, 15). In no other way, after all, except through such a process embedded in history, could we come to have a personal stake in the outcome. This makes a naive, literal understanding of Eden as a static paradise into grist for the satirist:

> Adam, destined as he was for a life of glorified sloth, never amounted to a doer; work ethic had no place in the newly created world. Besides, the Lord had a poor opinion of work which, characteristically, he inflicted upon the First Parents as punishment and curse.[18]

On the contrary. In truth, according to the Creator's plan for the universe, some assembly was required – and in fact a great deal. Creating our universe in six days was simply an impossibility, as much so as the proverbial building of Rome in one day. To be sure, God might have created instantaneously something that *looked* like our universe, much as a Cecil B. De Mille could call into existence a movie set that resembled ancient Rome. But the proverb about Rome is based in part on the fact that a real city is not just an arrangement of buildings, or even a crowd of people; it is an integrated community with a history extended through time, and its value in our eyes is inseparable from its time dimension and its history of organic growth. As John Haught expresses it,

> [e]volutionary theology would ... agree with Teilhard that the idea of an instantaneously complete creation is theologically unthinkable. Such a universe would be only an extension of God's own being; it would not be a world unto itself. It would have no internal self-coherence, no intrinsic autonomy, but would instead be a purely passive implementation of the divine will. It would be a frozen universe, one without a future and one incapable of supporting life since, by definition, living beings must continually transcend themselves.[19]

As for our universe, special creationists implicitly admit the necessarily artificial, "movie-set" nature of a six-day creation when they postulate that the world was created with an "appearance of age" – for example, that the light seemingly emanating from stars millions of light-years away was actually created *en route*, and has not really spent millions of years on its journey. This, of course, is just a "space age" version of the old arguments that Adam had a navel despite his never having been inside a mother's womb, or that fossils were created as such inside the rocks where they are found; and it equally implies a certain deceitfulness on the part of a Creator who would fill the "set" of creation with such "false fronts" at every turn. More plausible and palatable, especially to those who conceive of the divine nature as trinitarian (and hence as a community in itself), is a Creator who wills an authentic, organically- and historically-connected community of creatures.[20]

Like a real human community or a real universe, the Reign of God is something that by its very nature could not be brought into being by divine fiat. When Jesus went through cities healing the sick one by one, he could perhaps have raised his hand and cured all the sick of the world in an instant; but he did not. Instead, he urged his disciples to finish the job, promising that they would do even greater works than his (John 14:12). He had come, after all, not to establish universal health care on earth, but to establish the Reign of God, and to show how it was to be done. The man born blind owed his blindness to no sin; "rather, it was to let God's works show forth in him" (John 9:3). In the largest sense, the inherent limitations of our unperfected universe – born out of blind evolutionary forces, and still beset by moral blindness – derive from no one's sin, but will show forth the glory of God's work when the world is brought to its eschatological perfection.

This work of God comes about not by fiat but by invitation; and therefore the role of chance in the world's origins is no cause for scandal. To quote John Haught once more,

> ... divine love allows for a contingent universe, one not shaped by force. In such a world, chance or accidents can occur. Theology should not be surprised but should have expected that the world would be open to the kind of contingency and randomness we find in life's evolution. St. Thomas Aquinas argued that a universe totally dominated by necessity would not be distinct from God. It has to have elements of nonnecessity or contingency in order to be a world at all. "It would be contrary to the nature of providence and to the perfection of the world," he said, "if nothing happened by chance."[21]

Or, as Karl Schmitz-Moormann put it:

> The universe, though in certain aspects still a demonstration of the Almighty – the immensity of the universe with its billions of galaxies is obviously in need of an almighty Creator – is not in the first place a demonstration of God's almightiness. ... God's way of creating is not a demonstration of power, which would force everything called into being to go directly to God. ... God seems not to make things happen, but to allow them to happen.[22]

What is true of chance is also true of evil. Schmitz-Moormann has emphasized the evident importance to God of freedom of the creation, and the evolution of this freedom in a world called into being by God's love:

> ... we might thus speculate that God's intention in creating this world is not to establish a perfect order, to impose the divine will, but to call forth in love a creation that will one day become able to answer in love God's creative call.[23]

However:

> There cannot be any free evolution without necessary evils such as death or without statistically [un]avoidable evil. When things can go wrong, sooner or later some will go wrong. Only in a static and strictly determined world can evil be avoided. Illness, accidents, and untimely deaths are part of the price. We may be upset by seeing this price accepted by the Creator, but there is no rationally thinkable way to have the evolution of freedom without concomitant evil.[24]

John Haught adds that "the only kind of universe a loving and caring God could create in the first place is an unfinished one." If it were instantaneously finished, it could not be "something truly other than God and hence able to be the recipient of divine love."[25]

Indeed, this may take some getting used to: a view of reality in which the world's goodness is inseparable from its very imperfections, and the creation remains "truly other than God" even as it embodies its Creator's very creativity. In the words of philosopher Beatrice Bruteau:

> If there is to be a finite world that *grows*, one that develops and becomes more complex, more diversified, more interactive, and therefore more unified, and eventually more *conscious*, then it has to include chance, error, death, and pain. I think it is important that we see this and understand it. Otherwise, we may continue believing that these are "bad" things that "ought not" to be here, things that are "contrary to God's plan."
>
> Of course, a universe that was merely *created*, built by someone else from the outside, the way one would make a machine, could be totally planned and then constructed according to the plan and wouldn't need means for correcting itself, for gaining information about its environment and finding new ways to interact. But it would not image its Creator by being creative.[26]

Paradoxical though it may seem, this evolutionary view presents a more parsimonious and less jaundiced picture of human history than the logical alternatives – either that humans were specially created at a pinnacle of perfection from which they immediately "fell," only to begin a painful re-ascent with divine help; or else (as implied by acceptance of an evolutionary origin) that they followed a long "upward" path of progress from "lower" forms of life that was interrupted by the same "Fall" just as the threshold of human nature was reached. To me, it is far more consistent with the image of a unitary creative act and a consequently seamless creation to visualize human origins and human history as a story of generally "upward" progress (however slow, blind, halting, and sporadic), which led first to moral consciousness and only later to moral improvement.

11.3   A Good or a "Fallen" Creation?

This view of our origins and nature has less in common with the pessimism of St. Augustine than with the more optimistic view of St. Irenaeus, who after all stood closer to the Apostles in the chain of doctrinal transmission.[27] This view may also have the advantage of reconciling the traditional theology of salvation with the post-Vatican II emphasis on the goodness of the creation, as found in the writings of Thomas Berry, Matthew Fox, and many others. The latter trend of thought is often criticized as leaving little if any room in its optimistic worldview for sin.[28] Traditionally, Christian theologians described not only humanity but the entire universe as in some way "fallen" due to the sin of Adam. What I suggest is the somewhat paradoxical notion that the universe *as it came from the hand of the Creator* was both good and "fallen" at the same time.

I mean this in the sense that the aspect of the "Fall" which is *universal* to the whole creation is not to be understood as sinful or the result of actual sin, but merely as denoting that the world is imperfect or unperfected, though (with the help of grace) perfectible. In Holmes Rolston's apt phrase, sinful humanity should be seen as "failing rather than falling."[29] (Here we see once again the awkwardness of using the term "fallen" to describe something that has not in any meaningful sense "moved downward," but simply has yet to move further "upward." We cannot conclude from seeing a man at the foot of a ladder that he has fallen off it; he may never have been on it to start with.) Sin (moral evil) came into the world only with humans, but selfishness (a necessary ingredient and mechanism of creation-by-evolution, though one to be eventually transcended through our salvation) was present from the origin of life, together with death and other imperfections (physical evil). God, after all, said only that the created world was "very good," not that it was perfect.

Undeniably, our environment has suffered in countless ways from the sins of humanity (overpopulation, pollution, climate change, extermination of species, unsustainable exploitation of resources, and so on).[30] But it seems to me unhelpful to say that the "world" apart from human society and its immediate environs is in some theological sense "fallen." Selfishness is indeed ingrained in all life and in evolution, and as such it forms the historical substrate or raw material of our own sinfulness; but (like the booster rocket) it is more usefully spoken of as limited in its potential than as "fallen" in its condition. As theologian Craig Nessan correctly says, "Selfishness is not a fault among animals but a virtue insofar as it contributes to the successful propagation of genes."[31]

Another way to express this view of our imperfect world is that the critic should evaluate the painting as a complete composition, and not just (for example) the background details in isolation. The painter intended the background to serve as background; if it seems imperfectly drawn, even distorted, that may be intentional and may serve a purpose that can only be judged in the context of the complete work.

All this should come as at least a partial relief to the more guilt-ridden of us Catholics (and some other Christians!), those who believe "original sin" means that *all* the bad stuff in the world is somehow our fault: it's not, so God doesn't expect us to fix it all! As pointed out by Fr. William Reiser, "no matter how terrible the situation of the world, and no matter how serious they are about living their religion, Christians are not supposed to be driven people. Our belief that the world ultimately belongs to God, and that only the Spirit creates and redeems, protects us from being overburdened and crushed by our exposure to massive human suffering. There has to be room in our lives to celebrate and be festive, even though the world's liberation is so unfinished."[32] This should be a source of some comfort in both our individual spirituality and our pastoral work.

In this view, then, it is not human sin that brought about all the imperfections of the world, but more nearly the opposite; and those imperfections, in turn, were built into this world by its Creator: "Creation was made subject to futility, not of its own accord but by him who once subjected it" (Romans 8:20); "God has imprisoned all in disobedience that he might have mercy on all" (Romans 11:32). The inherent limitations of this material world set the stage for our sinfulness. The final decision, however, is always ours – free will and human culpability (given the availability of grace) are in no way excluded or diminished. "Say not: 'It was God's doing that I fell away' .... No man does he command to sin" (Sirach 15:11, 20a); "No one who is tempted is free to say, 'I am being tempted by God'" (James 1:13a). The blame and responsibility for the moral evil that we personally contribute to our world are ours alone, because this evil (unlike physical evil) stems from our individual human choices, made with full consciousness that we could choose differently.[33] What God *has* done is put us in a position where we must and can choose: between the selfish way of natural selection, and the selfless way of Christ, which alone can liberate us from this world's futility.

> I have set before you life and death, the blessing and the curse. Choose life, then, that you and your descendants may live, by loving the Lord, your God, heeding his voice, and holding fast to him. (Deuteronomy 30:19–20a)

> From a Christian perspective, Jesus Christ has revealed the contours of what it would mean for us to fully attain to the image of God. Jesus lived for God and for others with a self-less love that culminated in his death on the cross. Those who live "in Christ" press onward toward the future goal of a life transformed into the Christ-like image of God. To become like Christ would be the equivalent of becoming fully human.[34]

That unconscious organic evolution, which still goes on endlessly around us, and which made us so selfish that the total avoidance of sin is beyond our merely human power, has also raised us up, preparing us to become its own consciousness and conscience – a role into which we still struggle to grow. As the Catholic tradition has long repeated, "grace builds on nature"; and in the end, we each need Christ's saving action to overcome our original selfishness and answer his call. But there is more: human behavior is so deeply rooted in the entire evolution of the universe that the cosmic salvation glimpsed by Paul in Romans 8:19–23 is seen, still more clearly and more grandly, to include salvation, not *from* space, time, and matter, but salvation both in them and of them.

Notes

1.   Haught 2001, 51, 52.
2.   Ratzinger 1990, 89.
3.   Lonergan 1957, 667.
4.   Teilhard 1971, 193; emphasis in original.
5.   Mendenhall 2001, 147–148. Other violent biblical passages, notably the description of the Israelites' genocidal conquest of Canaan (Joshua 1–11), are apparently anachronistic misinterpretations and misrepresentations of the true history, read into the record centuries after the fact by writers of the monarchic period, who failed to grasp that premonarchic Israel had values and customs very different from their own violently nationalist and imperialist state. This "introduced terrible and tragic religious confusion into the biblical tradition, permanently etching in many people's minds the notion that Yahweh was, from the beginning, the god of one particular nation and one group of people" (Mendenhall 2001, 173).
6.   Mendenhall 2001, 131.
7.   Schoonenberg 1965, 42.

8. Duffy 1993, 331, expressing the views of Karl Rahner: "Sin is situated against a graced horizon. … Grace is in the end more powerful, eschatologically victorious. … Rahner's bright world of grace contrasts with the dark hued world of Augustine."

9. For example, Campbell 2000.

10. Williams 2001, 195–196.

11. Williams 2001, 197.

12. Williams 2001, 192.

13. Ephesians 1:4–14, 3:9–11; 2 Timothy 1:9–10; 1 Peter 1:18–20; cf. Campbell 2000, 3: "for a deeply loving God we can hardly be second best; [hence] a classical understanding of original sin is in trouble."

14. Campbell 2000, Chap. 6.

15. Cf. Barth 1962, de Rosa 1967. As Herbert Haag says with reference to Romans 5:12–21, "a literal understanding of [the account of the Fall] does not belong to the object of the Pauline teaching any more than the literal understanding of the story of Jonah is the object of Jesus' teaching [in Matthew 12:40]" (Haag 1969, 96).

16. Mendenhall 2001, 100.

17. Mesters 1974, 26, 89.

18. Rudofsky 1977, 14.

19. Haught 1998a, 576.

20. See, for example, Schmitz-Moormann (1997, 125–135), Bruteau (1997), and Edwards (1999) for development of an evolutionary theology of the Trinity.

21. Haught 1998a, 577; Aquinas, *Summa Contra Gentiles* III, 72, 74.

22. Schmitz-Moormann 1997, 122.

23. Schmitz-Moormann 1997, 144.

24. Schmitz-Moormann 1997, 144. The late author's collaborator, Fr. J. F. Salmon, SJ, agreed with me (pers. comm., 22 June 1998) that the word "avoidable" was probably intended to read "unavoidable." Cf. the quote from Teilhard in Chapter 14 here.

25. Haught 2002, 546.

26. Bruteau 1997, 125; emphases in original.

27. In Calvinist terms, the position taken here is closer to the "supralapsarian" view identified with Irenaeus and Schleiermacher than with the "infralapsarian" position associated with Augustine; Allik 1989.

28. The work of Pierre Teilhard de Chardin has been similarly criticized; for a rebuttal of this criticism, however, see H. de Lubac 1968, 135–139.

29. Rolston 1999, 300.

30. See Wright and Kill 1993 for one of many theological examinations of this topic now available.

31. Nessan 1995, 112.

32. Reiser 1997, 203.

33. This is just the opposite of the traditional view, as expressed by McGrath (1988, 125): "The doctrine of justification by faith results in a realist approach to Christian ethics, which recognizes that the pursuit of self-interest is an inevitability because of the total permeation of human nature by original sin." Rather, the permeation of human nature by sin is inevitable because evolution has been driven by the pursuit of self-interest. Recognition of this results in an even more realistic approach to ethics and to the doctrine of justification by faith.

    C. Nessan (1995, 114–115) points out that an evolutionary perspective can reconcile, and build on, Paul Tillich's ontological concept of sin (we are existentially estranged from our "essence" or potential) and Reinhold Niebuhr's stress on human responsibility.

34. Nessan 1995, 116.

CHAPTER TWELVE

Reprise: What about suffering?

What is going on in evolution ... is the world's suffering along with the groaning
Spirit of God toward new creation. Nature itself bears the shape of the cross. It
also, therefore, bears the promise of resurrection.

John F. Haught[1]

12.1 Are There Fates Worse Than Death?

Perhaps by this point the Christian who is skeptical of Darwinian evolution is
willing to concede a certain logical coherence to the foregoing. Yet no mere intellectual assent seems capable of expunging his or her gut feeling that a good God
would not tolerate the suffering that an evolutionary universe must entail. What
more can be said to assuage this existential anxiety?

As was done above (section 4.11) in replying to the objection that Darwinian
evolution is "cruel" and "wasteful," we must clarify what we mean by terms such as
"suffering." When we think of suffering in nature, the plight of the prey animal
naturally comes first to mind – although there are many unpleasant ways for
animals to die that do not involve predation or parasitism: starvation, genetic and
other congenital disorders, noninfectious diseases, complications of giving birth,
and physical accidents, for instance.

But I don't think that it is really this suffering as such that bothers us the most.
Most people, for example, think it is justifiable to inflict pain on animals in the
course of important medical research that cannot be done any other way. In fact,
we seem ready to tolerate almost any amount of suffering in ourselves or others, so
long as it serves some *purpose*. Suffering and dying for one's country, family, religion, ethical principles, and so on, are even praised and encouraged. The real
horror is *futility*; that is, suffering (or even just life) without purpose – the "vanity"
of Ecclesiastes. The myth of Sisyphus, eternally rolling his stone uphill again and
again, is a classic view of hell as pointless make-work. Cyclical repetition, devoid of
reason and hope, is our ultimate nightmare. A cyclical view of existence can even
characterize entire cultures, as described in section 7.1 – with such demoralizing
consequences as a "desire ... to refuse history" and a "terror of ... the meaning-
lessness of profane existence" on the part of archaic thought,[2] and Eastern religions' revulsion at a material world seen as endlessly repetitive, unholy, and even
illusory.

This sense of futility is what creation is groaning in anticipation of release from in
Romans 8:18–23. We progress-minded Westerners (imbued with the biblically-
inspired optimism noted in section 7.1) all want to move forward, to be a part of
some genuine advance, and not to be mired in everlasting standstill or futile repetition. But modern evolutionists are quite right in pointing out, *contra* superficial
teleological thinking, that evolution does not necessarily or automatically produce

"progress" in most individual lineages. (Many would deny it *ever* produces progress, though I disagree; see section 7.2 above). Since, in any case, the overwhelming bulk of evolution is not leading the evolving organisms anywhere beyond their next meal or their next mating season, and since (as writers like Michael Ruse emphasize) most of them meet with unpleasant ends along the way, it would seem there is plenty for creation to groan about.

A time-honored response to this existential agony is simply that of faith. Job can accept his suffering because of the "monumental evidence of reason and good will" displayed in creation – he has faith that God's wisdom, though unfathomable, can be trusted.[3] This, incidentally, is that same trust in God, both grounded in and explaining the constancy of nature, that originally undergirded the scientific impulse.

However, a more explicit key to creation's release from its subjection to futility is now available in the New Covenant – which promises that this subjection is "not without hope" (Romans 8:20). This key is perhaps best seen when Romans 8:18–23 is juxtaposed with John 16:21 (when a woman has borne her child, she no longer remembers her pain). If the evolution of intelligent life, capable of freedom and love, and the realization of the Reign of God are sufficient purposes for the creation as a whole (as I think they are), then all else finds its purpose in its contribution to those ends. Every creature's death that results from natural selection improves the adaptation of its own lineage; every death without exception feeds other organisms, continues the flow of energy and nutrients in the biosphere, and keeps the whole process of life and evolution going. The creation, which finds its consciousness in humanity (and in whatever other intelligent life there may be on other planets), both senses its suffering through us and recognizes through us that its suffering has not been in vain; and in the end it will "no longer remember its pain." Despite all the pangs of this cosmic birth, in hindsight (as Carlos Mesters[4] points out) the lasting damage done by evil will amount to no more than a scratch on the heel (Genesis 3:15).

And lest there be any doubt, it is also spelled out for us *how* we are delivered from this futility that we see in so much of human and evolutionary history: "Realize that you were delivered from the futile way of life your fathers handed on to you, not by any diminishable sum of silver or gold, but by Christ's blood beyond all price: the blood of a spotless, unblemished lamb chosen before the world's foundation and revealed for your sake in these last days" (1 Peter 1:18–20).

As it is, the world has actually accomplished something by its labor and groanings: it has brought forth life, in amazing diversity, and intelligent life to boot; and at least on this planet, all those living things are not just figuratively but literally each other's brothers and sisters – in an unbroken chain from the first burst of primordial energy, to the first bacterium, to us and to Jesus himself. The very atoms of our bodies were manufactured in stars that formed and exploded eons ago, scattering their substance as the dust from which our own solar system and its inhabitants were made. In fact, we could not have been made – our own multibillion-year evolution could not even have begun – until after these earlier generations of stars had come into being and passed away.[5] And that was only the beginning. "Life in human beings has an age of more than three billion years: from the beginning the chain has never been interrupted. Every human being is alive with a life that started shortly after the formation of the earth. In a precise sense, every human being incorporates the condensed history of the universe from the beginning of the formation of protons to the formation of the brain."[6]

As Darwin said, "There is grandeur in this view of life."[7]

12.2   Is There an Alternative?

Yes, countless creatures have had to suffer and die along the evolutionary way. But a universe in which an animal could never be killed, for example, by lightning would probably be a universe in which there could be no lightning, or electricity, or weather, or electrons, or physical laws anything like the ones we know – including evolution (and thus not even the animal itself). Probably such a universe could not even be fashioned out of matter and energy.

Every year, thousands of people are killed by earthquakes and volcanoes – a classic reason to doubt the goodness of God. The devastating Lisbon earthquake of 1755 shook the Christian faith of millions, and occasioned Voltaire's famous satire on orthodox beliefs, *Candide*. But earthquakes and volcanoes are signs and necessary byproducts of a geologically-active planet; they result from movements of the plates forming Earth's crust, which create the diverse and beautiful topography of our world and make possible the diversity of its flora and fauna, including us. If the movements of molten rock in Earth's interior ever ceased, our planet's protective magnetic field (like that of Mars) would also cease to exist, and the solar wind would gradually blow our atmosphere away into space, ending life here as we know it.

We know from daily experience that anything made of parts can come apart (like a fracturing crustal plate of the Earth, or a building collapsing in an earthquake), and that the more moving parts something has, the more prone it is to break down. Every atom in creation is made up of smaller particles, quarks, "superstrings," or other entities, all in motion; and nothing in the known universe has more of these moving parts more complexly organized than a human body.

When we think about it, everything we call "physical evil," every instance of suffering and death, is the result of some unwelcome change or damage on the molecular level. The rupture of molecular bonds that propagates into a broken bone; the tissue and cell damage done by the teeth of predators and by speeding vehicles or bullets; the chemical or radiological damage done to our cells by poisons; the microscopic assaults of viruses, bacteria, protozoans, and prions; the death of brain cells that results in Alzheimer's disease; the oxygen starvation of cells that causes heart attacks and strokes; the damage to DNA that leads to birth defects or cancer – all these misfortunes and more are rooted in, and readily understandable as, the simple coming apart of our basic molecular building blocks. Our very sense impressions and emotions are mediated by, and inseparable from, chemical reactions in specific cells of our nervous system. Molecular biology has now revealed in unprecedented detail that what is true of inanimate objects – their fundamental physical and chemical breakability – is even more acutely true of us living things, whose functions and malfunctions are more varied and complex than previous generations ever imagined.

So long as we and worlds are made in this way – so long as physicality is synonymous with multiplicity of parts – it is impossible that breakdowns of every imaginable sort could be avoided. God could no more make an unbreakable physical universe than a square circle. So I think that the physical "evil" of animal suffering is inseparable in principle from even a good creation, just as the real evil of sin is inseparable from a creation in which intelligent creatures have free will. God doesn't need to make excuses for this. It's part of the price we pay for all that is desirable in creation; and taking the package as a whole, it's worth the price.

But I must emphasize: it's not all "price"; there is an "up"-side to this physical breakability, and we find it in genetic mutations. As explained before, these are errors made in copying the genetic material. Most are harmful or neutral, a few are beneficial – but even the beneficial ones start out as *errors*, and the copying process tries to minimize errors. Therefore each beneficial mutation – each potential forward step in evolution – is *both* fortuitous, and an accident (an "evil") that a perfect copying system would have prevented. *A perfectly error-free copying process could not result in evolution*. In preventing degradation of the copies, it would simultaneously preclude any improvement in the copies. The possibility of progress would be frozen to death.

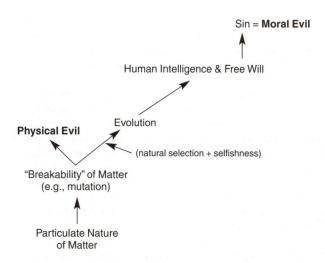

Figure 12.1 **The common origin of, and the causal relation between, physical and moral evil. Both are rooted in the inevitably "breakable" nature of particulate matter, which is manifested in many ways (including genetic mutations). "Physical evil" typically arises out of or consists of some simple "breakage" or unwelcome change in material objects, often on the molecular level. Mutations are a special class of such events (usually harmful, sometimes helpful) on which natural selection can act to produce evolution, together with evolution's inevitable corollary of selfish behavior. Products of this evolution include our intelligence and free will, which we have predictably used to create actual sin (moral evil).**

Thus there is a vital payoff to physical evil – but also even to the moral evil that results from human traits such as aggression. After all, the moral dimension of our consciousness, and moral evil, evolved out of the physical world and physical evil (see Figure 12.1), just as learned behavior and ultimately culture evolved out of instinctual behavior. But this phrase "evolved out of" does not imply that the older traits have been left behind, or even that they no longer serve a constructive purpose. Consider these words of primatologist Frans de Waal:

> Our human societies are structured by the interplay between antagonism and attraction. Disappearance of the former is more than an unrealistic wish, it is a misguided one. No one would want to live in the sort of society that would result, as it would lack differentiation among individuals. A school of herrings is a good example of an aggregation predominantly based on attraction: the fish move together without any problems, but they have no social organization to speak of. If certain species, such as humans, reach a high degree of social differentiation, role division, and cooperation, this occurs because the cohesive tendency is counteracted by internal conflict. Individuals delineate their social positions in competition with others. We cannot have it both ways: a world in which each individual attains his or her own identity, and a world without clashing individual interests.[8]

It need hardly be underlined that this ancient tension was and remains a prerequisite even to that harmonious complementarity among the differentiated members of the Body of Christ of which St. Paul spoke (1 Corinthians 12:4–30; Romans 12:4–8; Ephesians 4:11–16).

In the midst of our suffering, God "not only provides and protects (like a father) but also … suffers with us so that something new may be born as a result of this suffering (like a mother)."[9] We come into the world bawling our heads off, complaining of our discomfort, and completely oblivious to the decades of life and hours of labor our mothers have gone through to bring us to this point. Later, we complain that God does nothing about the suffering we encounter in the world – equally oblivious (cf. Hosea 11:3–4) to the billions of years of bringing-to-birth that were needed to produce creatures capable of such complaints, and also capable of doing something ourselves, as members of the Body of Christ, to mitigate the suffering. We need to take a larger and more mature view.

A major reason for undertaking this inquiry has been to help those seeking answers in the face of tragedy. It seems natural for human beings confronted with random disaster to ask why God wills or permits this; and, receiving no convincing answer, to doubt God's beneficence or even existence. In Mark Twain's pessimistic story *The Mysterious Stranger*, an old woman declares her faith that not a sparrow falls to the ground without God's seeing it. "But it falls, just the same," replies Satan. "What good is *seeing* it fall?" It is bad enough to suffer the loss of possessions, health, life, or loved ones, without losing one's faith as well. That, at least, is avoidable.

Let us once more consider the relationship between the very young child and the parent. The child lives in a seemingly irrational world in which the parent is all-powerful. An unpleasant event, such as a treat denied, a shot administered by a doctor, or even an illness or natural disaster, is something arbitrarily willed or tolerated by the parent or something that the parent failed to prevent; and so the child may blame the parent for the consequent suffering. It is only as we grow older that we realize that some of those "misfortunes" against which we railed – such as the vaccination – had in fact a logic to them that a child was unable to comprehend. We even come to realize that there are limits to a parent's power to prevent really bad things from happening.

One of the greatest advances in our intellectual maturation as a species was the discovery of evolution. Only now are we beginning to realize how things work in an evolutionary, material world. Take the simple fact that all material things have moving parts, and all things with moving parts are subject to breakdowns. This is a law of nature whose necessity not even God, the lawmaker, could evade: God's decision to create a material world could only be a decision to create breakable things, and ultimately broken ones. And as was noted above, nothing in the known universe has more moving parts and more ways to break down than a human being. A parent – or God – could protect a child completely from "physical evil" only by not bringing that child into existence at all.

The case of moral evil is really no different. None of us would willingly give up free will, even though selfishness threatens its exercise with perversion at every turn. Without that original selfishness, however, life could not have evolved and we would not exist. God's decision to create material beings with free will could only be a decision to create sinners.

Applicable to both physical and moral evil, then, is the punch line of Jesus' parable of the weeds and the wheat (Matthew 13:24–30): "pull up the weeds and you might take the wheat along with them. Let them grow together until harvest." God's ways are not like ours, impatient as we are for what we fancy to be "justice." We are like the heretic-hunting Catholic abbot Arnaud Amaury, who in 1209 ordered the massacre of the suspect townspeople of Béziers, saying, "Kill them all; the Lord will recognize his own!" Jesus, in contrast, says: "*Save* them all; the Lord will recognize his own!" Not only human sinners, but even natural phenomena of which we disapprove, may play such important roles in the divine plan that uprooting them may cause disruption beyond our imagining.

Although the inherent limitations of the material universe are not the result of an "enemy"'s sabotage (cf. Matthew 13:28), the constraint they place on God's action is the same. Just as an immediate divine curb of sinners would take away our free will and our meaningful participation in bringing about the Reign of God, so God could intervene to prevent natural mishaps or ameliorate nature's "cruelties" only at the cost of taking back all the control of events that had originally been delegated to natural laws. So why delegate it in the first place? To make the "kinder and gentler" world of nature that critics of evolution would like, such interventions would be needed literally countless times every second.

Neither could the critics be appeased by God's preventing only the "worst" tragedies. (For all we know, maybe God already does! According to Judeo-Christian tradition, after all, God sets limits to Satan's mischief in the world.) If no child ever died of cancer and the worst suffering known to us were a stubbed toe, we would still cry to heaven against the injustice done to our bruised digits. Or if, instead, we really were spared all physical and mental discomfort and lived in a permanent state of anesthetized bliss, the result would not resemble Eden so much as Aldous Huxley's *Brave New World*. Until the "harvest" of the Last Day, then, God must refrain from either breaking or binding up the bruised reeds of this world (Isaiah 42:3–4) in ways that might compromise the greater good of an autonomous creation.

Though God does not at once take away the suffering, still we believe that this is the God revealed in the life of Jesus, who abhorred suffering, relieved it at every opportunity, and rejected the idea that it was fit punishment for sin (for example, Matthew 5:45, Luke 13:4–5, John 9:2–5). This is a God who hates suffering, who would not tolerate it if there were any alternative – and who *will* do away with it in the end.

How? We don't know. The argument is made[10] that it is too anthropocentric to justify the casualties of evolution by the eventual appearance of us: surely, the countless individuals and species that perished along the way could not have been used by a loving God as mere means to an end, but must be valued for their own sakes and must still be in some way "redeemed." Will God somehow make it up to these creatures, in some resurrection or heaven of their own? Are we to play some mysterious part in this, not just as co-creators of God's Kingdom but as "co-redeemers" and healers of nature? This has not yet been revealed to us, but such speculations cannot be excluded. We know only that compassion moves us to desire some such happy ending, and we believe that God is not to be outdone in compassion. Some will doubtless argue that leaving the resolution of this question to the "end times" leaves our theodicy incomplete; but I would say that theodicy has done enough by explaining the data actually before us – by demonstrating that *up to now* the Creator has had no alternative, and hence needs no defense. Given this conclusion, it seems admissible to trust that, in the unknown "end times" to come, God will do whatever compassion may require.

12.3   A Humble or a Disciplinarian God?

Theistic evolutionists sometimes make the mistake of saying that God *chose* to create by means of evolution, when in fact no other choice was available. "Special creation" of things as they are today was not a practical alternative: no more could Mr. De Mille have shut off his cameras, walked away from his movie set of ancient Rome, and expected it to come to life as a real city. Pinocchio, and Pygmalion's Galatea, come to life only in storybooks; God the Father no more made Adam directly from clay than did the apocryphal boy Jesus bring clay birds to life. That was not an option.

Failure to recognize this fact is the reason why the notion of the "humility of God," now much discussed among theologians, is so readily misunderstood – especially from the viewpoint of theodicy, which asks: How can a God who is both almighty and benevolent tolerate evil? Seemingly, the creator of this suffering world cannot be both; so if we insist on a benevolent God, we must accept one whose powers are limited.

A self-humbling God, who cedes power over the world to the world's own laws, seems like just such a weak God. Process theology, however, plausibly holds that a God who acts through persuasion can actually exercise far greater influence on events, and hence greater power, than one who uses brute force. This is because a world with the freedom to help create itself has much more integrity and value than a puppet-like universe that is coerced into being; and the Creator is greater to the extent that the world created has greater value.[11] God's willingness to let the world make its own mistakes is not weakness, but a pure expression of God's love – like that of the good parent who longs for the child not just to exhibit approved behavior, but to develop a strong, healthy, *inner guide* to behavior. "The dominant intuition here is of a God whose power and effectiveness is expressed in the *longing* for the self-coherence and autonomy of that which is other than God."[12] This God is the father who allows the Prodigal Son – his creation – the freedom to run through his inheritance; who accepts the pain of separation this entails; who longs for his return; and who rejoices with him in the end (Luke 15:11–32).

Why, then, does evil remain? Not because God has gratuitously given up the power to prevent it. The key to the paradox is simply to realize that banishing evil from an autonomous world involves a contradiction, and is therefore impossible, even for God. (Thus Thomas Aquinas: "whatever implies contradiction does not come within the scope of divine omnipotence, because it cannot have the aspect of possibility. Hence it is more appropriate to say that such things cannot be done, than that God cannot do them."[13]) On the other hand, a non-autonomous world, even one without evil, is not worth creating. The "power" to do the impossible is illusory; hence there is no meaning in saying that God "surrenders" it. Inability to do that which intrinsically cannot be done is no real limitation on God's power.[14] (Recall, too, what was said in section 9.2.2: *whatever statement we make about the divine* – such as "God is all-powerful" – *must immediately be qualified by its negation*.)

Just as inadequate to explain evil as is God's "choosing" to create by evolution are the many arguments made over the centuries to the effect that suffering and death are somehow spiritually good for us: that we learn something from them, that they build character, that their acceptance shows our obedience to the Creator, that without them we would not appreciate the gift of life. Such a view is found even in Hebrews 12:5–11 and in St. Irenaeus.[15] All these assertions may be true; but to the extent they imply that God deliberately created suffering and death for just these purposes, they are seriously misleading. Such "benefits" should be seen as byproducts, at best, of laws necessary to this or any physical universe – and not as the fruits of training gratuitously inflicted on us by a divine drill instructor.

But if God didn't want us to suffer, it seems like He/She could easily have equipped us with more ways to avoid it. As a thoughtful acquaintance of mine argues: "Humans are on the verge of godlike power, with those technologies we are likely to have in 50–100 years. So, why didn't God just start out by giving humans godlike powers, such as those? Instead of making humans go through millennia of suffering before finally reaching an advanced, near-godlike stage, why didn't He start humans out with advanced knowledge of technology, political science, etc.? Any loving parent wants to give his children as much of a head start as possible, especially to prevent extreme suffering."

I don't think this would work, for a number of reasons; but we don't really need to speculate about why God might or might not choose to create in such a manner. In fact, the human race has plenty of real-world experience, and experimental data, concerning gods who give godlike status to their human creatures. In many times and cultures, human rulers have literally been regarded as divine or divinely anointed (or treated as if they were), and their children and heirs have been raised as little gods from infancy, coddled with privilege and deference. The results have been almost uniformly regrettable: little monsters who (if not too warped to function at all) are capable of little but degeneracy and despotism.

As a result, absolute monarchs and dictators have had mixed success in founding dynasties. The abilities of the founders are seldom manifested in even their immediate offspring, and where abilities are present, they are all too often choked by a too-deferential upbringing. The usual outcome, within a few generations, is degeneration. (The late, unlamented sons of former Iraqi dictator Saddam Hussein are a recent and particularly nasty example.) Hence the more enlightened rulers have tried hard to raise "normal" children, by having them strictly disciplined by tutors, or even schooled with children of mere nobles or commoners – in other words, *without* godlike status or powers.

This may sound like an argument for the idea that "suffering builds character"; but I don't think it's really about suffering. Even when crown princes go through military school with ordinary mortals, they don't encounter much suffering, as the rest of the world understands suffering, and they are not unaware of who they are and what station they are destined to occupy. If anything in the experience builds character, I suspect it is the chance to see what they can do on their own (at least "on their own" to a limited degree), with the inescapable advantage of their exalted position suspended as far as possible. Suffering may or may not build character (and we know it can just as often destroy character), but the absence of challenge can certainly destroy character, or stunt its growth. Character requires both discipline and autonomy. It has to grow from within (it can't be conferred by fiat), it takes time to grow, and it grows best in those who are allowed to find out for themselves, by trial and error, what is in them. It grows when they are able to define themselves as persons distinct from the power that created them.

Perhaps this is one reason why hereditary monarchy (that extreme expression of warped social Darwinism) has gradually given way to democracy. Humans learned the hard way that their rulers couldn't automatically pass on character or ability to their descendants; in fact, a privileged upbringing tended to have the opposite effect. So, once hereditary rule was no longer needed to ensure peaceful succession of governments, why have biological descent enter into it at all? Better, perhaps, a society of equals in which (ideally) all have a chance to develop in the absence of a privileged ruling class, and manifest merit is rewarded.

As for humanity as a whole, I think this means that God could not have made us with a technological silver spoon in our collective mouth. Without having to make it on our own both as individuals and as a species, we would have been denied the chance (inescapable in the natural order of things) to discover our own abilities and limits, and to become persons in our own right, fit for a relationship with our Creator.[16] In the spiritual life, "the Charity which keeps life never coddles it. The maturing of our personality, its full transformation in God, could hardly be achieved unless we were left in an apparent independence; to suffer, accept, deal with circumstances as real incarnate spirits, subject to all the vicissitudes of physical life. Our courage and loyalty must be tested by a genuine experience of solitude and darkness, if all our latent possibilities are to be realized."[17]

Even among us ordinary humans there are limits to the dictum that "Any loving parent wants to give his children as much of a head start as possible." A recent newspaper article provides the example of a Seattle couple, former Microsoft employees, who made millions from their stock options. Having thought hard about their family values and the challenge of this wealth, Mr. Rosenblatt said, "he and his wife have decided to limit their sons' inheritance. The couple is now deciding how much to give to philanthropy and how much to leave for their sons. 'We definitely want our kids to work and not just at a dilettante level,' he said. 'We want them to have to struggle.'"[18]

To sum up these points: Has God made the world more challenging than it needed to be, just to build character in us? My answer: no. But (and this is a separate issue) given how challenging it *necessarily* is, it would certainly have short-circuited the development of our character (and would probably have been unworkable in many other ways as well) if God had intervened to spare us from even the severest challenges.

From all this we can see that suffering (on every scale from a stubbed toe to the Nazi Holocaust) is even more intrinsically a part of the human condition than we ever suspected. We could dodge it only by not existing at all; and God could shield us from it only by not creating us at all. Can this be a source of comfort to the afflicted? Is it comforting to the sick child to know that its parent can do nothing to prevent or cure the illness? Is it comforting to the adult to realize that human suffering and death cannot be altogether prevented, even by God? In itself, no. But the first step in finding comfort is to stop looking for it in the wrong places.

The Book of Job – one of our earliest and most eloquent meditations on suffering – seems to end on a similarly comfortless note. Though Job's suffering is finally relieved, it is never satisfactorily explained to him. "Where were you when I laid the foundations of the world?" thunders God in response to Job's questions – with shocking sanctimony in the eyes of the reader, who is in on the dirty secret of God's little wager with Satan. As the Almighty rubs it in with a point-by-point outline of the complexities of creation and Job's ignorance thereof, the poor man is browbeaten into silence (Job 38–42).

But if we read this ancient text with modern scientific understanding, it is almost eerie how close God actually comes to giving Job what we would regard as a straight answer, by making reference to the nuts and bolts of creation. Indeed, if God saw fit to revise the Book of Job for us today, perhaps only a few added words would suffice to make the reason for suffering fully clear to the modern mind: *If you HAD been there at the creation – if you did know what went into the making, the evolving, of your world – then you would see that it could not be otherwise.* Here God stands revealed, not as an arbitrary and inscrutable tyrant, but as a solicitous and empathetic parent who acknowledges, however regretfully, that children cannot be entirely spared the pains of life. John Haught expresses it well:

> Evolutionary science ... demands that we give up once and for all the tyrannical images we may have sometimes projected onto God. The real stumbling block to reconciling faith and evolution, therefore, is not the sufferings in nature and human history, but our failure to have acquainted ourselves sufficiently with the

startling image of a God who seeks the world's freedom and who shares fully in the world's pain.[19]

While we live, we are subject to "the powers of this world."[20] Only when we have accepted the reality and limitations of life in a material universe, and have dispelled some of the confusion about what we can reasonably expect of God, can we then see clearly that the ultimate comfort God offers us lies in "new heavens and a new earth where, according to his promise, the justice of God will reside" (2 Peter 3:13). This will be a dominion somehow built on different principles from the Darwinian world, and a dominion we ourselves are invited to help God build. "He shall wipe every tear from their eyes, and there shall be no more death or mourning, crying out or pain, for the former world has passed away" (Revelation 21:4).

Yes, this mysterious dominion will be fully realized only in the distant future, but it is not mere "pie in the sky." It is also here and now, active in changing our world, and already well advanced in its construction – "The reign of God is already in your midst" (Luke 17:21).[21] And when, with God's help, we have entered this new existence, God will no longer remember our sins (Isaiah 43:25, Jeremiah 31:34), and we will no longer remember our pain.[22] "You will suffer in the world," promises Jesus. "But take courage! I have overcome the world" (John 16:33).

Notes

1. Haught 2001, 59–60.
2. Eliade 1954, 91–92.
3. Jaki 1974, 150–151.
4. Mesters 1974, 113.
5. Gribbin and Gribbin 2000.
6. Schmitz-Moormann 1997, 52.
7. Darwin 1959, Chapter XIV, sentence 270.
8. De Waal 1989, 234–236.
9. Sonnenberg 1995, 2.
10. For example, Southgate 2002.
11. Haught 2000, 40–43, 113–114; cf. Edwards 1999, 36–44; Thomas Aquinas, *Summa Theologiae*, I, q. 105, a. 5, *Summa Contra Gentiles*, III, 73, 74. See Bruteau 1997 for a thoroughgoing portrayal, rich in scientific detail as well as theological insight, of the universe as both "self-creating" and a true Incarnation of the Trinity.
12. Haught 2001, 118; emphasis added.
13. Aquinas, *Summa Theologiae*, Ia, q. 25, a. 3.
14. The same argument is made by C. S. Lewis (1962, Chap. 2).
15. As presented by Hick 1966; cf. Allik 1989. See Murchie 1978 for another example. Williams (2001, 176–179) also stresses this idea as her "secondary" solution to the problem of evil. Her "central" solution, like mine, is that the existence of free creatures able to be co-creators with God is adequate recompense for the unavoidable evils this entails. Given this, which she correctly calls "the only answer required to solve the problem of evil," I think her "secondary" solution is superfluous as well as misleading. Furthermore, as Tracy (1998, 526) points out, if all natural suffering is for the best, we should not try to prevent it; or rather: "if the moral lives of finite persons are to include ethically significant responses to natural suffering, then some of that suffering must be

pointless."

16. It may be noted (referring back to section 4.13) that those whose sense of dignity is offended by the thought of descent from "mere animals" are evidently more in sympathy with the attitudes of hereditary nobility and caste systems than with modern democracy, in which we are no longer encouraged to look to our ancestry for our sense of worth!

17. Underhill 1991, 80.

18. *The Washington Post*, Aug. 3, 2003, p. A14.

19. Haught 2001, 127.

20. Cf. John 14:30; Romans 7: 20–24; Galatians 4:3, 9; Ephesians 6:12; Colossians 2:20–21.

21. This view is readily compatible with the "metaphysics of the future" argued for by Haught (2000, Chap. 6). It does not, however, imply that our present existence is of lesser value in God's eyes, or that our lives today are "just" a stage on the way to the Kingdom God really wants – cf. Campbell 2000, 51, 71.

22. I mean that we will see our past sufferings in their proper perspective, like the mother in John 16:21, not that our memories will be erased. Campbell (2000, 56, 81–82) correctly stresses that our memories are integral to our individual identities, now and in eternity.

CHAPTER THIRTEEN

Teilhard's synthesis and its fruits:
a critique

Evolutionary science … provides the occasion for a renewed and expanded cosmic Christology.

John F. Haught[1]

13.1 Teilhard and Original Sin

It is not possible to do justice in setting forth an evolutionary view of Christianity (or a Christian view of evolution) without discussing the work of the French Jesuit paleontologist, theologian, and mystic Pierre Teilhard de Chardin (1881–1955). His work is the cornerstone of contemporary evolutionary theology, which continues to find inspiration in Teilhard's thought. Indeed, given that his writings on this subject date back at least to 1920, and that the most important ones have been generally available in print (and widely discussed) since before 1970, it is surprising and unfortunate that they have not yet transformed Christian theology even more than is the case.

Teilhard's thoughts on original sin and related topics are most clearly expressed in the collection of essays published as *Christianity and Evolution* (1971), which I myself encountered only after developing most of the ideas outlined above. While I generally agree with his overall vision, there are some aspects of his discussions of original sin which I think should be expanded and modified, and indeed brought into more harmonious relationship with the rest of his synthesis.

To Teilhard, original sin "simply symbolizes the inevitable chance of evil … which accompanies the existence of all participated being. Wherever being *in fieri* [in process of becoming] is produced, suffering and wrong immediately appear as its shadow: not only as a result of the tendency towards inaction and selfishness found in creatures, but also (which is more disturbing) as an inevitable concomitant of their effort to progress."[2] "As a statistical effect of chances, [evolution] can advance in its tentative constructions only by leaving behind it at all levels (inorganic, organic, and psychic) a long trail of disorder, suffering and error ('evolutive' evil)."[3] "Physical and moral disorder, of one sort or another, must necessarily be produced spontaneously in a system which is developing its organic character, *so long as* the system is incompletely organized."[4] In such a system, "it is absolutely inevitable ('fatalistically determined'): (1) that local disorders appear … and (2) that, from level to level, collective states of disorder result from these elementary disorders (because of the organically interwoven nature of the cosmic stuff). Above the level of life, this entails suffering, and, starting with man, it becomes sin."[5] Original sin, to Teilhard, is thus no more than a "universal law of imperfection which operates in mankind *in virtue* of its being '*in fieri*'."[6]

In other words, for Teilhard, the physical and moral disorder in the universe is an unfortunate but unavoidable by-product of the evolutionary way in which the universe is (indeed, had to be) created. Suffering and evil might be said to be inertia, friction, or entropy writ large. Hence, evil in the broadest sense is not something fundamentally extrinsic to God's creation, introduced gratuitously by some mischievous agent, but rather an inseparable part of the evolutionary universe. "We often represent God ... as being able to draw from non-being a world in which there is no damage, no breakage. This is a conceptual fantasy, and makes it impossible to solve the problem of evil."[7] "In this new setting, while evil loses nothing of its poignancy or horror, it ceases to be an incomprehensible element in the structure of the world and becomes *a natural feature*."[8] "In these circumstances, evil is not an unforeseen accident in the universe. It is an enemy, a shadow which God inevitably produces simply by the fact that he decides on creation. New being, launched into existence and not yet completely assimilated into unity, is a dangerous thing, bringing with it pain and oddity. For the Almighty, therefore, to create is no small matter: it is no picnic, but an adventure, a risk, a battle, to which he commits himself unreservedly."[9] In a note to this passage, Teilhard suggests that sin is to progress as smoke is to fire.

The congruence of Teilhard's thinking with much of what has been said above is clear.[10] However, three further observations are relevant.

First, Teilhard's vision is more ambitious and all-encompassing than my own original contributions here; that is, he ventures to explain not merely the suffering of living beings, but all forms of disorder in the inanimate universe as well, and he does so by means of a single, unified principle. His solution to the problem (already incorporated in the foregoing chapters) is thus more general than my proposal concerning original sin alone.

Second, however, in regard to a special case of this more general problem (namely, "original sin" as applied to humans), where Teilhard speaks only in rather abstract generalities, I propose a specific and concrete biological mechanism (an evolutionary heritage of selfish behavior enforced by natural selection) and distinguish this from the more fundamental basis of physical evil (the "breakability" of matter in general).

Third, whereas Teilhard seems to see selfishness and other forms of evil as purely negative phenomena having no constructive role or redeeming value in themselves, I argue that the natural, amoral selfishness which drives organic evolution has positive value insofar as it is the *sine qua non*, on the biological level, of the good creation. That black, nasty stuff in the bottom of our ship is not bilgewater, but the very fuel oil that drives the ship forward. Or, in a different metaphor: for Teilhard, selfishness is merely part of the stone debris left on the floor of the Sculptor's studio; for me, it is the Sculptor's very chisel.

These three differences in our viewpoints are neatly displayed in the following passage: "From this point of view original sin, considered in its cosmic basis (if not in its actualization in history, among the first human beings), tends to be indistinguishable from the sheer mechanism of creation – in which it represents the action of the negative forces of 'counter-evolution'."[11] Here we see original sin portrayed as (1) cosmic in scope, having a basis not restricted to animate beings, but also not clearly distinguished from phenomena on the animate level; (2) intimately related to the "mechanism of creation," which however is not defined or described in more concrete detail; but (3) a purely negative and destructive phenomenon, practically synonymous with entropy, rather than a contributing part of the "mechanism of creation" itself.

It may be wondered why Teilhard did not address in more detail the nature of this "mechanism of creation." Part of the answer, no doubt, is that his interest lay more in the eschatological aspects of the subject than in the details of process and mechanism. However, I suspect that his scientific training also disinclined him to examine closely the mechanisms of natural selection, or to take seriously their potential to play an important role in his synthesis. It is well known that Continental, and particularly French, biologists have traditionally taken a much more skeptical view of the importance of selection in evolution than have Anglo-American scientists.[12] The historical predilection of many French evolutionists for vitalistic and/or finalistic explanations probably sowed the seeds of, and certainly helped to nurture, Teilhard's finalistic thought (although he managed to avoid the pitfalls of crude vitalism). In a similar way, the prejudice prevailing in France against accepting Darwinian selection as the dominant directing force in evolution seems likely to have led him away from considering the possibility that genetically-determined "selfish" behavior might be essential to the creativity of organic evolution. This, at least, is a hypothesis for Teilhardian scholars to consider.

In any case, Teilhard's failure to hit on evolutionary selfishness as a reformulation of "original sin" in no way vitiates his synthesis. Rather, this reformulation provides a refinement of his vision and a missing piece of his puzzle that, in my opinion, renders his overall synthesis more robust and internally consistent than ever. The soul of Teilhard's thought – an extension of the ideas of (among others) St. Paul and St. Ignatius Loyola – is its radical valorization of matter and its recognition of the actively creative potential built into the very stuff of the universe. This view is only enhanced and confirmed by the realization that an aspect of life as despised as its inherent selfishness is in fact at the heart of its ability to progress. In Teilhard's system, the selfishness and consequent suffering that are inseparable from life are something of a loose end, retaining a hint of gratuitousness and arbitrariness, in the sense that they play no constructive role in cosmogenesis: they are a dead end, a sink for positive energy, a mere shadow cast by the light of God's creative love – rubble on the studio floor. Instead, in this reinterpretation of selfishness, Teilhard might perhaps have been as delighted as Milton's Adam to find God able to bring good even out of evil.[13]

13.2 Evolutionary Theology Today

As this book is not a history of theology, I will not attempt an exhaustive analysis of Teilhard's influence on subsequent theological thought (although an important strain of this thought, that of Schoonenberg and his followers, has been touched on in section 10.2 above). Teilhard's influence, however, has been considerable; and it is particularly relevant to call attention to the fruit that his work has borne in the 1990s and beyond: an entire new field of investigation, evolutionary theology, which at long last sees evolutionary science as a source of useful ideas and inspiration, and not just as a source of theological headaches. For all its promise and excitement, however, this field has yet to put the puzzle pieces together properly and solve completely the problem of original sin. Here I will consider some examples from this rapidly-growing body of work.[14]

One recent writer in the Teilhardian tradition was Karl Schmitz-Moormann, himself a noted Teilhardian scholar, who argued in his book *Theology of Creation in an Evolutionary World* that love – specifically, the "loving call of God" bringing about ever-increasing union among the elements of the universe – might, "in theology, be considered the driving force of creation and so of evolution."[15] This is an appealing idea, and one echoed still more recently by another heir of Teilhard, Jerry Korsmeyer, in *Evolution and Eden: Balancing Original Sin and Contemporary Science*. However, neither writer makes clear exactly how "love," or a response to God's persuasion, might account in a concrete way for the union of entities below the human level. In fact, given all that has been said above, in the case of subhuman life this idea would seem to be flatly contradicted: the driving force of evolution is clearly selfishness and not "love" among competing organisms.

It was partly for this reason, I suspect, that Schmitz-Moormann vehemently rejected the Darwinian emphasis on selfishness as an important mechanism of evolution. (I had the privilege of meeting Schmitz-Moormann not long before his death in 1996, and we enjoyed several marathon arguments on this subject.) Moreover, in his book's longest endnote, he went out of his way to attack "Darwinian dogmatists" who seek (as I have done) to explain evolution by mutation and natural selection alone.[16] He believed (mistakenly, in my opinion; see section 4.2 above) that Neo-Darwinian explanations reduce to the claim that evolution happens largely by "pure chance." Revealingly, out of the entire range of modern scientific thought – much of which he reviewed in some detail, and of which he had an impressive command – he found no other body of theory to be deserving of such harsh rejection as Neo-Darwinism.

I am not prepared, however, to conclude that the dominance of selfishness on the concrete and mechanistic level of biology is completely at odds with the idea of "love" as a unifying force when viewed from a theological perspective. This seems to me no more of a contradiction than the fact that different laws and physical forces are dominant at different scales of nature: whereas the weak, strong nuclear, and electromagnetic forces structure the "microcosmos," gravity is the organizing force of the universe on the grandest scales. Gravity also exists on the subatomic level, but is quantitatively insignificant and therefore not apparent in its effects. Moreover, the understanding of gravity provided by general relativity is not yet reduced to a quantum-mechanical explanation like the other three forces.

A similar effect of scale is observable among biological phenomena. Theoretical ecologist Robert Ulanowicz argues, for example, that "events and laws in the realm of ecology are *granular*, not universal. Models of events at any one scale can explain matters at another scale only in inverse proportion to the remoteness between them. ... [T]he assumption of granularity is not that laws are necessarily violated at remote scales, but merely that they become ineffective at controlling remote events relative to agencies that are more immediate to those happenings."[17] The laws of Mendelian genetics, for instance, are of scant use in explaining the ecological interactions among species.

So, by analogy, it may also be that unifying "love" (however understood) is mysteriously present (though not apparent or explicable, and not useful as a scientific explanation) on the level of subhuman biology and even cosmology. Schmitz-Moormann practically says as much himself: "The dominant force of evolution is only dimly visible on the earlier, lower levels of evolution, though it clearly is distinguishable as the force of union. On the human level ... it becomes the decisive force."[18] It is thus analogous to, if not identical with, the "inwardness" of inanimate matter which Teilhard postulated (as well as similar ideas advanced by Alfred North Whitehead and Hans Jonas[19]).

Thus, the classic dilemma of grace versus freedom, or predestination versus freedom,[20] may be understandable as a manifestation of the underlying tension between divine love or grace on the one hand and evolutionary selfishness on the other. I offer these speculations to suggest that the apparent inconsistency between Schmitz-Moormann's and Korsmeyer's views and my own is no necessary obstacle to a unified evolutionary theology of creation.

The authors just discussed exemplify the gratifying fact that Teilhard's ideas have finally been brought fully into the mainstream of Christian theology, where they are blending with other, mutually-supportive strains of thought such as process theology and the theology of the humility of God. A still more recent and attractive synthesis of these ideas is found in John Haught's book *God After Darwin: A Theology of Evolution*, which I have already cited several times.

Although highly satisfactory in many ways, Haught's theology of evolution still leaves some details to be smoothed out. Ironically (in view of his conviction that theology must take seriously the conclusions of science), these wrinkles seem to result in one case from adhering too closely to scientific thinking, and in another case from not following science far enough.

A strength of Haught's book is that he has covered several important aspects of evolutionary theology far better than I could do – for example, the metaphysical context appropriate for evolutionary theology. He espouses a "metaphysics of the future" in which perfection is situated only in the eschatological future, toward which God (spoken of by Karl Rahner as the "Absolute Future") invites and draws all of creation.[21] Haught notes that only this sort of metaphysics (which is found notably in the work of Whitehead) is truly consonant either with the future-oriented biblical themes of hope and promise, or with science's understanding of evolution. A major reason is that only a metaphysics of the future makes room for genuine novelty to appear in the course of history – a trait that Haught rightly sees as essential to any proper notion of evolution.

Despite some difficulties (which Haught readily concedes) in conceptualizing and explaining what is meant by this kind of metaphysics, I find the idea intuitively appealing. But it seems to me he allows his adherence to Whitehead's ideas to overly limit his own argument. Significantly, he praises Whitehead's thought for "remaining consistently faithful to scientific discovery"[22] – implying, perhaps, that by not bringing more overtly religious concepts into his metaphysics than Whitehead does, he will make it more palatable to the naturalistically-minded. This may be a worthy goal, but the hitch comes when Haught seeks to specify the Creator's ultimate aim for the creation. This ends up being expressed in Whiteheadian terms as "more and more intense versions of ordered novelty, another word for which is 'beauty.' God's will, apparently, is for the maximization of cosmic beauty."[23]

The problem is that this kind of God is no more nor less than Haldane's God, the one with the "inordinate fondness for beetles." "Cosmic beauty," the beauty of endless diversity, both living and nonliving, is an aim that could fall within even the limited horizon of the materialist – which is not a high aim for a theology to aspire to. Nor do I think it would be an adequate response to say that higher emergent properties of life – intelligence, self-consciousness, free will, love – enhance diversity and "beauty" and hence are implicit in this word. The biblical God of love is not adequately revealed if described as merely a god of "beauty"; the kind of universe that Haught seems to envision as God's ideal sounds more to me like an art gallery than like the Reign of God that Jesus so passionately proclaimed. While possibly less jarring to the agnostic or atheistic scientist, the emphasis on the aesthetic (which particularly colors Haught's Chapter 8, in contrast to the other, more biblically-based parts of his book) lends an air of cool detachment to a God whom the Bible instead reveals as a burning fire of love and justice. Seemingly forgotten here is Haught's admission, two chapters before, that "the notion of a metaphysics of the future has an irreducibly religious origin."[24]

As a result, Haught's theodicy fails to completely erase the image of a callous God. He says that "all the suffering, struggle, loss, and triumph in evolution are finally endowed with eternal meaning. *Whatever occurs* in the evolving universe can contribute – at least in the long run – to the *beauty* that takes shape in the compassionate embrace of God."[25] This, surely, leaves questions unanswered. Is the suffering of creatures an inevitable part of evolution, or is it deliberately willed by a God for whom sheer variety of experience (including unpleasant experience) is an aesthetic end in itself? Would it not be better to speak of God as one who wills the maximization of love and justice, rather than as an aesthete, the compassion of whose embrace may be subject to doubt by the sufferer, or the uncharitable reader?

Even when the biblical imperative to "love justice" is mentioned some pages later, it too is seemingly rationalized on merely aesthetic grounds: "Incorporating those who are disadvantaged, or reaching out to minorities banished from social and political life, adds nuance and contrast that brings aesthetic depth to human community."[26] While the good is of course beautiful, what is lacking is a clearer acknowledgment that community is *good* for more reasons than just its "beauty." "God longs for the well-being, self-coherence, and aesthetic adventurousness of the cosmos"[27] – but does not "well-being" take priority, especially if it conflicts with "aesthetic adventurousness," which could even be construed to include sin?

Haught is correct that "[t]he notion of God as defenseless and vulnerable love provides ... an *ultimate* explanation of nature's evolutionary character ... without having to candy over the deviations, disorder, and tragedy that Darwinian science has uncovered."[28] But, in my view, he has not fully demonstrated *how* this is true, because he has not taken into account all that science has revealed about the inevitability of evil. This is where he has not followed science far enough; and it detracts from his discussion of original sin at the end of Chapter 8.

A follower of the "cultural-transmission" school (as all the evolutionary theologians writing today seem to be), Haught understands original sin as resulting from our birth into cultural milieux that pressure us "to acquiesce in an indifference to God's creative cosmic aim of maximizing beauty."[29] As for any genetic aspect of the problem, he asserts (without giving a supporting rationale) that "even though the potential to do evil is already a part of our genetic makeup, it is theologically inappropriate to identify original sin *simply* with the instincts of aggression or self-ishness that we may have inherited from our nonhuman evolutionary ancestry. Even though these tendencies are part of our evolutionary legacy, the *substance* of 'original sin' is the culturally and environmentally inherited deposit of *humanity's* violence and injustice that burdens and threatens to corrupt each of us born into this world" (emphasis added).[30]

"Simply" is a key word in this passage; Haught means that original sin is not *purely* a matter of genetic determinism. This is true enough; but I have tried to show above that the "substance of original sin" is indeed partly the genetically-inherited *and* partly the culturally-inherited deposit of *prehuman* selfish behavior. This seems to be a blind spot for all theologians of the "cultural- transmission" school. They do not ask a question that inevitably occurs to an evolutionary biolo-gist: If original sin is merely a matter of our birth into a corrupting human culture, what was the corrupting culture that greeted the *first* humans ever born, when no *human* culture yet existed?

Obviously, it was prehuman culture,[31] together with our genetic heritage of self-ishness (which is also the ultimate source of culturally-learned selfish behavior). But theologians have not yet taken account of the fact that prehuman culture existed; they are fearful of yielding too much ground to genetic influences on human behavior; and, perhaps, they are not eager to talk about the "first" humans under any circumstances, given their lack of a theologically satisfactory alternative to Adam and Eve.[32] I have argued that these fears and hesitations are unfounded, and that prehuman cultural and genetic influences on our behavior can be factored into the human equation without undermining our free will. In this way, I think, biology can add a necessary dimension to our understanding of original sin, and bring the promising synthesis of evolutionary theology into closer congruence with both scientific consensus and biblical faith.

Another important recent work, Patricia Williams's *Doing Without Adam and Eve: Sociobiology and Original Sin*, has already been discussed briefly above (Chapter Nine, note 6; Chapter Twelve, note 15). Her conclusions hardly differ from my own, and the differences seem to be largely semantic; approaching the issue as she does from a philosophical standpoint, her work is a useful complement to the present one.

A pattern of development, or at least a spectrum of opinion, can be seen in this evolving body of literature. Teilhard paid no real attention to evolutionary mecha-nisms, whereas Schmitz-Moormann (while embracing the idea of evolution itself) went out of his way to dispute the Neo-Darwinian account of how evolution works. Later evolutionary theologians, however, such as Jerry Korsmeyer, John Haught, and Denis Edwards (see section 10.2 above), seem comfortable enough with the scientific account of the process, though they still express reservations about the extent to which human sinfulness can be said to have any genetic basis. In this they reflect the pervasive influence of Schoonenberg and subsequent Catholic theolo-gians, who insist that sin has been propagated through cultural transmission, as already discussed. Donald Campbell, Gerd Theissen, and Philip Hefner go farther in acknowledging a major role for genetic inheritance, but too hastily and sanguinely draw the line between selection-driven evolution and selection-defying virtue at the border of culture and/or religion. Gabriel Daly, Patricia Williams, and I seem to belong in yet a further category, inasmuch as we acknowledge and emphasize both the evolutionary, genetic precursors of sin and the social and cultural means by which it is perpetuated, as well as the pervasion of our culture and even much of our religion by evolutionary selfishness. I read this pattern as one of increasingly comprehensive appropriation of scientific conclusions by theology, and increasing use of the scientific data as a source of theological insight.

Is this a prudent path for theology to follow? Or is theology in danger of accommodating itself too closely to the scientific consensus of the day, only to be embarrassed by a shift in that consensus on the morrow – as has happened before? (Jesuit astronomer George Coyne reportedly quipped, "The theology that marries the science of today will be the widow of tomorrow."[33]) Certainly there is still much healthy debate about the details of evolutionary biology; but I am confident that the essentials of the argument I present here are based not on tentative details but on the most robust conclusions of evolutionary science: the facts of cosmic and organic evolution, and the dominant roles of selfish behavior and natural selection in producing adaptation. Advances in this science there will surely be, but I expect them to take the form, not of the Copernican revolution in astronomy, but of the Einsteinian "revolution" in physics: in other words, they will represent not a reversal of what was thought before, but a more comprehensive synthesis that will build on and extend the current theory. Darwinian evolution is here to stay, and theology has already begun to recognize it as a development to be welcomed.

Notes

1. Haught 2001, 64.
2. Teilhard 1971, 40; contrast with the passage from Korsmeyer 1998, 123, quoted above in section 8.2.3!
3. Teilhard 1971, 218.
4. Teilhard 1971, 149; emphasis in original.
5. Teilhard 1971, 195.
6. Teilhard 1971, 51; emphasis in original.
7. Teilhard 1971, 33.
8. Teilhard 1971, 82; emphasis in original.
9. Teilhard 1971, 84–85.
10. Here I disagree with a statement of Harold Morowitz, who sees a "sharp and direct" contrast between Teilhard's views and that of sociobiologists who assert "that the study of animal societies is critical to understanding human behavior" (Morowitz 1985, 24). This is because Teilhard stresses the evolutionary discontinuity represented by the appearance of reflective thought ("noogenesis"), whereas at least some sociobiologists deny that this was such a big deal and stress instead the similarities of humans and other primates. But clearly, even by Morowitz's telling, this is a mere difference in emphasis. There are elements of both continuity and discontinuity in any "threshold effect" such as this, and while one or another proponent of a given view may err by overemphasizing one facet of reality to the exclusion of another, we need not see in this an irreconcilable disagreement.

11. Teilhard 1971, 150.
12. Boesiger 1980; Limoges 1980.
13. Cf. J. Milton, *Paradise Lost*, book 12, lines 469–476.
14. Other writers in this fertile field besides those discussed here include Paul Brockelman, Beatrice Bruteau, Mary Conrow Coelho, Diarmuid O'Murchu, David Toolan, and Cletus Wessels.
15. Schmitz-Moormann 1997, 124.
16. Schmitz-Moormann 1997, 171–172.
17. Ulanowicz 2003.
18. Schmitz-Moormann 1997, 135.
19. See Haught 2000, Chap. 10.
20. Cf. Schmitz-Moormann 1997, 139–145.
21. Haught 2000, Chap. 6.
22. Haught 2000, 126.
23. Haught 2000, 42.
24. Haught 2000, 89.
25. Haught 2000, 128; emphasis added.
26. Haught 2000, 134.
27. Haught 2000, 136.
28. Haught 2000, 137; emphasis in original.
29. Haught 2000, 138.
30. Haught 2000, 139.
31. Cf. Whiten et al. 1999, Whiten and Boesch 2001.
32. This lack of a better idea is frankly admitted in the official supplement and modification to the relatively progressive "Dutch" Catechism of 1966: "The Church remains attached to the monogenist perspective, and this attitude is wise. For it knows in fact that the traditional formulas about Adam and Eve and the human race fallen in Adam contain a truth of the history of salvation which has been entrusted to it – even though these formulas are not to be understood literally. But the Church is not able to affirm the same thing with regard to the polygenist formulas. Hence it preserves the traditional formulas and asks that they be preserved as the only ones which certainly safeguard the faith. But it does so without closing the door to questions which are raised by scientific findings." (Dhanis and Visser 1969, 537).
33. I owe this quote to my friend Peter Dodson, who explains that Coyne said this in response to the question of what theological conclusions he drew from the Big Bang. Coyne's answer: none!

CHAPTER FOURTEEN

Summary and conclusion

I gladly pay homage to Teilhard's priority by basing a short summary of my thesis on a quotation from his work. In a 1947 essay entitled "Reflections on original sin," he noted that, in an evolutionary universe,

> The problem (the intellectual problem) of evil disappears. In this picture, physical suffering and moral transgressions are inevitably introduced into the world not because of some deficiency in the creative act but by the very structure of participated being: in other words they are introduced as the *statistically inevitable by-product* of the unification of the multiple. In consequence they contradict neither the power of God nor his goodness. Is the game worth the candle? Everything depends on the *final* value and beatitude of the universe – a point on which we may well trust ourselves to God's wisdom.
> [Footnote] In a general way, this amounts to saying that the problem of evil, insoluble in the case of a static universe (i.e. a "cosmos"), no longer arises in the case of a (multiple) evolutive universe (i.e. a cosmogenesis). It is strange that so simple a truth should still be so little perceived and stated.[1]

Thus did Teilhard understate his breathtaking claim that the great, brooding Problem of Evil, which for thousands of years has burdened and vanquished the best minds of philosophy and theology, is nothing more than a pseudoproblem – an optical illusion of the mind, which vanishes into thin air the moment one shifts one's point of view. And he was right, as right as he was bold. How could this be? Were the wisdom and insight of all who went before surpassed by those of Teilhard? No, and still less by my own. What has occurred here is a simple paradigm shift, of the sort familiar in all branches of knowledge. The thinkers who were and still are defeated by the problems of evil and theodicy have merely been lacking an essential piece of the puzzle: a deep understanding (and not a mere acknowledgment) of the fact that the world has not simply been created by divine fiat, but has *evolved*. Seen from that promontory of knowledge, the world looks entirely different: not every option was available to the Creator.

The "problem of evil," in short, is no different from the objections raised in every grade-school catechism class whenever the topic of God's power comes up: "Can God make a square circle?"[2] "Can God make a rock so big he can't lift it?" Or (we can now add) "Can God make a world in which bad things don't happen?" The answer, in each case, is: "No, because that would involve a logical contradiction." The real problem has been that, before the (relatively recent) discovery of evolution, we never realized that such an ideal world would involve contradictions.

These contradictions stem basically from two things: free will and the composite nature of matter. The role of free will is easily grasped: it has always been clear that moral evil, or sin, results from bad choices by people, and that God had to leave us room to make bad choices so that we would also be able to make good choices. Only slightly less obvious was the fact that physical evil (accident, disease, death) is

181

in every case a result of things coming apart or breaking down in some physical, mechanical way; and since all things material, from subatomic particles to (especially) us, are made of separate, moving parts ("multiple" in Teilhard's terminology), they will inevitably come apart sooner or later.

What was not at all obvious, until we learned to see the world as a product of evolution, was this: there is a *continuity*, a *connection*, between the simple breakability of physical things on the one hand, and our own intelligence and free will on the other. It is precisely matter's inherent tendency to breakdown and disorder (mutation in the genetic material, for example) that is used by Darwinian natural selection as a source of raw material to build ever more complex living things, and ultimately intelligent ones. The process takes an immensely long time and involves the deaths of immense numbers of living things; but the result is a world of living things that are (a) beautifully diverse, (b) authentically related to one another by real genealogical ties, and (c) capable (in us) of entering into a personal relationship with their Creator.

Is the gain worth the pain? Not if there was an easier way to do the job; but the alternative is an illusion. If God had created the universe all finished and ready-made, as we once believed, it would simply not work as we see it working today, for a host of physical and biological reasons. It would not even be a real, organically-grown, dynamic universe such as we know, but only a static simulation of one, like a movie set. In particular, it would not be a world of real relationships – passionate relationships, deeply felt (by both God and us) because deeply rooted in a real history of change – relationships among God and the other persons who inhabit this world.

When we confront suffering and death, therefore, we can take some comfort in knowing that God is not incompetent or callous, but that there was simply no other way to make the sort of world God evidently wanted. When we are benumbed by the thought of the billions of years evolution needed to fashion our self-conscious intelligence, we are assured by science that nature offers no quicker recipe. If there were a better way, a workable shortcut, I think we can be sure that God would have thought of it. But this is something we could never have grasped intellectually without knowing something of the actual history of our world and how it evolved.

But if the key to the riddle of suffering and evil is as simple as the mere breakability of physical objects, why were the great thinkers of the past stumped for so long by it? They knew well enough that things were made of parts, and could come apart, even before they knew about molecular biology or evolution. I suspect, however, that a major obstacle to this insight was the habit of thinking referred to above as Gnosticism, which continues to subtly influence even orthodox Christians. If you start out with low expectations of matter, and with the assumption that spirit, especially God's Spirit, can overcome any limitation of mere matter, then all options seem open, including the perfection of a primordial Eden. If the world is now a mess, some creature must bear the blame, and Adam is a convenient Fall guy.

Instead of saying that matter is evil and spirit good, though, we must recognize that elements of what we tend to call "good" and "evil" are present in both. The material creation was pronounced good by the Creator, even though it includes physical "evil" as well as the instinctive selfishness that tempts us to commit acts of moral evil. Our spiritual faculties (including free will) make moral evil possible: it does not exist apart from them, just as physical "evil" does not exist in the absence of living things that can suffer from it.[3] But these faculties also make possible positive acts of virtue, and are needed to morally transcend our natural (= material) selfishness. The Gnostics thus erred in simplistically equating material with evil and spiritual with good,[4] but they also intuited an important truth insofar as moral evil has its historical roots in the material realm, to which selfishness belongs. This is probably true even of sins that do not involve desire for tangible, material things but rather desire for abstract things, such as the sin of pride, which grows out of an individual habit of selfishness first nurtured in the material realm. (Real altruism, or at least an approximation to it, likewise grows out of a habit of, and abstraction from, reciprocal altruism.) Unfortunately, the Gnostics saw an unbridgeable chasm between the "evil" of matter and anything good, where there are really only the contrasting ends of a causal chain.

The example of the Incarnation is the ultimate rebuttal to Gnosticism, in that it demonstrates the value the Creator places on the material realm, even to the extent of actually becoming a part of it (Philippians 2:6–8). Authentic, Incarnational Christianity is a perennial scandal to the Gnostic way of thinking. Christ's self-humbling, self-emptying embrace of our physical nature forces us to take seriously the significance of matter in the scheme of things – just as God took it seriously. The great artist does not hold his medium in contempt; his glory lies in being limited by it while managing to realize his vision in spite of its limitations. We may feel scandalized that we were brought forth from cold, impersonal matter by the brutality of natural selection. But let us recall that when Michelangelo entered his studio, he found before him nothing but a cold, impersonal block of marble; and taking up his cold, impersonal tools, he brutally hammered and fragmented it until he had carved his "Pietà" – stone now no longer impersonal, and even imbued with a mysterious inner warmth.

Teilhard grasped this Incarnational, evolutionary vision in most of its essentials. In emphasizing the importance of selfishness in the process of evolution by natural selection, I have merely fleshed out his outline in some particulars. In so doing, I hope I have clarified the concrete nature of what has been called original sin (or better: "original selfishness"), defined biologically as the innate imperative to perpetuate and benefit oneself whatever the cost to others, and theologically as "that need for salvation by Christ which is universal to all human beings and acquired through natural generation." Our evolutionary selfishness, which inclines us to sin, is universal to all humans because it is inherited by us through natural generation from the very first forms of earthly life, not merely from any supposed "first man." Our collective moral guilt, however – "the sin of the world" (John 1:29) – is but the sum of our individual, freely-made immoral choices (actual sins), and thus dates only from our origin(s) as moral agents ("human beings"); it need not, and does not, imply that we originated from a single human couple. Our need for salvation is thus composite in nature: the (primordial) source of its universality is radically decoupled, logically and temporally, from the (relatively recent) source of its moral character. The two sources, however, are *organically connected* by a long chain of causality via the mechanism of Darwinian evolution: we, with our intelligence and free will, arose from inevitably "selfish" ancestors, and this original selfishness inevitably hobbles our moral choices.

To recapitulate the entire argument, in a few words: Because God is selfless love, the world had to have its own autonomy, free of divine compulsion. For the world to be autonomous and capable of generating novelty, there had to be room for chance or accident. Because matter is made of parts, it is inherently breakable; this is the fundamental source of natural (physical) "evil." Because errors in copying genetic material (mutations) are consequently unavoidable, natural selection has variation on which to work. Because selection automatically favors traits that promote self-preservation and self-replication, all organisms are necessarily selfish. Because our inherited evolutionary selfishness (= original selfishness or original "sin") inclines us to favor ourselves over others, we (using the free will conferred by our evolved intelligence) often choose to sin; thus moral evil evolves out of physical "evil." Because perfect unselfishness cannot arise through this natural process, we are all in need of supernatural grace to build on our evolved nature, and in need of a supernatural example to help us transcend what natural, Darwinian evolution can produce – that is, we need salvation by Christ. This universal human need for salvation, arising out of our biological nature, is what the Christian tradition has defined as original "sin." Its evolutionary origins, and the inevitability of evil in a material creation, are now clear.

This is a clarification that surely would have been made earlier and by others, had it not been for the tragic, decades-long suppression of Teilhard's work and that of other creative Catholic theologians. Intended to safeguard the Catholic faith, this suppression has needlessly perpetuated obstacles to that very faith, such as a distorted understanding of original "sin" long since made obsolete by discoveries in science.

Some readers will no doubt be put off by my audacity here in giving such a cut-and-dried, analytical, "left-brain" answer to the age-old riddles of evil and original sin. Aren't these mysteries of faith, Deep Things of God, which are not to be reduced to facile, "scientific" explanations?

My reply is, quite simply: No, they are not. Mystery, in the theological sense, is present wherever God is present, because God is infinite and our understanding is finite – and there is still mystery aplenty in God's creation of this stupendous world, in God's unconditional love for us sinful mortals, and in God's response to the evil we create. But, by definition, God is not present in sin. The doctrine of original sin was never a statement about God; it was only an anthropological statement, a statement about human beings, their sinfulness, and the natural (not divine!) origins of evil. Therefore it has never been a "mystery" in a strict theological sense, but only a *problem* – one lying wholly within the created order, and hence fair game for the natural scientist. In the end, this is what accounts for the fact, noted by Chesterton, that original sin stands alone among classic Christian doctrines in being empirically verifiable. I have sought to show that it is not only verifiable but verified, and in what way. This I offer as a scientist's contribution to theology – if you will, a clearing of some scientific underbrush that has hindered theology's advance.

Still, perhaps not quite all the loose ends are tied up. This inquiry into the evolutionary roots of our sinfulness has led to a conclusion that may be unwelcome in various ways to some, but is unwelcome in one particular way to the scientist in me. It has brought into sharp focus a gulf that separates the creation from its Creator. The process of evolution, by the very nature of its mechanisms, is ordered toward the short term and the individual; yet Christians and other religionists are supposed to think in terms of a future eternity and to seek the good of the other and of the community. Even aside from the necessity that the finite creation must be qualitatively different from the Infinite, is there not a more jarring incompatibility here than we should expect?

As a scientist, I would like to find a seamless continuity, a theoretical unification, between the means of evolution and what we humans value as our highest ends and ideals. We scientists, after all, are trained to seek parsimony in all our theorizing, and to invoke the fewest possible principles in our explanations of phenomena. By this criterion, however, there is a certain irreducible messiness in supposing that we owe our origins largely to selfishness, but are in the end asked to renounce and transcend that same selfishness. On this supposition, the universe would seem to be governed by two different and contradictory principles, one gradually taking over from the other at that uncomfortable stage of evolution where we now find ourselves.

And yet, the reality of this very discontinuity is stressed throughout the Scriptures and has always been seen as a fundamental observation of Christian anthropology: there is something in our human nature that is incompatible with, even at war with, the Reign of God. "The flesh lusts against the spirit and the spirit against the flesh; the two are directly opposed. This is why you do not do what your will intends" (Galatians 5:17). Until recently, this refractory something in our nature was explained, lamely, by "Adam's sin." Now that we know it has deeper roots, roots coextensive in fact with the whole history of creation, the question returns with some force though in a new form: not "Why is there moral evil?" or "Why is there physical evil?" or even "Why did God choose to create, knowing that material creation cannot be free from mishap?," but rather "Why is the selfless love shown by God's decision to create, and the love we are called to imitate, not more evident in the workings of all God's creation?"

One answer was suggested above: that, as seen in the case of the four fundamental forces of physics, the universe manifests different and sometimes opposite organizing principles on different scales. Different forces of attraction or repulsion are prominent, depending on the stage of cosmic evolution, the scale of observation, and the local conditions; but all the forces exist and act simultaneously. Even on the grandest scale, the expansive force of the Big Bang is in tension with the opposing force of gravity, notwithstanding whatever underlying unity of the four basic forces there may be.

Likewise there is in life a certainly unavoidable, but also useful tension between antagonism and attraction, between conflict and cohesion, between individual self-actualization and the common good. Someone wisely coined the phrase "creative tension" to describe this familiar but paradoxical fact. Perhaps no energy source other than this kind of tension could power creation all the way through to its designed end in the Reign of God. Perhaps love alone, unmixed with adversity, is not enough after all. Perhaps good can only be appreciated in contrast with evil, life in contrast with death, altruism in contrast with selfishness; and from this appreciation may grow the desire and ultimately the decision to act in favor of the good.[5]

The scientist's instinct for parsimony is, after all, only a research strategy and a working assumption: nature is not always parsimonious, and counterbalancing forces are commonplace – especially in evolution, where all adaptations are compromises among conflicting selective pressures. A deeper look at reality reveals that discontinuities and contradictions are vital, perhaps to the harmony, but more importantly to the unpredictability, of the creation, which is a dynamic process and not a static equilibrium. Creation cannot be truly creative if it is completely predictable. Further, if the Creator means to have (in Martin Buber's terms) an "I-Thou" relationship with the creation, then implicit in this relationship must be some sort of radical discontinuity, even unlikeness, between the two, just as surely as the relationship requires in a different sense that the human creature be made in God's image.

There is a thin line between this creative tension and the old matter–spirit dualism that is one of pagan antiquity's more troublesome legacies. In describing what evolutionary theology can contribute in the somewhat different context of environmentalism, John Haught incidentally points out a way to defuse this problem:

> A complete discontinuity between "this present age" and "the age to come" would hardly be consistent with the good news of the coming of God's reign; such discontinuity would amount to a denial of the inherent goodness of creation and of God's incarnation in our present world. Just as believers can assume some continuity between their personal identities now and a glorified existence in the "age to come," they may also be permitted to assume that the coming of God's reign transforms or transfigures, and does not abandon or obliterate, the natural world whose life-forms have come about by way of the process of Darwinian evolution.
>
> An evolutionary perspective allows us to see that the biblical distinction between "this present age" and the "age to come" is not nearly so ecologically problematic as it might otherwise seem. A problem arises only when we forget the temporal-historical bearing of these expressions and translate them imaginatively into "the natural world" on the one hand and the "supernatural world" on the other. ... In transfigured status, ... the present cosmos along with all of its prior evolution will continue to remain deeply implicated in the world's eventual eschatological fulfillment.[6]

The Christian belief in the "resurrection of the body" implies just this sort of transfiguration of our world, not the abandonment of it. What form will the "new heavens and ... new earth" (Isaiah 65:17, 66:22; 2 Peter 3:13; Revelation 21:1), and our material bodies, take in the age to come? That has not been revealed to us; all we have to go on is the promise embodied in the resurrected Christ: "we shall be changed" (1 Corinthians 15:52). "Dearly beloved, we are God's children now; what we shall later be has not yet come to light. We know [only] that when it comes to light we shall be like him ..." (1 John 3:2). In this promise resides our faith and our hope.

Meanwhile, evolution undergirds this faith and hope in one respect above all. Beyond any seeming discontinuities between means and ends, between creaturely selfishness and divine love, evolution points to a profound and ultimate *unity* in all that is. It testifies that we creatures are *not* unrelated bits of stuff thrown together in one pot – separately created, by the same God to be sure, but linked in no more intimate way. Joined by common descent from the earliest life on Earth, offspring of a planet itself a product of cosmic evolution, our bodies made indeed from the very stardust scattered in the universe's dawn, we are truly one with the whole creation. Such a unified creation, moreover, must stem from a unitary creative act – the act of a single Creator. To the believer, then, the fact of evolution proclaims above all that *God is one*.

Science continues to make discoveries that are relevant to theology, and theologians must be free to work out the ramifications of these discoveries and remove the obstacles to faith that our ignorance needlessly creates. Believers need have no fear of advances in scientific knowledge. If Christianity contains an authentic revelation mixed in with all the inevitable human error, then advances in our knowledge should tend to resolve rather than increase the difficulties, and make clearer the truth that was there all along. I am struck by how the evolutionary worldview has exactly the latter effect, shedding new light on a doctrine that has always been among the most baffling: original sin. Those churchmen who suppressed this growth in our understanding of our faith stand revealed as those whose own faith was weak. Let this not be repeated.

Notes

1. Teilhard 1971, 196; emphasis in original. In this context, Teilhard calls attention to Matthew 18:7: "It is inevitable that scandal should occur."
2. My friend Tom Sheahen points out that there are mathematical ways (such as using cylindrical rather than Cartesian coordinates) to make a circle "square"; so I had better specify that I am referring strictly to Cartesian circles!
3. Rolston 2003.
4. An echo of this error can perhaps be found in some modern theologians' equations of the biological (including natural selection) with evil and the social, cultural, or religious with good; see notes 28 and 32 to Chapter 9 above.
5. Cf. Clarke 1996.
6. Haught 2000, 152–153.

Response to Part Four

Monika K. Hellwig

It is probably not fruitful to discuss the question of Adam's identity here beyond what was said in the response to Part Two. Any discussion of a remote ancestor, human or prehuman, who might be traced or conjectured may be otherwise of interest, but it has no relevance to an understanding of the doctrine of original sin. The relationship of the doctrine to the suffering of the innocent is along the lines briefly suggested concerning the tradition about "preternatural gifts" in the response to Part Two above. There is no difficulty in acknowledging that physical death and some kinds of suffering are intrinsic to being a living body. The Christian claims are about the way death is experienced as throwing a shadow of fear backwards over the whole of life, and about the way suffering is unnecessarily multiplied, perception and understanding are clouded, and values tend to slip out of the proportionate order of priority.

A Catholic theologian need not dispute Domning's contention that instincts of survival and propagation from prehuman development survive in the human species and erupt in violence, greed, domination, dishonesty, and deception. Christian tradition is replete with warnings that we must be aware of and discerningly critical of our "animal instincts" which can betray us into irrational and irresponsible behavior, distorting our judgments and disordering our priorities and relationships.

What the Catholic theologian cannot grant is a reduction of the doctrine of original sin to the above. There is more at stake than a continuing evolution. There is distortion and infidelity in human history. Human persons are capable of recognizing cruelty and violence for what they are, capable of understanding the importance of truth and honesty for community life, and capable of controlling their own behavior. They are not compelled to follow their instinctual drives. The distortions, injustices, and deceits of human history do not call simply for further evolutionary development but for conversion, reversal, and redemption.

The vocabulary of the fall and salvation/redemption cannot really be critiqued except in terms of the contexts and historical debates in which the metaphors and other figures of speech arose to be adapted for use in theological argument. It is simply not possible to discuss them in terms of whether they are scientifically meaningful to modern minds. The language of religious beliefs is a language of hints and suggestions and leaps of imagination, creating a different order of symbolism and a larger range of analogy than the language of science which attempts to be exhaustively descriptive. One cannot simply lift terms and propositions out of one and place them in the discourse of the other.

The genius of Teilhard de Chardin is that he made a mystical synthesis that somehow transcended both in the realm of prethematic vision and contemplation. When challenged to explain how he integrated the doctrine of original sin into his vision he was never able to satisfy his questioners that he had adequately done so. His contribution to reconciling the Christian vision of reality with an evolutionary understanding was far-reaching and critical but it was left to others to fashion a coherent theology.

Rejoinder

Daryl P. Domning

I have ventured a critique of the contemporary consensus among Catholic theologians that I have called the "cultural-transmission" view of original sin. In response, Monika Hellwig points out that the true function of the doctrine in Christian theology is not to explain the (pre)historical origins of sin and evil, but to stress that all human beings are *in need of salvation* from the captivity (unfreedom) of sin. In addition, the doctrine serves to raise our awareness (1) that evil and suffering can and should be resisted; (2) that evil springs from within us as well as from outside; and (3) that the Creator is willing and able to save us from our sinful situation. Further, given the risk inherent in the exercise of free will, it is naturally inevitable that humans will do evil; hence no supernatural explanation (or even historical account) of the origins of sin is logically needed. With all of this I agree; and I also agree that the systematic exigence *in theology* is to clarify our present moral situation and not our remote beginnings.

I feel, however, that theologians – especially given their own "present situation" at the start of the twenty-first Christian century – cannot so easily dissociate themselves from concern with our beginnings. Too much Christian catechesis, for too many years, has put forward Adam and Eve as real historical personages, and the Garden of Eden as the cradle of our real beginnings. Likewise with the vocabulary of the "Fall" and "redemption": it is not scientists but catechists who continue to drag these terms out of their ancient contexts into discussions of the present day. And modern minds, formed in a scientific age, continue to seek meaning in them – anachronistically and misguidedly, perhaps, but they have little alternative in the absence of figures of speech more suited to modern theological argument.

In fairness, theologians do not always control the official teachings of their Churches, and many theologians have tried hard to come up with more satisfactory formulations of this doctrine. But they have not entirely succeeded; and there are still some Catholic theologians who defend the literalist version, which remains more or less enshrined in the official *Catechism*. The fact is that the Church has long claimed to know something about our beginnings that it did not know. The fact that this claim should never have been made – that the suggestive language of religious beliefs should never have been confused with the descriptive language of science – does not change the reality that the claim was made, continues to be made by some, and continues to confuse and disturb many believers.

Hence my challenge to these outmoded ideas, even while I appreciate that the more progressive theologians no longer accept them. If the systematic exigence of clarifying our beginnings, and those of evil itself, lies in the domain of the scientist rather than that of the theologian, well and good; I accept the challenge. But is it true that the scientist's conclusions will have no immediate relevance to the redemption, or to an understanding of the doctrine of original sin? Hellwig rightly observes that evolutionary theory has many interesting consequences for our understanding of God, the act of creation, and our own moral responsibility as participants in this ongoing creation. In particular, she notes that the discernment of our proper goals and roles in this creative process "requires a great detachment from self-interest" – the very self-interest, or *original selfishness*, that I have identified with original "sin." Is it not relevant to redemption to properly identify and name that from which we need to be redeemed? Does the understanding of original sin gain nothing from the scientific perspective set forth in this book? The reader must decide.

As for "reduction" of original sin to our animal instincts, I agree that this should not be understood to imply that further evolution can fix what's wrong with what evolution up to now has done. On the contrary: I insist that the divine call to conversion, and divine aid in reversing our instinctive Darwinian priorities, were and are absolutely essential to our salvation.

Indeed, we need all the help from divine revelation we can get, and not even Genesis 1–3 has outlived its salvific usefulness. With due allowance for its mythic and poetic nature, the story of the Garden still offers us profound insights into our human nature and the human situation. Bible scholars continue to mine from it gems like the allegory (pointed out by Hellwig) of Eve as the mothering community or tradition that has become instead the misleading temptress. This beautifully encapsulates the views of the Schoonenberg school, which are (as I have said) deeply true and valuable as far as they go. Surely this is a large part, and maybe all, of what the doctrine of original sin originally sought to express. But somewhere along the line it became misunderstood as a statement of our historical origins, and now we are hooked on history, for better or worse. Fortunately we now have independent sources of knowledge about our real history; and whereas the misunderstanding made things worse, for theologians and laity alike, sorting out the historical from the theological bits in the light of evolution can only make things better, for all of us.

Bibliography

Scripture quotations are from the *New American Bible*.

Acker, J. 2000. "Creationism and the Catechism." *America* 183(20): 6–9.

Ackerman, J. 1998. "Dinosaurs take wing." *National Geographic* 194(1): 74–99.

Allik, T. 1989. "Matthew Fox: on the goodness of creation and finitude." *Listening* 24: 54–72.

Alszeghy, Z. 1967. "Development in the doctrinal formulation of the Church concerning the theory of evolution." pp. 25–33 in J. Metz (ed.), *The evolving world and theology. Concilium*, vol. 26.

Alszeghy, Z. and M. Flick. 1967. "An evolutionary view of original sin." *Theology Digest* 15: 197–202.

Alters, B. J. and S. M. Alters. 2001. *Defending evolution: a guide to the creation-evolution controversy*. Jones and Bartlett Publishers, Boston, MA.

Anderson, B. W. 1984. "Creation in the Bible." pp. 19–44 in P. N. Joranson and K. Butigan (eds.), *Cry of the environment: rebuilding the Christian creation tradition*. Bear & Company, Santa Fe, NM.

Anderson, R. P. and C. O. Handley, Jr. 2001. "A new species of three-toed sloth (Mammalia: Xenarthra) from Panamá, with a review of the genus *Bradypus*." *Proceedings of the Biological Society of Washington* 114(1): 1–33.

Ayala, F. J. 1995. "The myth of Eve: molecular biology and human origins." *Science* 270: 1930–1936.

Ayala, F. J. 1998. "Evolution and the uniqueness of humankind" [address to the US Catholic bishops]. *Origins* 27(34): 565–574.

Ayala, F. J. 2001. "Chance and necessity: adaptation and novelty in evolution." pp. 231–261 in: J. B. Miller (ed.), *An evolving dialogue: theological and scientific perspectives on evolution*. Trinity Press International, Harrisburg, PA.

Barlow, G. W. 2000. *The cichlid fishes: nature's grand experiment in evolution*. Perseus Publishing, Cambridge, MA.

Barnes, L. G., D. P. Domning, and C. E. Ray. 1985. "Status of studies on fossil marine mammals." *Marine Mammal Science* 1(1): 15–53.

Barth, K. 1962. *Christ and Adam: man and humanity in Romans 5*. Collier Books, New York.

Barton, N. 2000. "The rapid origin of reproductive isolation." *Science* 290: 462–463.

Behe, M. J. 1996. *Darwin's black box: the biochemical challenge to evolution*. The Free Press, New York.

Bekoff, M. 2002. "Virtuous nature." *New Scientist* 175(2351): 34–37.

Bennett, C. H., M. Li and B. Ma. 2003. "Chain letters and evolutionary histories." *Scientific American* 288(6): 76–81.

Berra, T. M. 1990. *Evolution and the myth of creationism: a basic guide to the facts in the evolution debate*. Stanford University Press, Stanford, CA.

Berta, A., C. E. Ray, and A. R. Wyss. 1989. "Skeleton of the oldest known pinniped, *Enaliarctos mealsi." Science* 244: 60–62.

Birkhead, T. 2000. *Promiscuity: an evolutionary history of sperm competition.* Harvard University Press, Cambridge, MA.

Blackstone, N. W. 1997. "Argumentum ad ignorantiam" [review of Behe 1996]. *Quarterly Review of Biology* 72(4): 445–447.

Boadt, L. 1984. *Reading the Old Testament: an introduction.* Paulist Press, Mahwah, NJ.

Bodensieck, J. (ed.). 1965. *The encyclopedia of the Lutheran Church.* Augsburg Publishing House, Minneapolis.

Boehm, C. 1997. "Egalitarian behaviour and the evolution of political intelligence." pp. 341–364 in: A. Whiten and R. W. Byrne (eds.), *Machiavellian intelligence II: extensions and evaluations.* Cambridge University Press, Cambridge.

Boesiger, E. 1980. "Evolutionary biology in France at the time of the evolutionary synthesis." pp. 309–321 in E. Mayr and W. B. Provine (eds.), *The evolutionary synthesis: perspectives on the unification of biology.* Harvard University Press, Cambridge, MA.

Bradie, M. 1994. *The secret chain: evolution and ethics.* State University of New York Press, Albany.

Brown, R. E. 1985. *Biblical exegesis and church doctrine.* Paulist Press, Mahwah, NJ.

Bruteau, B. 1997. *God's ecstasy: the creation of a self-creating world.* Crossroad Publishing Co., New York.

Byrne, K. and R. A. Nichols. 1999. "*Culex pipiens* in London Underground tunnels: differentiation between surface and subterranean populations." *Heredity* 82: 7–15.

Camazine, S. 2003. "Patterns in nature." *Natural History* 112(5): 34–41.

Campbell, A. F. 2000. *God first loved us: the challenge of accepting unconditional love.* Paulist Press, Mahwah, NJ.

Campbell, B. G. and J. D. Loy. 1996. *Humankind emerging.* 7th ed. HarperCollins, New York.

Campbell, D. T. 1975. "The conflict between social and biological evolution and the concept of original sin." *Zygon* 10(3): 234–249.

Cann, R. L., M. Stoneking, and A. C. Wilson. 1987. "Mitochondrial DNA and human evolution." *Nature* 325: 31–36.

Carroll, R. 1997. *Patterns and processes of vertebrate evolution.* Cambridge University Press, New York.

Carson, H. L. and D. A. Clague. 1995. "Geology and biogeography of the Hawaiian Islands." pp. 14–29 in W. L. Wagner and V. A. Funk (eds.), *Hawaiian biogeography: evolution of a hot spot archipelago.* Smithsonian Institution Press, Washington.

Cheney, D. L. and R. M. Seyfarth. 1990a. "In the minds of monkeys." *Natural History* 99(9): 38–47.

Cheney, D. L. and R. M. Seyfarth. 1990b. *How monkeys see the world: inside the mind of another species.* University of Chicago Press, Chicago.

Chesterton, G. K. 1905. *Heretics.* John Lane, New York and London.

Chesterton, G. K. [1909] 1924. *Orthodoxy.* Dodd, Mead & Co., New York.

Clark, W. R. 1996. *Sex and the origins of death.* Oxford University Press.

Clarke, W. N. 1996. "Living on the edge: the human person as 'frontier being' and microcosm." *International Philosophical Quarterly* 36(2): 183–199.

Clifford, A. M. 1998. "Biological evolution and the human soul: a theological proposal for generationism." pp. 162–173 in: T. Peters (ed.), *Science and theology: the new consonance*. Westview Press, Boulder, CO.

Coates, M. I. and J. A. Clack. 1991. "Fish-like gills and breathing in the earliest known tetrapod." *Nature* 352: 234–236.

Connor, J. L. 1968. "Original sin: contemporary approaches." *Theological Studies* 29: 215–240.

Copley, S.D. 2000. "Evolution of a metabolic pathway for degradation of a toxic xenobiotic: the patchwork approach." *Trends in Biochemical Sciences* 25(6): 261–265.

Daeschler, E. B. and N. Shubin. 1998. "Fish with fingers?" *Nature* 391: 133.

Daly, G. 1989. *Creation and redemption*. Michael Glazier, Wilmington, DE.

Darwin, C. [1859] 1959. *The Origin of Species by Charles Darwin: a variorum text* (M. Peckham, ed.). University of Pennsylvania Press, Philadelphia.

Darwin, C. 1871. *The descent of man, and selection in relation to sex*. 2 vols. John Murray, London.

Darwin, F. (ed.) 1887. *The life and letters of Charles Darwin, including an autobiographical chapter*. 2 vols. D. Appleton & Co., New York.

Dawkins, R. 1989. *The selfish gene*. New edition. Oxford University Press.

Dewey, J. 1910. *The influence of Darwin on philosophy and other essays in contemporary thought*. Henry Holt and Co., New York.

Dhanis, E. and J. Visser. 1969. The supplement to A New Catechism. ... On behalf of the Commission of Cardinals appointed to examine A New Catechism. pp. 511–574 in: *A New Catechism: Catholic Faith for Adults with Supplement*. Seabury Press, New York.

Diamond, J. 1993. *The third chimpanzee: the evolution and future of the human animal*. HarperPerennial, New York.

Dominey, W. J. and L. S. Blumer. 1984. "Cannibalism of early life stages in fishes." pp. 43–64 in G. Hausfater and S. B. Hrdy (eds.), *Infanticide: comparative and evolutionary perspectives*. Aldine Publishing Co., New York.

Domning, D. P. 1978. "Sirenian evolution in the North Pacific Ocean." *University of California Publications in Geological Science* 118: xi + 176.

Domning, D. P. 1987. "Sea cow family reunion." *Natural History* 96(4): 64–71.

Domning, D. P. 1999. "The earliest sirenians: what we know and what we would like to know." In: E. Hoch and A. K. Brantsen (eds.), [Abstracts of the Second Conference on] Secondary Adaptation to Life in Water. Sept. 13–17, 1999. Geologisk Museum, Copenhagen, Denmark: 12–13.

Domning, D. P. 2000. "The readaptation of Eocene sirenians to life in water." In: *Proceedings of a Conference on Secondary Adaptation to Life in Water. Historical Biology* 14: 115–119.

Domning, D. P. 2001. "The earliest known fully quadrupedal sirenian." *Nature* 413: 625–627.

Domning, D. P. 2002a. "New 'intermediate form' ties seacows firmly to land." *Reports of the National Center for Science Education* (Berkeley, CA) 21(5–6): 38–42. [Bears printed date "2001."]

Domning, D. P. 2002b. "The Two Standards: a fork in the road of evolution." *Christian Life Communities Harvest* 35(1): 6–8.

Domning, D. P. and H. Furusawa. 1995. "Summary of taxa and distribution of Sirenia in the North Pacific Ocean." *The Island Arc* 3(4): 506–512.

Duffy, S. J. 1988. "Our hearts of darkness: original sin revisited." *Theological Studies* 49: 597–622.

Duffy, S. J. 1993. *The dynamics of grace: perspectives in theological anthropology.* Liturgical Press, Collegeville, MN (A Michael Glazier Book; New Theology Studies, vol. 3).

Dugatkin, L. A. and H. K. Reeve (eds.). 1998. *Game theory and animal behavior.* Oxford University Press, New York and Oxford.

Duke, R. C., D. M. Ojcius, and J. D. Young. 1996. "Cell suicide in health and disease." *Scientific American* 275(6): 80–87.

Duquoc, C. 1978. "New approaches to original sin." *Cross Currents* 28: 189–200.

Durant, J. R. 2001. "A critical-historical perspective on the argument about evolution and creation." pp. 263–278 in: J. B. Miller (ed.), *An evolving dialogue: theological and scientific perspectives on evolution.* Trinity Press International, Harrisburg, PA.

Dusheck, J. 2002. "The interpretation of genes." *Natural History* 111(8): 52–59.

Duve, C. de. 1995. *Vital dust: life as a cosmic imperative.* BasicBooks, New York.

Duve, C. de. 1996. "The constraints of chance." *Scientific American* 274(1): 112.

Dyson, F. J. 2001. "Why is life so complicated?" pp. 139–153 in: J. B. Miller (ed.), *An evolving dialogue: theological and scientific perspectives on evolution.* Trinity Press International, Harrisburg, PA.

Edwards, D. 1998. "Original sin and saving grace in evolutionary context." pp. 377–392 in: R. J. Russell, W. R. Stoeger, and F. J. Ayala (eds.), *Evolutionary and molecular biology: scientific perspectives on divine action.* Vatican Observatory, Vatican City, and Center for Theology and the Natural Sciences, Berkeley, CA.

Edwards, D. 1999. *The God of evolution: a trinitarian theology.* Paulist Press, Mahwah, NJ.

Eisenberger, N. I., M. D. Lieberman, and K. D. Williams. 2003. "Does rejection hurt? An fMRI study of social exclusion." *Science* 302: 290–292.

Eliade, M. 1954. *The myth of the eternal return; or, cosmos and history.* Bollingen Series XLVI, Princeton University Press, Princeton.

Ellis, G. F. R. 1998. "The thinking underlying the new 'scientific' world-views." pp. 251–280 in: R. J. Russell, W. R. Stoeger, and F. J. Ayala (eds.), *Evolutionary and molecular biology: scientific perspectives on divine action.* Vatican Observatory, Vatican City, and Center for Theology and the Natural Sciences, Berkeley, CA.

Farber, P. L. 1994. *The temptations of evolutionary ethics.* University of California Press, Berkeley.

Fitzmyer, J. A. 1968. "The Letter to the Romans." pp. 291–331 in: R. E. Brown, J. A. Fitzmyer, and R. E. Murphy (eds.), *The Jerome biblical commentary.* vol. II. *The New Testament and topical articles.* Prentice-Hall, Inc., Englewood Cliffs, NJ.

Floyd, C. 2000. "Virtuous species: the biological origins of human morality. An interview with Frans de Waal." *Science & Spirit* 11(1): 14–16.

Fossey, D. 1983. *Gorillas in the mist.* Houghton Mifflin, Boston.

Futuyma, D. J. 1995. *Science on trial: the case for evolution.* Second edition. Sinauer Associates, Sunderland, MA.

Futuyma, D. J. 1998. *Evolutionary biology*. Third edition. Sinauer Associates, Sunderland, MA.

Gastaldo, R. A. and W. F. Tanner (conveners). 1984. The evolution–creation controversy: perspectives on religion, philosophy, science and education – a handbook. Proceedings of a symposium … *Paleontological Society Special Publication* No. 1: 1–155.

Gaster, T. H. 1969. *Myth, legend, and custom in the Old Testament*. Harper & Row, New York.

Gewirth, A. 1993. "How ethical is evolutionary ethics?" pp. 241–256 in: M. H. Nitecki and D. V. Nitecki (eds.). *Evolutionary ethics*. State University of New York Press, Albany.

Ghiselin, M. T. [1969] 1984. *The triumph of the Darwinian method*. University of Chicago Press.

Gibbs, W. W. 1996. "Programming with primordial ooze." *Scientific American* 275(4): 48, 50.

Gingerich, P. D. 2001. "Rates of evolution on the time scale of the evolutionary process." *Genetica* 112–113: 127–144.

Godfrey, L. R. (ed.) 1983. *Scientists confront creationism*. W.W. Norton, New York.

Godfrey, S. J. and C. R. Smith. 2005. *Paradigms on pilgrimage: creationism, paleontology, and biblical interpretation*. Clements Publishing, Toronto.

Goodall, J. 1986. *The chimpanzees of Gombe: patterns of behavior*. Belknap Press, Harvard University, Cambridge, MA.

Goodenough, U. 1998. *The sacred depths of nature*. Oxford University Press, New York and Oxford.

Gould, S. J. 1980. *The panda's thumb: more reflections in natural history*. Norton, New York.

Gould, S. J. 1997. "Nonoverlapping magisteria." *Natural History* 106(2): 16–22, 60–62. (Reprinted in Miller 2001.)

Gould, S. J. 1998. "The paradox of the visibly irrelevant." *Natural History* 106(11): 12–18, 60–66.

Graham-Rowe, D. 2002. "Radio emerges from the electronic soup." *New Scientist* 175(2358): 19.

Gribbin, J. and M. Gribbin. 2000. *Stardust: supernovae and life – the cosmic connection*. Yale University Press, New Haven, CT.

Grzimek, B., et al. (eds.). 1973. *Grzimek's animal life encyclopedia*. Van Nostrand Reinhold, New York.

Gutiérrez, G. 1991. *The God of life*. Orbis Books, Maryknoll, NY.

Haag, H. 1969. *Is original sin in Scripture?* Sheed and Ward, New York.

Haught, J. F. 1998a. "Evolution's impact on theology" [address to the US Catholic bishops]. *Origins* 27(34): 574–577.

Haught, J. F. 1998b. "Evolution, in nature and Catholic thought." pp. 180–185 in: M. Fiedler and L. Rabben (eds.), *Rome has spoken: a guide to forgotten papal statements, and how they have changed through the centuries*. Crossroad Publishing. Co., New York, NY.

Haught, J. F. 2000. *God after Darwin: a theology of evolution*. Westview Press, Boulder, CO.

Haught, J. F. 2001. *Responses to 101 questions on God and evolution*. Paulist Press, Mahwah, NJ.

Haught, J. F. 2002. "In search of a God for evolution: Paul Tillich and Pierre Teilhard de Chardin." *Zygon* 37(3): 539–553.

Hauser, M. D. 1997. "Minding the behaviour of deception." pp. 112–143 in: A. Whiten and R. W. Byrne (eds.), *Machiavellian intelligence II: extensions and evaluations*. Cambridge University Press, Cambridge, MA.

Hausfater, G. and S. B. Hrdy (eds.). 1984. *Infanticide: comparative and evolutionary perspectives*. Aldine Publishing Co., New York.

Hefner, P. 1993. "Biological perspectives on the Fall and original sin." *Zygon* 28: 77–101.

Hellwig, M. K. 1992. *The Eucharist and the hunger of the world*. Second edition. Sheed and Ward, Kansas City, MO.

Hick, J. 1966. *Evil and the God of love*. Revised edition. Harper and Row, New York.

Hölldobler, B. and E. O. Wilson. 1994. *Journey to the ants: a story of scientific exploration*. Harvard University Press, Cambridge, MA.

Hopson, J. A. 1987. "The mammal-like reptiles: a study of transitional fossils." *American Biology Teacher* 49(1): 16–26.

Hopson, J. A. 1994. "Synapsid evolution and the radiation of non-eutherian mammals." pp. 190–219 in: D. R. Prothero and R. M. Schoch (eds.), *Major features of vertebrate evolution. Short Courses in Paleontology* No. 7. The Paleontological Society, Pittsburgh.

Hrdy, S. B. 1977. *The langurs of Abu: female and male strategies of reproduction*. Harvard University Press, Cambridge, MA and London.

Hughes, L. R. (ed.) 1992. *Reviews of creationist books*. Second edition. National Center for Science Education, Berkeley, CA.

Hunter, S. B. 1998. "The newer anti-evolutionists: introducing Greg Koukl." *Reports of the National Center for Science Education* 17(5): 17, 20.

Huxley, J. 1931. *What dare I think? The challenge of modern science to human action & belief*. Harper & Brothers, New York.

Huxley, J. 1953. *Evolution in action*. Harper & Brothers, New York.

Huxley, J. 1957. *Religion without revelation*. Mentor Books, New York.

Huxley, T. H. [1894] 1993. "Evolution and ethics." pp. 29–80 in: M. H. Nitecki and D. V. Nitecki (eds.). *Evolutionary ethics*. State University of New York Press, Albany.

Jacobs, L. 1971. Article on "Sin." *Encyclopedia Judaica*, vol. 14. Keter Publishing House Ltd., Jerusalem.

Jacquet, L. 1989. "Original sin: a new look at the oldest sin in the book." *US Catholic* 54: 6–12.

Jaki, S. L. 1974. *Science and creation: from eternal cycles to an oscillating universe*. Science History Publications, New York.

Jeeves, M. 1998. [Lecture at the Woodstock Theological Center, Georgetown University, Washington, DC] *Woodstock Report* No. 53: 10–11.

John Paul II, Pope. 1985. "Foi chrétienne et théorie de l'évolution." *La Documentation Catholique* 82: 783–784.

John Paul II, Pope. 1988. "Message of Pope John Paul II to the Reverend George V. Coyne, S. J., Director of the Vatican Observatory." P. M11 in: R. J. Russell, W. R. Stoeger, and G. V. Coyne (eds.), *Physics, philosophy and theology: a common quest for understanding*. Vatican Observatory, Libreria Editrice Vaticana, Vatican City.

John Paul II, Pope. 1996. "Message to Pontifical Academy of Sciences on evolution" (revised translation). *Origins* 26(25): 414–416.

Johnson, E. 1996. "Does God play dice? Divine providence and chance." *Theological Studies* 57: 3–18. (Reprinted in Miller 2001.)

Johnson, T. C., C. A. Scholz, M. R. Talbot, K. Kelts, R. D. Ricketts, G. Ngobi, K. Buening, I. Ssemmanda, and J. W. McGill. 1996. "Late Pleistocene desiccation of Lake Victoria and rapid evolution of cichlid fishes." *Science* 273: 1091–1093.

Kelley, P. H., J. R. Bryan, and T. A. Hansen (conveners). 1999. The evolution-creation controversy II: perspectives on science, religion, and geological education. *Paleontological Society Papers* 5: ix + 242.

Kepnes, S. 2000. "'Turn us to you and we shall return': original sin, atonement, and redemption in Jewish terms." pp. 293–304 in: T. Frymer-Kensky, D. Novak, P. Ochs, D. F. Sandmel, and M. A. Signer (eds.), *Christianity in Jewish terms*. Westview Press, Boulder, CO.

Kitcher, P. 1982. *Abusing science: the case against creationism*. MIT Press, Cambridge, MA.

Klein, R. G. 1999. *The human career: human biological and cultural origins*. Second edition. University of Chicago Press, Chicago.

Knoll, A. H. and R. K. Bambach. 2000. "Directionality in the history of life: diffusion from the left wall or repeated scaling of the right?" pp. 1–14 in: D. H. Erwin and S. L. Wing (eds.), *Deep time: Paleobiology's perspective*. *Paleobiology* 26(4), Supplement.

Koretsky, I. A. and P. Holec. 2002. A primitive seal (Mammalia: Phocidae) from the early Middle Miocene of Central Paratethys. *Smithsonian Contributions to Paleobiology* 93: 163–178.

Korsmeyer, J. D. 1998. *Evolution and Eden: balancing original sin and contemporary science*. Paulist Press, Mahwah, NJ.

Koza, J. R., M. A. Keane, and M. J. Streeter. 2003. "Evolving inventions." *Scientific American* 288(2): 52–59.

Kruuk, H. 1972. *The spotted hyena: a study of predation and social behavior*. University of Chicago Press, Chicago.

Kuhl, S. C. 1998. "Darwin's dangerous idea ... and St. Paul's: God, humanity, responsibility, meaning in the light of evolutionary findings." pp. 76–104 in: R. Brungs and M. Postiglione (eds.), Creation AND evolution: proceedings of the ITEST workshop, October, 1997. ITEST Faith/Science Press, St. Louis, MO.

Laden, G. 1998. "The naked truth: the fallacy of genetic Adam and Eve." *Reports of the National Center for Science Education* 17(5): 22–24.

Lewis, C. S. 1962. *The problem of pain*. Macmillan, New York.

Limoges, C. 1980. "A second glance at evolutionary biology in France." pp. 322–328 in E. Mayr and W. B. Provine (eds.), *The evolutionary synthesis: perspectives on the unification of biology*. Harvard University Press, Cambridge, MA.

Lipson, H. and J. B. Pollack. 2000. "Automatic design and manufacture of robotic lifeforms." *Nature* 406(6799): 974–978.

Lombroso, C. 1887. *L'homme criminel*. F. Alcan, Paris.

Lonergan, B. J. F. 1957. *Insight: a study of human understanding*. Philosophical Library, New York.

Lott, D. F. 2002. "Plains song: bison and life on the 'American Serengeti'." *Natural History* 111(8): 44–51.

Lovejoy, C. O. 1988. "Evolution of human walking." *Scientific American* 259(5): 118–125.

Lowenstein, J. M. 1982. "Twelve wise men at the Vatican." *Nature* 299: 395.

Lubac, H. de. 1968. *The religion of Teilhard de Chardin*. Image Books, New York.

Margulis, L. and D. Sagan. 2001. "The beast with five genomes." *Natural History* 110(5): 38–41.

Marshall, C. R. 2001. "Darwinism in an age of molecular revolution." pp. 67–96 in: J. B. Miller (ed.), *An evolving dialogue: theological and scientific perspectives on evolution*. Trinity Press International, Harrisburg, PA.

Masani, P. R. 1985. "The thermodynamic and phylogenetic foundations of human wickedness." *Zygon* 20(3): 283–320.

Matsumura, M. (ed.) 1995. *Voices for evolution*. National Center for Science Education, Inc., Berkeley, CA.

Mayr, E. 2001. *What evolution is*. Basic Books, New York.

Mazin, J.-M. and V. de Buffrénil (eds.). 2001. *Secondary adaptation of tetrapods to life in water. Proceedings of the international meeting*, Poitiers, 1996. Verlag Dr. Friedrich Pfeil, Munich.

McDermott, B. O. 1977. "The theology of original sin: recent developments." *Theological Studies* 38: 478–512.

McGrath, A. E. 1988. *Justification by faith: what it means to us today*. Zondervan Academic Books, Grand Rapids, MI.

McShea, D. W. 2001. "The hierarchical structure of organisms: a scale and documentation of a trend in the maximum." *Paleobiology* 27(2): 405–423.

Meléndez-Hevia, E., T. G. Waddell, and M. Cascante. 1996. "The puzzle of the Krebs cycle: assembling the pieces of chemically feasible reactions, and opportunism in the design of metabolic pathways during evolution." *Journal of Molecular Evolution* 43: 293–303.

Mendenhall, G. E. 1970. "The Hebrew conquest of Palestine." pp. 100–120 in: E. F. Campbell, Jr. and D. N. Freedman (eds.), *Biblical Archaeologist Reader* 3. Doubleday, Garden City, NY.

Mendenhall, G. E. 2001. *Ancient Israel's faith and history: an introduction to the Bible in context*. Westminster John Knox Press, Louisville, KY.

Mesters, C. 1974. *Eden: golden age or goad to action?* Orbis Books, Maryknoll, NY.

Miller, J. B. (ed.). 2001. *An evolving dialogue: theological and scientific perspectives on evolution*. Trinity Press International, Harrisburg, PA.

Miller, K. R. 1999. *Finding Darwin's God: a scientist's search for common ground between God and evolution*. Cliff Street Books, New York.

Mitchell, E. D., Jr., R. R. Reeves, and A. Evely. 1986. "Bibliography of whale killing techniques." *Reports of the International Whaling Commission*, Special Issue 7: 1–161.

Mitchell, R. W. and N. S. Thompson (eds.). 1986. *Deception: perspectives on human and nonhuman deceit*. State University of New York Press, Albany.

Molesworth, H. D. 1969. *The golden age of princes*. G. P. Putnam's Sons, New York.

Monod, J. 1971. *Chance and necessity: an essay on the natural philosophy of modern biology*. Alfred A. Knopf, New York.

Moore, A. L. 1889. *Science and the faith: essays on apologetic subjects*. Kegan Paul, Trench, Trubner & Co., London.

Moore, R. 2002. "Racism and the public's perception of evolution." *Reports of the National Center for Science Education* 22(3): 16–18, 23–26.

Morowitz, H. J. 1985. *Mayonnaise and the origin of life: thoughts of minds and molecules*. Charles Scribner's Sons, New York.

Morris, D. 1986. *Catwatching*. Crown Trade Paperbacks, New York.

Morris, J. D. 1996. "Is there such a thing as creationist counseling?" *Back To Genesis* (Institute for Creation Research) No. 85: page d.

Morris, J. D. 2004. "Is believing in evolution the same kind of thing as believing in gravity?" *Back To Genesis* (Institute for Creation Research) No. 183: page d.

Murchie, G. 1978. *The seven mysteries of life: an exploration in science and philosophy*. Houghton Mifflin, Boston, MA.

Murphy, N. 1998. "Supervenience and the nonreducibility of ethics to biology." pp. 463–489 in: R. J. Russell, W. R. Stoeger, and F. J. Ayala (eds.), *Evolutionary and molecular biology: scientific perspectives on divine action*. Vatican Observatory, Vatican City, and Center for Theology and the Natural Sciences, Berkeley, CA.

National Academy of Sciences. 1999. *Science and creationism: a view from the National Academy of Sciences*. Second edition. National Academy Press, Washington, DC.

Nessan, C. L. 1995. "The fall from dreaming innocence: what Tillich said philosophically in light of evolutionary science." pp. 104–117 in: F. J. Parella (ed.), *Paul Tillich's theological legacy: spirit and community*. Walter de Gruyter, Berlin and New York.

Nesse, R. M. and G. C. Williams. 1998. "Evolution and the origins of disease." *Scientific American* 279(5): 86–93.

Neuner, J. and J. Dupuis. 1975. *The Christian faith in the doctrinal documents of the Catholic Church*. Christian Classics Inc., Westminster, MD.

Niebuhr, R. [1941–43] 1964. *The nature and destiny of man: a Christian interpretation*. 2 vols. Charles Scribner's Sons, New York.

Niebuhr, R. 1960. *Moral man and immoral society: a study in ethics and politics*. Charles Scribner's Sons, New York.

Nitecki, M. H. and D. V. Nitecki (eds.). 1993. *Evolutionary ethics*. State University of New York Press, Albany.

Nowak, M. A., R. M. May, and K. Sigmund. 1995. "The arithmetics of mutual help." *Scientific American* 272(6): 76–81.

Ong, W. J. 1960. "Evolution and cyclicism in our time." pp. 125–148 in W. J. Ong (ed.), *Darwin's vision and Christian perspectives*. Macmillan, New York.

Packer, C. 1994. *Into Africa*. University of Chicago Press, Chicago.

Packer, C. and A. E. Pusey. 1997. "Divided we fall: cooperation among lions." *Scientific American* 276(5): 52–59.

Pagels, E. 1988. *Adam, Eve, and the Serpent*. Random House, New York.

Pennock, R. T. 1997. "Naturalism, creationism and the meaning of life: the case of Philip Johnson revisited." *Creation/Evolution* 16(2): 10–30.

Pennock, R. T. 1999. *Tower of Babel: the evidence against the new creationism*. MIT Press, Cambridge, MA.

Pennock, R. T. (ed.). 2001. *Intelligent design creationism and its critics*. Bradford Books/MIT Press, Cambridge, MA.

Petit, C. W. 1998. "Touched by nature: putting evolution to work on the assembly line." *US News & World Report* 125(4): 43–45. July 27, 1998.

Pius XII, Pope. 1950. *Humani generis*. [English translation: The encyclical "Humani generis" with a commentary (by) A. C. Cotter, S. J. Weston College Press, Weston, MA, 1951.]

Platnick, N. I. and H. D. Cameron. 1977. "Cladistic methods in textual, linguistic, and phylogenetic analysis." *Systematic Zoology* 26(4): 380–385.

Pojeta, J., Jr. and D. A. Springer. 2001. *Evolution and the fossil record*. American Geological Institute, Alexandria, VA.

Polis, G. A. 1984. "Intraspecific predation and 'infant killing' among invertebrates." pp. 87–104 in G. Hausfater and S. B. Hrdy (eds.), *Infanticide: comparative and evolutionary perspectives*. Aldine Publishing Co., New York.

Pope, S. J. 1994. *The evolution of altruism and the ordering of love*. Georgetown University Press, Washington, DC.

Pope, S. J. 2001. "Agape and human nature: contributions from Neo-Darwinism." pp. 417–436 in: J. B. Miller (ed.), *An evolving dialogue: theological and scientific perspectives on evolution*. Trinity Press International, Harrisburg, PA.

Price, B. 1990. *The creation science controversy*. Millennium Books, Sydney.

Price, P. W. 1996. *Biological evolution*. Saunders College Publishing, Fort Worth, TX.

Rachels, J. 1990. *Created from animals: the moral implications of Darwinism*. Oxford University Press, Oxford and New York.

Rahner, K. [1958] 1965. *Hominisation: the evolutionary origin of man as a theological problem*. Herder and Herder, New York.

Rahner, K. 1967. "Evolution and original sin." pp. 61–73 in J. Metz (ed.), *The evolving world and theology*. *Concilium*, vol. 26.

Ratzinger, J. 1990. *'In the beginning …': a Catholic understanding of the story of creation and the Fall*. Our Sunday Visitor Publishing Division, Huntington, IN.

Ratzinger, J. and V. Messori. 1985. *The Ratzinger report: an exclusive interview on the state of the Church*. Ignatius Press, San Francisco, CA.

Raup, D. M. 1991. *Extinction: bad genes or bad luck?* W. W. Norton & Co., New York.

Reiser, W. 1997. *To hear God's word, listen to the world: the liberation of spirituality*. Paulist Press, Mahwah, NJ.

Rendell, L. and H. Whitehead. 2001. "Culture in whales and dolphins." *Behavioral and Brain Sciences* 24: 309–382.

Rennie, J. 2002. "15 answers to creationist nonsense." *Scientific American* 287(1): 78–85.

Reznick, D. N., F. H. Shaw, F. H. Rodd, and R. G. Shaw. 1997. "Evaluation of the rate of evolution in natural populations of guppies (*Poecilia reticulata*)." *Science* 275: 1934–1937.

Ridley, M. 2001. "The mechanism of evolution." pp. 53–65 in: J. B. Miller (ed.), *An evolving dialogue: theological and scientific perspectives on evolution*. Trinity Press International, Harrisburg, PA.

Rolston, H., III. 1999. *Genes, genesis and God: values and their origins in natural and human history*. Cambridge University Press.

Rolston, H., III. 2003. "Naturalizing and systematizing evil." pp. 67–86 in: W. B. Drees (ed.), *Is nature ever evil? Religion, science, and value*. Routledge, London and New York.

Ronshaugen, M., N. McGinnis, and W. McGinnis. 2002. "*Hox* protein mutation and macroevolution of the insect body plan." *Nature* 415: 914–917.

Rosa, P. de. 1967. *Christ and original sin*. Bruce Publishing Co., Milwaukee, WI.

Rosenberg, K. R. and W. R. Trevathan. 2001. "The evolution of human birth." *Scientific American* 285(5): 72–77.

Rottschaefer, W. A. 1997. "Evolutionary ethics: an irresistible temptation: some reflections on Paul Farber's The Temptation of Evolutionary Ethics." *Biology and Philosophy* 12: 369–384.

Rudofsky, B. 1977. *The prodigious builders*. Harcourt Brace Jovanovich, New York and London.

Ruse, M. 1986. *Taking Darwin seriously: a naturalistic approach to philosophy*. Basil Blackwell, Oxford.

Ruse, M. 1994. "Evolutionary theory and Christian ethics: are they in harmony?" *Zygon* 29(1): 5–24.

Ruse, M. 1999. "Going to extremes: the design question." *Science & Spirit* 10(4): 12–13, 23.

Sargent, T. D., C. D. Millar, and D. M. Lambert. 2000. "The 'classical' explanation of industrial melanism: assessing the evidence." *Evolutionary Biology* 30: 299–322.

Schmidt, W. H. 1984. Article on the word *br'*. pp. 336–339 in: E. Jenni and C. Westermann (eds.), *Theologisches Handwörterbuch zum Alten Testament*. Band I. Chr. Kaiser Verlag, Munich, and Theologischer Verlag, Zurich.

Schmitz-Moormann, K. (in collaboration with J. F. Salmon). 1997. *Theology of creation in an evolutionary world*. Pilgrim Press, Cleveland, OH.

Schoonenberg, P. 1965. *Man and sin*. Sheed and Ward, London and Melbourne.

Schoonenberg, P. 1967. "Original sin and man's situation." *Theology Digest* 15: 203–208.

Schopf, J. W. 1998. *Evolution! Facts and fallacies*. Academic Press, San Diego.

Scotchmoor, J. and F. K. McKinney (eds.). 1996. *Learning from the fossil record*. *The Paleontological Society Papers* 2: 1–329.

Scotchmoor, J. and D. A. Springer (eds.). 1999. *Evolution: investigating the evidence*. *The Paleontological Society, Special Publication* 9: 1–406.

Shanks, N. and K. H. Joplin. 2000. "Of mousetraps and men: Behe on biochemistry." *Reports of the National Center for Science Education* 20(1–2): 25–30.

Shermer, M. 1997. *How to debate a creationist: 25 creationists' arguments and 25 evolutionists' answers*. Skeptics Society, Altadena, CA.

Sherwin, F. 2004. "The *dogma* of evolution." *Acts & Facts* (Institute for Creation Research) 33(2): 5.

Sigmund, K. 1993. *Games of life: explorations in ecology, evolution, and behaviour*. Oxford University Press, Oxford.

Sigmund, K., E. Fehr, and M. A. Nowak. 2002. "The economics of fair play." *Scientific American* 286(1): 82–87.

Skehan, J. W. and C. E. Nelson. 2000. *The creation controversy & the science classroom*. NSTA Press, Arlington, VA.

Smuts, B. 2000. "Common ground: studies of the social and emotional lives of forest apes reveal the evolutionary roots of human nature." *Natural History* 109(10): 78–83.

Sober, E. 1993. "Evolutionary altruism, psychological egoism, and morality: disentangling the phenotypes." pp. 199–216 in: M. H. Nitecki and D. V. Nitecki (eds.). *Evolutionary ethics*. State University of New York Press, Albany.

Sober, E. and D. S. Wilson. 1998. *Unto others: the evolution and psychology of unselfish behavior*. Harvard University Press, Cambridge, MA and London.

Sonnenberg, J. 1995. "A newly-minted woman theologian reflects on the Pope's letter on women and ordination." *New Women, New Church* (Women's Ordination Conference), vol. 17(4–6) and 18(1–2), May 1995: 2.

Southgate, C. 2002. "God and evolutionary evil: theodicy in the light of Darwinism." *Zygon* 37(4): 803–824.

Steele, E. J., R. A. Lindley, and R. V. Blanden. 1998. *Lamarck's signature: how retrogenes are changing Darwin's natural selection paradigm*. Perseus Books, Reading, MA.

Strahler, A. N. 1987. *Science and earth history: the evolution/creation controversy*. Prometheus Books, Buffalo, NY.

Sturmbauer, C., S. Baric, W. Salzburger, L. Rüber, and E. Verheyen. 2001. "Lake level fluctuations synchronize genetic divergences of cichlid fishes in African lakes." *Molecular Biology and Evolution* 18(2): 144–154.

Tattersall, I. 1993. *The human odyssey: four million years of human evolution*. Prentice Hall General Reference, New York.

Tattersall, I. 1995. *The fossil trail: how we know what we think we know about human evolution*. Oxford University Press, New York and Oxford.

Tattersall, I. and J. H. Schwartz. 2000. *Extinct humans*. Peter N. Nevraumont/ Westview Press, Boulder, CO.

Taubes, G. 1998. "Evolving a conscious machine." *Discover* 19(6): 72–79.

Teicher, M. H. 2002. "Scars that won't heal: the neurobiology of child abuse." *Scientific American* 286(3): 68–75.

Teilhard de Chardin, P. 1971. *Christianity and evolution*. Harcourt Brace & Co., San Diego and New York.

Theissen, G. 1985. *Biblical faith: an evolutionary approach*. Fortress Press, Philadelphia.

Thewissen, J. G. M. (ed.). 1998. *The emergence of whales: evolutionary patterns in the origin of Cetacea*. Plenum Press, New York and London.

Thewissen, J. G. M., E. M. Williams, L. J. Roe, and S. T. Hussain. 2001. "Skeletons of terrestrial cetaceans and the relationship of whales to artiodactyls." *Nature* 413: 277–281.

Thomson, K. S. 1980. "The ecology of Devonian lobe-finned fishes." pp. 187–222 in: A. L. Panchen (ed.). *The terrestrial environment and the origin of land vertebrates*. Systematics Association Special Volume 15. Academic Press, London.

Thomson, K. S. 1994. "The origin of the tetrapods." pp. 85–107 in D. R. Prothero and R. M. Schoch (conveners). *Major features of vertebrate evolution. Short Courses in Paleontology* No. 7. The Paleontological Society, Pittsburgh, PA.

Thornhill, R. 1979. "Adaptive female-mimicking behavior in a scorpionfly." *Science* 205: 412–414.

Tracy, T. F. 1998. "Evolution, divine action, and the problem of evil." pp. 511–530 in: R. J. Russell, W. R. Stoeger, and F. J. Ayala (eds.), *Evolutionary and molecular biology: scientific perspectives on divine action*. Vatican Observatory, Vatican City, and Center for Theology and the Natural Sciences, Berkeley, CA.

Tudge, C. 2002. "Why science should warm our hearts." *Reports of the National Center for Science Education* 22(1–2): 41–44 (reprinted from *The New Statesman*, Feb. 26, 2001).

Twain, M. 1969. *The mysterious stranger*. Edited by W. M. Gibson. University of California Press, Berkeley and Los Angeles.

Ulanowicz, R. E. 2004. "Ecosystem dynamics: a natural middle." *Theology and Science* 2(2): 231–253.

Underhill, E. [1934] 1991. *The school of charity: meditations on the Christian Creed*. Morehouse Publishing, Harrisburg, PA and Wilton, CT.

Vandervelde, G. 1975. *Original sin: two major trends in contemporary Roman Catholic reinterpretation*. Rodopi NV, Amsterdam.

Van Schaik, C. P., M. Ancrenaz, G. Borgen, B. Galdikas, C. D. Knott, I. Singleton, A. Suzuki, S. S. Utami, and M. Merrill. 2003. "Orangutan cultures and the evolution of material culture." *Science* 299: 102–105.

Vermeij, G. J. 1987. *Evolution and escalation: an ecological history of life*. Princeton University Press, Princeton, NJ.

Waal, F. de. 1982. *Chimpanzee politics: power and sex among apes*. Harper & Row, New York.

Waal, F. de. 1986. "Deception in the natural communication of chimpanzees." pp. 221–244 in R. W. Mitchell and N. S. Thompson (eds.). *Deception: perspectives on human and nonhuman deceit*. State University of New York Press, Albany.

Waal, F. de. 1989. *Peacemaking among primates*. Harvard University Press, Cambridge, MA.

Waal, F. de. 1996. *Good natured: the origins of right and wrong in humans and other animals*. Harvard University Press, Cambridge, MA.

Waal, F. de and F. Lanting. 1997. *Bonobo: the forgotten ape*. University of California Press, Berkeley.

Wakefield, J. 2001. "Complexity's business model." *Scientific American* 284(1): 31, 34.

Westermann, C. 1984. *Genesis 1–11: a commentary*. Translated by J. J. Scullion. SPCK, London.

Whiten, A. and C. Boesch. 2001. "The cultures of chimpanzees." *Scientific American* 284(1): 60–67.

Whiten, A. and R. W. Byrne (eds.). 1997. *Machiavellian intelligence II: extensions and evaluations*. Cambridge University Press, Cambridge.

Whiten, A., J. Goodall, W. C. McGrew, T. Nishida, V. Reynolds, Y. Sugiyama, C. E. G. Tutin, R. W. Wrangham, and C. Boesch. 1999. "Cultures in chimpanzees." *Nature* 399: 682–685.

Wiedenhofer, S. 1991. "The main forms of contemporary theology of original sin." *Communio* 18: 514–529.

Wiley, E. O. 1981. *Phylogenetics: the theory and practice of phylogenetic systematics*. John Wiley & Sons, New York.

Williams, G. C. 1993. "Mother Nature is a wicked old witch." pp. 217–231 in: M. H. Nitecki and D. V. Nitecki (eds.). *Evolutionary ethics*. State University of New York Press, Albany.

Williams, P. A. 2001. *Doing without Adam and Eve: sociobiology and original sin.* Fortress Press, Minneapolis, MN.

Wilson, D. S. 1998. "Game theory and human behavior." pp. 261–282 in L. A. Dugatkin and H. K. Reeve (eds.), *Game theory and animal behavior.* Oxford University Press, New York and Oxford.

Wiseman, J. A. 2002. *Theology and modern science: quest for coherence.* Continuum Publishing Co., New York and London.

Wong, K. 2002. "The mammals that conquered the seas." *Scientific American* 286(5): 70–79.

Wright, N. G. and D. Kill. 1993. *Ecological healing: a Christian vision.* Orbis Books, Maryknoll, NY, and CODEL, Inc., New York, NY.

Wright, R. 1994. *The moral animal: evolutionary psychology and everyday life.* Random House, Inc., New York.

Zimmer, C. 1998. *At the water's edge: macroevolution and the transformation of life.* The Free Press, New York.

Zimmer, C. 2001a. "Alternative life styles." *Natural History* 110(4): 42–45.

Zimmer, C. 2001b. *Evolution: the triumph of an idea.* HarperCollins, New York.

Zimmerman, A. 1998. *Evolution and the sin in Eden: a new Christian synthesis.* University Press of America, Lanham, MD.

Index of scripture references

HEBREW SCRIPTURES

Genesis
1	22, 25, 130
1–2	21, 94
1–3	4, 75, 83–84, 86, 96, 107, 140, 191
1:22	91
1:26	55
1:31	92
2	85
2–3	22, 70, 95, 139, 146, 150, 152
2:5–7, 19	21
2:7	36, 60
2:7–8, 15	154
3	11–12, 14–15
3:1	108
3:15	161
3:16	78

Exodus
4:22	131
12:38	130
15	130
24:4–8	125

Leviticus
19:18, 33–34	122–123
24:10	130

Numbers
11:4	130

Deuteronomy
30:19–20	158
32	130

2 Kings
22:20	92

Job
book of	53, 161
38–42	169

Joshua
1–11	158

Ecclesiastes
book of	160

Sirach (Ecclesiasticus)
15:11–20	108, 158

Isaiah
1:2	131
6:8–12	153
11:1–9	152
26:12, 18	153
42:3–4	166
43:1	130
43:19–21	130
43:25	170
55:8	125
64:7	36
65:17	186
66:22	186

Jeremiah
7:3ff.	125
18:2–6	36
31:9	131
31:31–34	127, 170

Hosea
11:1	131
11:3–4	164
13:7–9, 16	150

Amos
9:1–4	150

NEW TESTAMENT

Matthew
1	129
3:9	35, 128
5:5	132

5:43–44	129		9:3	155
5:43–48	124		13:34	125
5:45	166		14:12	155
6:1–4	125		14:30	171
7:12	123		15:13	106
9:5–6	35		15:15	110
10:34–39	124		16:21	161, 171
12:40	159		16:33	170
13:24–30	165		17:14	125
13:28	165			
15:4–6	123		Acts	
16:2–3	61		10:34	112
18:7	187			
18:23–35	56		Romans	
19:12	129		5	97, 139
19:21–24	129		5:7–8	126
19:21–26	124		5:8	150
19:24–26	153		5:12–19	139
22–23	133		5:12–21	159
22:37–40	122		5–8	133
26:28	125		6:3–11	145
			7:15	152
Mark			7:20–24	171
1:15	125		7:22–23	153
3:31–35	129		8:14–15	132
3:32–35	124		8:18–23	160–161
9:38–40	125		8:19–23	158
			8:20	157, 161
Luke			8:29–39	66
1:78–79	153		9:4	131
6:35	124		9:21	36
9:23–24	124		11:32	157
10:25–37	122		12:4–8	164
12:54–56	61			
13:4–5	166		1 Corinthians	
14:12–14	125–126		1:18–20	126
14:26	124, 129		1:27	132
15:11–32	167		12:4–30	164
17:21	147, 170		15	139
			15:22–23	13
John			15:46	151
book of	125		15:52	186
1:12	130			
1:17	133		2 Corinthians	
1:29	183		5:17	124
3:17	151			
5:17	107		Galatians	
6:41–66	126–127		3–6	133
7:53–8:11	129		4:3–5	118
8:23	127		4:3–7	132
9:2–5	166		4:3, 9	171

4:22–31   132
5:14   124
5:17   185

Ephesians
1:4–14   159
3:9–11   159
4:11–16   164
6:12   171

Philippians
2:6–7   57
2:6–8   183

Colossians
1:19–20   125
2:12   145
2:20–21   171

1 Timothy
book of   139

2 Timothy
1:9–10   159

Titus
2:11–14   151

Hebrews
12:5–11   167

James
1:12–15   108
1:13   158

1 Peter
1:18–20   159, 161

2 Peter
3:13   170, 186

1 John
3:2   186

Revelation
21:1   186
21:4   170

Index of subjects

Abelard, Peter 13, 152
absolute monarchy 134–135, 168
actual sin 118, 140–141, 145, 149, 157, 163, 183
adoption 128–132
aggression 5, 58, 102, 104, 164, 178
aging 80, 82
altruism 28, 48–50, 56, 67, 92, 102, 104–107, 115–116, 119–121, 123, 125–127, 134, 151–152, 183, 186
anthropic principle 110
apes 41, 45, 49, 58–59, 71–72, 102–103, 106, 121, 134, 150
apoptosis 79, 107
Athanasius, St. 152
atheism 63–64, 70, 88–89, 110
atonement 152
Augustine of Hippo, St. 13, 20, 97, 116, 143, 145, 147, 156, 159
autonomy 35, 65, 85, 110, 112, 149, 154, 166–168, 184

Baptism 145, 148
beauty 177
Béziers, massacre of 165
Bible 5, 83, 86–87, 121, 128, 151, 177
breakability of matter 162, 163, 165, 173, 182, 184
Bruteau, Beatrice 133
Bunam, Rabbi Simcha 60

Calvin, John 70, 123
Campbell, Donald T. 132, 134, 179
cannibalism 103
Chesterton, G. K. 4, 108, 184
commandments 121–122
community 12–15, 54, 66, 92, 95–98, 120, 126, 130–131, 133, 154, 177, 182, 185, 188, 191
complexity 33–34, 38–39, 42, 58, 69, 82, 90–93, 106, 112
concupiscence 143, 145, 148
Conrad, Joseph 50
Conway Morris, Simon 112–113

cooperation 29, 48–49, 50, 68, 103–107, 115, 119–120, 164
covenant 86, 122, 125, 127–128, 130–132, 161
creationism 1, 6, 41, 46, 54, 58, 63, 65–69, 83, 85, 87–89, 113, 118, 154
cross of Jesus 126, 134, 152, 158, 160
cruelty 52–53, 115, 165
cyclic universe 83–84, 87, 160

Daly, Gabriel 132, 179
darkening of intellect 47–48, 61–62
Darwin, Charles 2, 24, 39, 75, 87–88, 101, 107
Darwinian fitness 28, 35, 129
death 3, 14, 26, 47, 51, 53, 61, 75, 77–84, 92, 97, 107, 109, 113–114, 118, 134, 139, 153, 155–158, 160–162, 167, 169–170, 175, 181–182, 186, 188
deceit 63, 102–103, 115–116, 119–120, 154
deism 110
dignity 12, 54–60, 171

Eden 4–6, 20, 84–85, 146–147, 150, 152–154, 182, 190
Edwards, Denis 178
entropy 35, 52, 173–174, 182
essentialism 25, 42, 44, 55, 58, 60, 87
evil 1, 5, 6, 12–13, 16, 59–60, 63, 70, 85, 92–93, 96–98, 107, 109, 117, 125, 132–134, 139–140, 148, 150, 152, 155, 157–158, 161–167, 170, 172–174, 177–178, 181–187, 190
evolutionary ethics 54–55, 108, 119, 125

Fall of Adam, 47, 139–140, 147, 149–150, 156–157, 159, 180, 182, 185, 188, 190
free will 5, 14, 34, 62–63, 98, 108, 117–118, 120, 141, 144, 157, 163, 165, 176–178, 181–184, 190
futility 84, 157–158, 160–161

Gaia hypothesis 109
game theory 4, 49, 105, 121

gametes *see* germ cells
genetic algorithms 28
genetic determinism 108, 133, 178
genotype 24, 144–145
germ cells 81, 115, 144
Gnosticism 59–60, 69, 110, 182–183
Goodall, Jane 102
Gould, Stephen Jay 27, 112–113
grace 139, 143–145, 147–149, 151, 157–159, 176, 184

Haldane J. B. S. 24, 177
Haught, John F. 7, 30, 34, 65, 67, 108, 176–178
Hebrews 84–85, 122, 129–131
Hefner, Philip 134, 179
history, valorization of 84–87, 146, 151, 182, 186
homology 31, 105
hope 6, 28, 62, 86–87, 89, 97, 151, 160–161, 176, 183, 186
Humani Generis 2–3, 20, 142, 147
humility of God 57, 60, 86, 110–111, 127, 134, 166, 176–177, 183
Huxley, Aldous 165
Huxley, T. H. 109

image of God, humans made in 55, 57, 66, 69, 126, 139, 158, 186
Incarnation 30, 56, 60, 133, 153, 170, 183, 186
inclusive fitness 28
industrial melanism 43, 68
infanticide 50, 102–103
information theory 33, 114
inheritance of acquired characters 40
intelligence 24, 55, 58–59, 65, 90–91, 94–95, 109–110, 112–113, 115, 117, 119, 121, 133, 141, 161, 163, 177, 182, 184
intelligent design 39, 63, 65, 67, 75
intelligent designer 27, 33, 136
intentionality 108
intermediate fossils 46, 68
Irenaeus, St. 156, 159, 167

John Paul II, Pope 1, 3, 57, 92
justice 115, 165, 170, 177
justification 145, 153, 159

kenosis *see* humility of God
kin selection 28–30, 48–49, 107, 123

Kingdom of God *see* Reign of God
Korsmeyer, Jerry 109, 175–176, 178

Lisbon earthquake of 1755 162
living fossils 44
love 31, 53–54, 58, 64, 66, 82, 86, 101, 106, 110, 122–126, 134, 152, 155, 156, 158, 161, 167, 174–177, 184–185, 187
Luther, Martin 148

macroevolution 37–38, 40–46, 68
meaning of life *see* purpose
microevolution 40, 42, 68
mind *see* intelligence
mitochondrial Eve 72–73
monogenism 3, 6, 71, 74, 95, 140–141, 143, 180, 183
morality 64, 106, 115, 117, 120, 136, 150, 170, 183
Morowitz, Harold 179
mutation 24, 36–37, 43, 52, 73, 81, 91, 111, 163, 175, 182, 184
myth 11, 84–85, 96, 146

natural selection 23–30, 32–40, 43–45, 48–49, 51–52, 54–55, 61–63, 65–66, 70, 76–78, 88–91, 101, 103, 105, 107, 111–114, 119, 124, 128, 133–134, 141, 149, 153, 158, 161, 163, 173–175, 179, 182–184, 187
naturalism, methodological and metaphysical 64
naturalistic fallacy 54
Niebuhr, Reinhold 159
Noah's Ark 72
novelty 34, 36, 112, 114, 176, 184

original sin, definitions of 118, 140–141, 148–149, 153, 172–173, 178, 183–184, 190–191
orthogenesis 24, 90

pain *see* suffering
Paul VI, Pope 3
Pelagianism 13, 144, 146–148
personalism 143–144
phenotype 25, 144–145
Pius XII, Pope 2–3, 140
polygenism *see* monogenism
preadaptation 27
pride 57, 60, 66, 102, 183

process theology 3, 166, 176
progress 2, 4, 16, 20, 39, 53–54, 84, 86, 89–92, 112, 153, 156, 160–161, 172–174
promise of God 66, 89, 96–97, 128–129, 132, 160–161, 170, 176, 186
punctuated equilibrium 44
purpose 51, 64–66, 70, 160–161

Rahner, Karl 3, 53, 71, 142, 144, 159, 176
Ratzinger, Joseph 4, 149
reciprocal altruism 29, 49, 120, 123, 127, 151, 183
recombination 25, 37, 80
reconciliation 5, 49, 106, 120
redemption *see* salvation
Reign of God 53, 124–125, 133, 147, 152–155, 161, 165–166, 170–171, 177, 185–186
revelation 3, 47, 55, 66, 121–122, 127, 152, 187, 191
Rolston, Holmes, III 132
Ruse, Michael 60, 64, 93, 132, 161

salvation 13, 31, 70, 86, 97–98, 123, 126, 128, 140–143, 145, 148–153, 156–158, 161, 183–184, 188, 190–191
Schmitz-Moormann, Karl 92, 175–176, 178
Schoonenberg, Piet 5, 142–146, 174, 178, 191
self-deception 62–63, 120
selfishness 30–31, 48–50, 56, 62, 67–70, 81, 101–110, 113, 116–121, 123, 127, 132–134, 139–145, 147–153, 157–159, 163, 165, 172–176, 178–179, 183–187, 191
self-organizing processes 111
sexual reproduction, evolution of 80, 114
situationalism 143–144
slavery 95, 104, 132
Social Darwinism 54, 89, 168

sociobiology 106, 128–129, 132–133, 179
somatic cells 81, 113–115
soul 2–3, 55, 57, 60, 69, 95, 141
species swarms 45
suffering 1, 14, 53, 70, 75–78, 87–88, 92, 97, 109, 110–111, 118, 134, 139, 151, 157, 160–170, 172–174, 177, 181–182, 188, 190

Teilhard de Chardin, Pierre 3, 4, 65, 140, 142, 147, 150, 154, 159, 172–176, 178, 181–184, 189
Theissen, Gerd 133–134, 179
theodicy 75, 87, 92, 164, 166, 177, 181
theory 32, 84
Thomas Aquinas, St. 4, 20, 67, 69, 116, 123, 155, 159, 167, 170
Tillich, Paul 159
time required for evolution 53, 182
Trent, Council of 21, 144–145, 147–148
Trinity 57, 126, 134, 154, 159, 170
trust in God 129, 161, 166
truth 60–61, 84–85, 187
Twain, Mark 164

unity of God 187

vestigial organs 45
Voltaire 162

Waal, Frans de 5, 106
wastefulness 51–53, 109
Whitehead, Alfred North 176
Williams, G. C. 109
Williams, Patricia A. 133, 170, 178–179

yetzer ha-tov and *yetzer ha-ra* 139

ZFY Adam 73